My Life
and Music

Photograph taken in New York in the 1940's.

My Life and Music

Artur Schnabel

DOVER PUBLICATIONS, INC.
NEW YORK
COLIN SMYTHE LTD.
GERRARDS CROSS, ENGLAND

The publishers wish to acknowledge the great
help they have received from Mr. K. U. Schnabel,
to whom all but one of the photographs used belong.
The Introduction is reproduced by kind permission
of Edward Crankshaw.
The English translation by César Saerchinger of
Reflections on Music is reproduced here by permission
of the Manchester University Press.

Copyright © 1988 by Colin Smythe Limited.
Reflections on Music copyright © 1934 Simon & Schuster, Inc.
Copyright renewed © 1962 by Karl Ulrich Schnabel.
My Life and Music copyright © 1961 Karl Ulrich Schnabel.
Copyright © 1970 by Colin Smythe Limited.

Published in Canada by General Publishing Company, Ltd., 30 Lesmill
Road, Don Mills, Toronto, Ontario.
Published in Great Britain by Colin Smythe Ltd.

This Dover/Colin Smythe edition, first published in 1988, is an
unabridged, slightly corrected republication of *My Life and Music &
Reflections on Music,* published by Colin Smythe Ltd. in 1970. *My Life and
Music* was originally published by Longmans, Green & Co., Ltd., London,
in 1961. *Reflections on Music* was originally published by Manchester
University Press, Manchester, in 1933, and in 1934 by Simon & Schuster,
Inc., New York. A list of illustrations has been added to the present edition.

Manufactured in the United States of America
Dover Publications, Inc., 31 East 2nd Street, Mineola, N.Y. 11501

Library of Congress Cataloging-in-Publication Data

Schnabel, Artur, 1882-1951.
    My life and music / Artur Schnabel.
        p.   cm.
    This Dover/Colin Smythe edition is an unabridged, slightly corrected
republication of My life and music & Reflections on music, published by
Colin Smythe Ltd. in 1970.
    ISBN 0-486-25571-9 (pbk.)
    1. Schnabel, Artur, 1882-1951.   2. Pianists—Biography.
3. Music—Philosophy and aesthetics.   I. Schnabel, Artur, 1882-
1951. Reflections on music. 1988.   II. Title.
ML417.S36A3   1988
786.1′092′4—dc19
[B]
                               87-27300
                                 CIP
                                 MN

British Library Cataloguing in Publication Data

Schnabel, Artur
    My life and music.
    1. Schnabel, Artur 2. Pianists—Biography
    I. Title II. Schnabel, Artur. Reflections on music
    786.1′092′4 ML417.S36

ISBN 0-86140-276-6

CONTENTS

ILLUSTRATIONS

FOREWORD

A DISCERNING writer and poet, Alan Denson, informed my wife recently that Artur Schnabel's 'My Life and Music' was out of print and strongly suggested the possibility of its re-publication because he felt that the value and power of the Master's thought should be available to the younger generation who only knew him through his records and consulted Edition. The idea immediately appealed to her and me, not only as an act of piety to the memory of our beloved friend but also because his views on music which have been of great interest to his contemporaries, should also be made available to succeeding generations.

These views provide a corollary to his records, for which public demand has continued on an unprecedented scale since his death. This is scarcely surprising. In Britain he was universally revered as a supreme musician, a worthy successor to Busoni and Joachim; while the impact he made on the musical life first of Germany and later of the U.S.A. still lives on, specially through the artists who were his pupils.

May we hope that the re-publication of this book will be of service to the many who wish to know about the intimate thoughts of this great man.

To the book has been added the speech which Artur Schnabel made on receiving his doctorate from the University of Manchester.

ROBERT MAYER

1970

INTRODUCTION

In 1945 Artur Schnabel was asked by Mr Robert Hutchins to lecture about music to senior students at the University of Chicago. Schnabel protested that he was a musician, not a lecturer—or, in his own words, a gardener, not a botanist; but at last he agreed to talk informally for twelve sessions about his own life and work and his thoughts about them.

He enjoyed the experience and put all of himself into it. I think he found it a happy occasion for clarifying his own ideas. All he had to do was to stand up and talk, using a fragile autobiographical thread on which to string his ideas about many things. Since he was talking most of the time anyway, when not actively engaged in playing or composing (he talked away, meditatively rumbling, even when climbing in the high Alps, or swimming in Lake Como, or, most alarming of all, crossing the road at Hyde Park Corner), it came quite naturally to him.

It should be remembered that these talks were addressed to a very young, naïve audience. Never less than deeply serious (for Schnabel never in his life 'talked down' to anyone: he was incapable of such a thing), he yet speaks here with a special and charming simplicity, punctilious to explain ways of life and of thought remote from his hearers' experience.

The talks were not intended for publication. But then, in a sense, nothing Schnabel ever did was for publication: even at his most formal concerts the effect was not of a virtuoso communicating to a vast audience, but, rather, of the public being allowed to watch and overhear the private communing of a profoundly engaged musician. He was one of those who, in any company, went on being himself. The company might be two or three friends on the terrace of a hillside tavern among the Italian lakes, a group of professional musicians in his New York apartment, a full-dress party after a concert, glittering with white waistcoats, or a packed house at the Albert Hall. It was all one. Whether Schnabel was arguing about world government, justifying his flight from the Vienna of Schnitzler and von Hofmannsthal, exploring the mind of Mozart, trying to explain his own most obscure compositions, or playing the Diabelli Variations to a dazed audience of three thousand in the Carnegie Hall, he was the same man doing the same thing. Kings might look at him, and so might cats; what he gave was invariably himself, and his life was basically an endless exploration into the truth of everything that came his way. Had he been a writer he would have been a great paradoxist. As a human being he was the man who could not see the Emperor's new clothes.

He never had a Boswell, which was a pity: he had in private conversation an apparently unlimited capacity for coining epigrams and apophthegms about everything under the sun: but they were not closed epigrams; they did not kill a subject, they opened it up. And they were made all the more striking because he possessed in a very high degree the musician's capacity for disassociating words and putting them together in new and often revealing combinations. This was useful in his teaching: 'Streaming—not dreaming' he would say of the slow movement of Brahms's B flat concerto. He was a dedicated punster and perhaps the world's most accomplished practitioner in that queer German sub-art, the *Schüttelreim*. Nevertheless these talks, of which a stenographic record was taken, give so well the general flavour of his conversation that it seems entirely proper to publish them as they were given—or almost as they were given.

Schnabel's use of the English language presented a special problem. It was flowing and highly graphic English, with a vocabulary which made the equipment of most Englishmen look shabby. But it abounded in mistakes of grammar: these are one thing in conversation, when the listener is carried along by the tide of words, the voice deep, full-toned and warm, punctuated by the even warmer chuckle. Some spoken words he never got right; 'melancholy' was a rumbling 'melahn'choly' to the end. Many of his inversions and some of his grammatical mistakes were quasi-deliberate, and wholly a part of him: some he would have corrected, given the opportunity. So it was decided to keep the individual flavour of his English, ironing out only, as he himself would have ironed out, the most crude and unnecessary mistakes of grammar. Everything else is as he said it.

At the end of each session there was a time for questions. Some of the questions were of a silliness beyond belief, and Schnabel shrugged them off. These have been excised. Others were fairly silly, but sparked off good answers. Some were good in themselves. All these have been kept. Most had no particular relevance to what Schnabel had been saying: they were just questions that people wanted to ask—such as: 'Why do you never play the Tchaikovsky concertos?' Because of this, and because the narrative, which was conceived as a consecutive whole, reads better without the interruptions, questions and answers have been grouped at the end, throwing a backward light on what has gone before. But in fact, for the musician, some of the best and most significant passages occur in these answers to questions.

It may be asked why I, no musician, should be introducing the talk of one of the world's greatest interpretative musicians. The answer to that, quite simply, is that Artur Schnabel needs no introduction as a musician from anybody at all; but that as a man he does. I had the privilege of Schnabel's closest friendship for twenty years, from 1931 until his death in 1951: this is my sole qualification for writing about him, but it seems to me sufficient. It was one of those friendships which come only to the exceptionally lucky, and then only once or twice in a lifetime. Close friendship does not necessarily mean close agreement about everything. On the contrary. But it is true to say that while Schnabel was alive no single idea came alive to me until I had tried it out on him. He was one of those men who are all of a piece: one set one's compass by him, even if only, as sometimes happened, to plot a divergent course.

For a long time, among some people, indeed, until his death, he had the reputation of being cerebral and unfeeling. Certain critics conceived an image of him which was a most perfect travesty of the man, and held to it stubbornly. This is the kind of thing that makes one extremely wary of accepting at secondhand any judgement about any human being. The legend arose, I suppose, largely because he made not the least concession to popularity. He played what he said he was going to play and never gave an encore. His programmes—and when he first began playing in London and New York recital programmes were far, far scrappier and more inane than they usually are today—were thought out and deeply serious in intent; they contained no show-pieces or light relief. His appearance on the platform was subdued to the music. He would face the audience, unsmiling, bow formally, a little curtly, and sit down at the piano. Seen from some way off, the square stocky figure, with the stiff grey hair, the stiff grey moustache, did indeed look a little forbidding. He did not throw himself about. He did not move his arms, his hands, except to get them from one part of the keyboard to another. He did not bend over the keys. He sat, quite relaxed, not on a stool but on a special high-backed chair, leaning as a rule slightly back: a series of immensely thundering octaves would be produced with no more apparent expenditure of physical effort than a single note, played contemplatively, *piano*. And when it was all over he stopped playing, bowed curtly, and went. From the back of a large concert-hall, a listener insensitive to musical art might be excused for imagining that there was a minatory look about him and a somewhat matter-of-fact approach.

But the people who wrote about him in this way were certain critics who had no excuse for errors of judgement of this kind. And what always struck me as being quite incomprehensible was the way they went on labelling Schnabel as a cerebral musician, year after year, when it was perfectly clear to them that many of their more distinguished colleagues, to say nothing of the swiftly growing audiences, were moved to tears by the unsurpassed profundity of controlled emotion evoked by that small, still figure. One would have thought they would have been impelled to try to find out what it was they were missing. And if they were incapable of hearing it in the music they could so easily have found it by looking closer at the man. He did not smile at the audience: he reserved his smiles for the composer. And nobody watching him from close by could for one moment have doubted that they were watching a man who was totally wrapt away from all the world, oblivious to the world, engaged in the most intimate of dialogues with the dead man whose poetry it was his calling to express. The eyes, looking straight ahead, reflected almost unbearably every changing mood. Sometimes, communicating desolation, they darkened and the whole body, quite motionless, seemed nevertheless to shrink into numbness. Or when all was well and whoever it was, Mozart, or Schubert, was happily chattering away, the grey head would be very slightly cocked, as though listening for the distant sounds of which the performance was the echo; when it was all tenderness the eyes and the mouth would smile, and the head would be shaken very slightly, as a man smiles and shakes his head at the innocence of children or first love.

'First hear, then play,' he would say; and this was precisely what he did. Before the fingers moved and the sound came at the beginning of a composition, you were aware of a gathering of force: the pianist was listening; he then played what he heard. And so it went on all through the most elaborate composition. Apart from the immediate impact of the profound simplicity and directness with which he played, I suppose most sympathetic listeners were first struck by the phenomenal evenness of his playing. A heaving crescendo of repeated chords was achieved with an exact gradation in the increase of sound which was a perfect mathematical progression—and the gradations were invariably the same in the repeats, and from one performance to the next. His trills—listen to the recording of the variations of Beethoven's Opus 111—were not mechanical devices: they were variations of feeling, and always the same variation in the same place. He had a dozen quite distinct trills and could achieve through these more urgency and variety of expression than most musicians could achieve through the light and shade of a complete movement. His pauses were organic: through them the music breathed. From repeat to repeat, from performance to performance, they were identical. When he played the *arietta* of Opus 111 time stood still; but if you put a stop-watch to it you would discover, incredulously, that it took no longer than the average performance. But this wonderful exactitude was not achieved by mathematical means; the steadiness came not from contriving, but from listening to sounds unheard by us, to the ideal which was always the ideal, and obeying their command. There was never the slightest hint of 'this is how I feel today', which can make other players give highly variable performances, sometimes, as we say, inspired, sometimes not; it was always: 'First hear, then play.'

Not that he never changed. Far from it! 'I should hope I had—I am fifteen years older!' he said once to a conductor who said after a rehearsal that Schnabel had a different idea of a certain concerto from when they had last played it together. He never began to be satisfied. He never rested until he got at the innermost truth of a given composition. That is to say, he never rested. One of the questions at the end of this book came from a student who asked why Schnabel played the music of only a handful of composers. He answered, fairly, that in the first place the question was wrong: in his youth he had played much contemporary music. He then went on to give his reasons for so rarely playing Bach in public. He finally said, 'I am attracted only to music which I consider to be better than it can be performed. Therefore I feel (rightly or wrongly) that unless a piece of music presents a problem to me, a never-ending problem, it doesn't interest me too much. For instance, Chopin's studies are lovely pieces, perfect pieces, but I simply can't spend time on them. I believe I know these pieces; but playing a Mozart sonata, I am not sure that I do know it, inside and out. Therefore I can spend endless time on it.'

It was significant and wholly characteristic that the music he spent most time with was the 'simplest', the sort of pieces children are given to play because they can manage the notes. I remember one late summer at Tremezzo on Lake Como when most of the pupils had gone away and Schnabel was preparing for a series of recitals—Mozart, Schumann and Schubert—which he was to give in London, seven in all, that autumn. (He never practised, of course, as practising is understood: he used to say sometimes that this was because he had been born lazy, but readers of the talks that follow will see just why he did not believe in practising. He *worked,* and his capacity for work was infinite.) The composition he was working on most was Schumann's *Kinderscenen.* It was blazingly hot and the grapes were being gathered in. While the housework went on inside the little villa, Schnabel sat alone in his darkened music room, with its two great Bechsteins (it was only later that he came to Steinways), curtains drawn against the blaze and the heat; and we would sit about on the terrace outside, with its heavenly view across to Bellaggio and the misty mountains beyond, while the air was filled with the poignant gravity of Schubert's posthumous B flat sonata, or the unbridled *Weltschmerz* of Schumann's *Fantasiestücke,* or the cool lucidity of one of Mozart's acceptances, achieved only in his music, of the human condition. But again and again, morning after morning, sometimes for hour after hour, he would go back and back again to the *Kinderscenen* of Schumann. There was something wrong; he had not penetrated that music as he knew he could. Above all there was something wrong with, of all things, *Träumerei*. He knew, and was cross because he knew. Nothing was said: it was simply that this extraordinary genius could not play to his liking a little fragment which every pianist learns in the nursery and then never thinks about again. One morning, just before lunch, he broke off and started again, and this time there was a shriek from the back of the house: 'Artur—you've got it!' Twice more he played it through. That was Therese, his wife, who had been the most celebrated singer of *Lieder* in Germany before anyone had heard of Artur Schnabel. 'What do you mean, I've got it?' 'You've been playing it wrong for forty years!' 'What do you mean, playing it wrong? Why didn't you tell me before?' 'What was the good? I told you then. Should I go on telling you every day?' 'Yes, you told me. I didn't understand you. Now I do.'

There are not many people who have the least idea either of the wonderful musicianship of Therese Behr Schnabel, who died in 1959, or of the debt her husband owed to her. She was older than him by several years, and it was she who, after his infant prodigy days, forced him on the German public by insisting that he appear as her accompanist. She had the most unerring musical tact of anyone I have ever known, and this came out in her singing even when she had no voice left at all. But above all it came out in her handling of her husband's genius; she *knew,* with the unconscious certainty of a blackbird or a born tennis player. He had to find out, to discover, and, of course, in the end, he discovered more than she knew, removing with infinite application layer on layer of opacity, so that his performance of, say, the Diabelli Variations in his last years was like looking at the sun without dark glasses.

His whole life, his whole conversation, was unending discovery, and it applied to everything he touched, or that interested him: there was only one tabu, and that was the second-hand. The whole of his teaching was bent to one end: to make his pupils think for themselves. You get some of this in his talks, above all in the answers to questions. There was only one thing forbidden: received authority, including his own. 'Tradition,' he would say—and this applied to tradition in piano playing as in everything else—'too often means a collection of bad habits.'

E.C.

My Life and Music

PART ONE

1

BEFORE I begin to talk on the subject I have chosen for our
meetings here, I wish to say a few introductory words. First of
all, I am sure that already I have revealed that the English
language is not—unfortunately for you—my mother tongue. I
had my first lesson in English at the age of thirty-eight. It was
offered to me by an old friend who even as a schoolboy in
Vienna was especially interested in English. He was already
trying then—and continued with the experiment all his life—
to translate Shakespeare's Sonnets into German. So I accepted
his offer with enthusiasm. He brought to my first lesson a little
book which, naturally, I expected to be a primer. Looking at
the title, I guessed that it must be something else, a kind of
reader. The title was *The Hunting of the Snark*. What 'hunting' meant I knew from English pictures, so I asked: 'What is
a snark?' 'I don't know,' was his reply. After that we both
agreed, without any harm done to our relationship, that another, less humorous type of teaching might be more practical
for my purposes. I engaged a professional teacher, an English
woman. Because my time for instruction was very limited, I
suggested that she should accompany me on my daily walks,
should let me try to speak English and should simply tell me
when I went wrong. My vocabulary was, of course, much
smaller than that of so-called Basic English, but through her
corrections it was rapidly widened. We did this for two months
or so, and that was my entire instruction in English. Perhaps
this is not the worst method of learning a language—for a
middle-aged person.

Not only is my English imperfect, but I am, actually, not
entitled to do what I am going to do here because I am 'only
a musician', as a gentleman once said when I complained at a
rehearsal about some arrangements on a platform. As quoted
to me by somebody who sat in the auditorium next to this
gentleman, his words were: 'What is he so fussy about? He
is only a musician.' I extended his criticism immediately to

3

Mozart, one of whose works I had to perform on that occasion, and was quite content.

When I received the invitation to take this chair, I remembered that I was 'only a musician' and wrote a letter, a few passages of which I shall read to you. 'That I esteem your invitation to be a guest instructor at your Institute a high honour and a true satisfaction, goes without saying. Allow me to add that this invitation, however, has also made me slightly uneasy. You credit me with abilities outside the sphere of my natural vocation. I, on the other hand, am quite certain of having no gifts other than some of those required by that vocation. The rather exclusive, and thus one-sided, department of the art of music in which I am employed demands my services as a, let me say, "direct" musician, one in charge of the production of music. The "indirect" musician, a fairly new calling, takes music to pieces, relates it to extra-musical conditions, proceeds methodically, analytically—for which I believe myself to have no talent whatsoever—and undertakes to represent music chiefly with words and figures. The "direct" musician, to express it in a not quite correct metaphor, is a gardener; the "indirect" musician a botanist. The art of music is abstract and transcendental (that makes the metaphor incorrect), and is never purposive or descriptive (which makes the attempt of translating it into words still more of a Sisyphean labour). The only medium by which to establish contact with musical ideas are tones. They are the medium of expression in which I have professional training. With words, above the average level of common usage, I am a dilettante. You expected me, I know, to speak of music. But quite apart from the insurmountable difficulty—as I see it—of presenting, or indicating, with a medium other than tones the essence, interior life, origin, spontaneity, or function of music, I have no training, no experience, and no ambition to do that. Anybody who communicates knowledge at the University of Chicago must, of course, be an expert—at least in the technique of communicating through words and figures. To acquire such a technique takes time. "Direct" music demands all my time. I imagine, certainly, that "experts" range from nonentities to validities. Yet, they are all experts. The amateur, even he with the most vivacious mind, has to stay at home.'

I have now to explain to you why I did not stay at home, why I am here, in spite of my unsuitability for this job. Well, the

4

reply to my letter was a deadly attack on my apprehensions, for it did not deny the risk involved and did not tie me to a programme. Thus, I agreed to attempt, unprepared, this excursion, on condition of mutual absolution should it end in failure. The next step was to consider a subject for this talking venture. Eventually I decided, after much thought and some discussions with friends, to give you a summary of my career as a musician. It started when I was seven years old; I am now sixty-three. I have chosen this subject not because I think of myself as somebody important, but only because my career has taken me from what I would call the last flowering of an individualistic age to the first unfolding of a collectivistic one. I have been almost everywhere where the art of music has a market. I have lived in many different countries. I have met very many people of great talent and some others of great reputation. Many of the things which I am going to tell you will be known to you already, but yet I think you might not be bored to hear them once more.

The career of a musician ought to be—it is, actually and in many ways—different from the careers of artists in other fields of art. All comparisons of the other arts with music are necessarily somewhat superficial. The art of music needs, essentially, not much contact with social groups, or concern with social problems. By the art of music I understand here the comparatively very young art of *absolute* music, and never applied or auxiliary music. This absolute, autonomous, independent music has developed into what is perhaps the most exclusive medium for the spiritual exaltation of the active individual in an intimate, private sphere of personal experience. Music is one of the performing arts with which, in exercise, one can be alone, entirely alone. Theatrical art is not comparable with music because the actor always reproduces or represents what is in everybody's orbit of experience. He uses language, the means of communication of all men. He can hardly act alone in his home. He needs an ensemble, and he is a part of visible human acts. Dancing can be abstract, or symbolical, but even then it remains sensual and technical. As a creative art also music is different from other arts, from the literary, the pictorial, the architectural. The writer describes and interprets what he has seen and experienced. The painter also describes, or at least he did before abstract painting appeared, though even this is not to be compared with music.

In the performance of music, if one uses the piano, one can actually play all the music composed for performance, and can be alone. I am inclined to assume that the 'Well-Tempered Clavier' was meant by Johann Sebastian to be heard just by the one person who plays it.

It is good to remember that music created in Germany and Austria after its emancipation from Italian and Dutch influences consisted more and more of types best suited to the sphere of *exclusive,* personal experience. Before the development and transition of music from auxiliary to absolute, it was chiefly in the service of the Church and the Court. It was, of course, also in use for some other social and domestic purposes. The autonomy of music led to its isolation from any function. Music became an end in itself. Chamber music (in the modern sense), the piano piece, the *Lied,* were—so far—the final forms of this process. Possibly it could not go further with the supplying of inspiring and elevating activities for the individual. Now we are already witnessing an attempt to transform this isolated type of music, following the trend toward collectivism, into a social function. It is a matter of opinion whether there are some values that will never be suited to mass circulation. I cannot conceive of the day—and, besides, I do not yearn for it—when everything will be for everybody. Some of the most delicate types of music are already conspicuously neglected. That is to be expected. And it is quite consistent that the most popular performer of music is now the orchestra. It has, in the meantime, increased to 100 pieces or more. Music might, in the next decades, become an attractive reservoir for the absorption of unemployed persons, and orchestras may swell to more and more players, even if only one portion really plays, while the others get paid for standing by. I am curious to see (if the years are given me) where this attempt to move an 'Ivory Tower' to a widening market will lead to.

Today, I would say, music has already suffered. I would, however, not say that public life has not been benefited. *It has,* and music is still great.

I announced that I would give you an account of my career. What I have said so far is clearly not a part of it, but rather a confession of faith. It is time to begin the narrative.

*　　　*　　　*

I was born in a small Austrian village, which belonged to the Austrian part of Poland. My parents were Austrian subjects whose religion was Jewish. The little village was a curious place. I have not too definite memories of the happenings during the first ten years of my life, but rather distinct ones of places and smells. My birthplace was tiny and rather poor—a kind of suburb to a small town. This small town was the twin to a somewhat larger town which one reached over a bridge, under which I never saw any water flow. The other town belonged to the Austrian province of Silesia. Socially these three places were very different. Bielitz was the name of the largest, as long as it belonged to Austria. After the First World War, it came to Poland and is now named Bielsko.

In Bielitz lived the so-called upper classes, which meant in that case a majority of non-Jews and non-Poles. They were rather haughty—snooty we would say now. The town, I have to admit, was undoubtedly much cleaner than the other two places, and therefore its smells are not so manifest in my memory as those of the others. The people in Bielitz were mostly Protestants.

Biala, its twin, was more of an agricultural centre. There were many Poles, but they were not considered, generally, real Poles. I remember that the contemptuous name given to these people within Austria was that of 'water Poles'—watered down Poles, so to say. They were mixed with the poorer Jews. It was a lively place. Bielitz was cleaner but its twin was more lively—thanks to the Poles and Jews and poverty, perhaps.

The people living in Lipnik, my birthplace, were apparently still poorer. I remember only one street; it was the whole place. The pride of it was the house of a liquor maker. His son became a musician, and later a dear friend of mine. They were the first well-to-do people with whom I came into contact. These details may not be quite correct, because I have no notes, no material at all which could help me in telling you all these things and those which will follow. A few years after I was born my parents moved to the clean town. In their religious observances they were mildly orthodox: many of my relatives, for instance my grandparents, were strictly orthodox. When my parents moved to Vienna afterwards, they became externally more and more assimilated, but their devotion never weakened.

Almost all these poor or middle-class Jewish families were

very ambitious to help their children to rise into a higher sphere of existence and experience. When I was six years old, my elder sister (I had two sisters) started to take piano lessons. My mother told me—I don't know how reliable this is—that I, without having lessons, succeeded in doing what she was taught much quicker than she. I simply went to the piano and did it. My sister's piano teacher thought that a boy who could do this must have musical talent, and she started teaching me. After a year she thought I should be taken to Vienna for a talent test by some experts, who would decide whether I had the equipment to become a professional musician. In the meantime I had a few lessons with two other—both male— piano teachers in Bielitz. I remember only one of them. He lived in the tower of a rather ugly castle, belonging to a Polish nobleman. During a lesson he would suddenly disappear through a trapdoor. This impressed and also frightened me. I now have a pretty good idea as to what he was doing during the ten minutes before he returned. I am sure he enjoyed a bottle of wine—I remember the smell.

At that time I also had my first tutor for general education. He was an old man with a white beard and was not too tidy. For a short time I learned Hebrew from him, but can hardly remember a single word of it.

In 1889, when I was seven, I was taken to Vienna to play for Professor Hans Schmidt. I also had some letters of recommendation to other Viennese people. I cannot say what impression Vienna made on me. After all, I was only a baby! Hans Schmidt was Professor at the Conservatory of the Society of Friends of Music, one of the most famous institutes in the world. He was the author of 'the thousand daily exercises' (or perhaps a few less). He also had a white beard. You, here and now, cannot imagine most men having beards; in my boyhood, however, beards were the rule. They were very decorative. The Emperor had most carefully trimmed whiskers, so everybody who wished to look serious and dignified also had whiskers or beards, including my father, my uncles, and so on. Professor Hans Schmidt accepted me as a pupil. Some other people heard me too—musicians and music lovers—and declared unanimously that I had the equipment to become a professional musician. Thus, from my seventh year on, I was considered a professional musician, by the decision of my patrons and my parents. They made me a pianist. I had no choice. I might, otherwise, have become a composer. Officially I have remained a pianist, although secretly I always did and still do compose. I neither deplore nor regret this destiny. The piano is a quite satisfactory instrument—for a musician. What I learned with Professor Schmidt, I cannot say—I simply don't remember. It was obviously not inspiring, or perhaps I was not yet sufficiently aware. My work with him lasted for two years. Then I was sent to another man—of him I shall speak later.

I was mentioned to some wealthy people who were keenly interested in helping young talent and my mother was summoned to see the heads of their charity departments. Three of these rich families supported me for the next eight years without ever asking, or expecting, to see me or to hear me. This was sheer luck. Up to my fifteenth year I got monthly allowances which my mother, or later on I myself, had to collect at their offices. Decades later I once met a descendant of one of my sponsors and told him that his grandfather had helped me to study music and to enjoy my boyhood—he hardly listened!

The leading music store in Vienna at that time was still the kind at which you could buy nothing else but music and, perhaps, music paper: there were no dolls, as you can find nowadays in music stores in America—in some you can even buy refrigerators. How strange, that our age of specialists should be less exclusive than the previous age. We combine, somehow, specialization with standardization. The man running this music store in Vienna, Albert J. Gutmann, was very enterprising and rather influential in the history of public musical life in the second half of the nineteenth century. All great musicians of the epoch kept personal contact with him, and the gatherings at his home, every Sunday afternoon, were internationally known—as a 'star parade', as one would now call it. On each of these occasions some music was performed, most often contemporary, to promote some young composer. He also sold pianos, in another shop, and arranged concerts. When I was eight he arranged a private concert for me, to arouse interest in my talent. It was given in the small hall connected with his piano salesrooms. I played the D minor concerto by Mozart, still considered a work accessible chiefly to children— traditional misconceptions of this sort have an astonishing longevity. My concert must have been quite successful. It prolonged and improved my chances of being supported continuously and sufficiently to cover the expenses of my own and my family's existence. My dear parents were ambitious but they were not greedy, so I was spared the fate of being an exploited prodigy. After this first semi-public performance I did not perform in public before I was fourteen. Then, of course, I was thought to be grown up—a musician, just like other musicians.

I remember very distinctly two other candidates for world fame in Vienna, a girl and a boy, both my age, who, unlike me, were exhibited as prodigies. Both came from a milieu similar to mine. This touches on a very interesting problem I should like to discuss another time. They both got much publicity: I did not get any. To this very day I have retained a certain reserve about publicity. I don't know exactly why I feel averse to it, but I felt so even when I was only seven years old. These two children played often at the Imperial Court. I never did, which, of course, disappointed my mother. It was always in the papers that one or other of my two young colleagues had played for the Emperor, played for the Archduke —I had not played for anybody. I remember that one day a friend of my family came and teased me, asking: 'Now, what about you? Did you see that Poldi Spielmann has again played before crowned heads and that Ilona Eibenschütz has composed a Polka and dedicated it to the Archduke So-and-so, and that it is displayed in the windows of Gutmann's store? Your name is not there.' My mother told me that I answered: 'What does the Emperor know about music?' Perhaps I did. My mother, in any case, had much imagination.

When I was nine, somebody advised my mother that for me to continue with that (allegedly) dry, uninspiring Professor Schmidt made no sense, that there was in Vienna a much superior teacher, a Professor Leschetizky. He did not teach at a conservatory. He had no official position. He lived rather aloofly and hardly appeared anywhere in public. He had not played in public for a long time. My mother took me to see him. My memory of this event is fairly clear. (I had advanced to the perceptivity of a nine-year-old human being.) I remember that I waited two hours in a small room before Leschetizky appeared. He was always late. If you came for a lesson at eleven o'clock, he began it at one o'clock. He, too, had a beard, though it was not yet quite white. His house seemed to have a much more inspiring atmosphere than my previous teacher's studio. We felt this immediately. It was not just the

10

atmosphere of a thousand daily exercises. Leschetizky asked me, after I played part of my repertoire for him, to sight-read. He opened, I remember, the piano score of *Cavalleria Rusticana* which had been published just a week before. My sight-reading must have satisfied him, for he accepted me as a pupil.

The first year his wife, Madame Essipoff, a then famous piano virtuoso, actually took care of my pianism and he heard me only on a few occasions. Madame Essipoff was very kind to me. I had to play studies and exercises, chiefly Czerny's, I remember. She used to put a coin on my hand, a silver coin almost as big as a silver dollar (a gulden) and if I played one Czerny study without dropping it, she gave it to me as a present. I think that was sweet of her. In the meantime, I have changed my way of handling the piano so radically that now if I were to play only a few tones the coin would drop. I don't think that the 'static' hand is a recommendable technique for the expression of music. For very young beginners, however, it might, temporarily, be the only method.

At Leschetizky's I established contact for the first time with an international crowd. He had pupils from countries all over the world, the majority from the United States. Paderewski had been one of his pupils. Their relations cannot have been too happy: this was clearly indicated by the hesitation of each to mention the other, and even more by what they said about each other when forced to say something. I have not read Paderewski's memoirs, but somebody reported to me that references to Leschetizky are rare in them and always cool. Maybe this report was not correct. I never found out what was at the bottom of their, let me call it, alienation. However, Paderewski, who has never denied being his pupil, was such a sensation, such a hero in the States, that American students flocked to Leschetizky.

Soon Leschetizky himself began instructing me. He said to me repeatedly throughout the years, and in the presence of many other people: 'You will never be a pianist. You are a musician.' Of course I did not make much of that statement, and did not reflect much about it; even today I cannot quite grasp it. However, he made the distinction.

11

2

I HAVE said that what I am summarizing here has not been prepared. These talks may therefore turn out to be like pieces of a Chinese puzzle. I shall supply the pieces, and you will have to put them together in order to get a picture. I hope they fit.

To continue with my story: I come back to my birthplace, Lipnik. It had neither a railway station, nor a post office of its own. When asked to give the data of my life for books of reference, biographical sketches, or such things, I add to the name Lipnik: Austria. At some time particularly conscientious people must have been curious to learn to which part of Austria Lipnik belongs. They must have consulted a map of Austria, one which was published before the First World War. There they could find two Lipniks in the Empire, both of which had railways stations and post offices and thus a place in an atlas: one in Czechoslovakia, the other in Carinthia. They preferred, for unknown reasons, the latter. My Lipnik was in the Polish section of northern Austria. She bore hardly any resemblance to her namesake in Carinthia (a southern province of Austria), with her gigantic rocks, glaciers, lakes, and a small alpine population famous for their virtuosity in yodelling. Their neighbours are Yugoslavs and Italians. To see myself more often than not labelled the 'Carinthian Pianist' naturally amuses me very much. Well, it is a historic error of little importance. The Austrian-Hungarian monarchy was, as you know, a motley array of fourteen nations, of which the majority had, more or less, the position or function of serfs. Some of the Austrian provinces had an almost colonial character. The masters and usufructuaries sat in Vienna, Prague and Budapest.

When I first came to Vienna, it seemed to me an immense place compared with what I had seen before. When I later saw Berlin, London and New York, Vienna of course seemed almost miniature. In the 'Gay Nineties' she was clearly in the

12

eleventh hour of her function as the 'Ballroom of Europe', as she was once cleverly named. For a time the Austro-Hungarian monarchy was so highly rated that a great foreign statesman said of her: 'if she did not exist, one ought to invent her'. She has since died, and her resurrection is, at present, not even dreamed of.

Vienna, around the *fin de siècle*, had certain well-defined categories of citizens. The tenor of social life there was given by the aristocracy which—centred around its peak, the Court —exercised all the high functions connected with a still old-fashioned court, and was generally and gladly accepted as the social *prima donna*. Second to the Court and aristocracy came the Church, the Army and the Administration. It was prover-bial that these noble bosses (with some exceptions of course) never overworked themselves. Not to work—in a common sense—was a part of *noblesse oblige*. I think this is quite an important fact. The less time was lost in work, the more was left for the only admissible competition: the desire to excel each other in the tasks of *noblesse*, based on solidity and refinement. Third came a titled group without century-old pedigrees. They were the lower layer of the aristocracy, com-posed mostly of men (or their descendants) who for outstand-ing achievements in the army or in the administration were chosen for promotion to noble rank. Long service—endurance —was counted as one of the achievements. Also a few mer-chants and bankers were on occasion rewarded in this way. In the second half of the nineteenth century even artists, scientists, doctors, educators and so on, were raised to nobility —presumably in the last phase of its fading glory. Then came three layers of *bourgeoisie*, and towards the bottom the varied groups below the white collar supremacy. Among them were wine-growers, for very good wine was grown in the close vicinity of Vienna. The wine-keller, in the winter, and espec-ially the wine-garden in spring and summer, were frequented by everyone. There the social categories mixed and, if suffi-ciently animated by the young wine, even fraternized for a few hours in the equality of intoxication. These gardens were often in front of the vineyards. The wine was served in carafes, from the cask. Song and women were never missing. It was the most intoxicating trio ensemble—leading to freedom-from-care.

The lower classes in Vienna were a rather rough crowd, in

13

contrast to the upper ones, who excelled in great charm and elegance. It was, I repeat, the eleventh hour of that culture which begins in the home and probably also ends there. A kind of effort to enjoy these last performances of that culture was quite striking. The upper classes in Vienna seemed to know that they were doomed. It was a last escape into sweet superficiality, into an aesthetically pleasant defeatism. One of the best characterizations of this decadence-conscious Vienna was given by her own people during the First World War. With an inclination to joke about their weaknesses, they parodied a German Army communiqué. The Germans reported: 'The situation is serious but not at all desperate.' The Viennese: 'The situation is desperate, but not at all serious.'

Life in such an atmosphere was not enjoyable for everyone. I, for one, did not feel entirely happy there. The spirit of defeatism gradually permeating the air hemmed in creative impulses and the healthy development of higher gifts, both not yet rare among the Viennese. The maxim: enjoy as much as possible the mannered elegance, as well as more robust pastimes, was not conducive to so-called serious ambitions. When my family moved to Vienna because of my assignment to the musical profession, we first lived in a sort of ghetto—a voluntary ghetto, not a compulsory one, as for instance in Czarist Russia. Very soon after, we moved to a somewhat less homogeneous quarter. I don't remember very much about the chosen ghetto: just the street, the synagogue and the grocer where I often went to get things for my mother. I remember that the herrings always smelled of kerosene, because the two commodities were kept in barrels next to each other. I remember also our family doctor, Doctor Ignatz Kreisler, the father of Fritz Kreisler, the famous violinist. I thus knew Fritz Kreisler, who is several years older than I, from my boyhood on. His father, the doctor, still alive in my memory, was an angelic man with a white beard, one of the kindest I remember.

After I had started, on Leschetizky's advice, my lessons with Madame Essipoff, someone told my mother that I ought also to have instruction in composition. So one day she took me to Mr Anton Bruckner. I remember exactly the little I saw of his home, also the street and even the number of the house. We went up one flight of stairs, knocked at a door, and heard the sound of slowly approaching slippers. A bald-headed man opened the door, just wide enough for me to peep in. I noticed a dusty hallway with some laurel wreaths piled up, and stacks of music. 'What do you want?' he asked. My mother explained: 'I want you to give lessons in theory to my son.' He grumbled: 'I don't teach children,' pushed us out and closed the door. This was my only personal acquaintance with Bruckner. Afterwards I saw him only from a greater distance.

Because of this futile interview with Bruckner, Leschetizky had to recommend another teacher in composition and theory for me. He mentioned a much less well-known composer. This new teacher was very pedantic, dry, and uninspiring. I must have shown some resistance—though I was in later years often praised for having always been a 'good' boy, patient, and if dissatisfied, chiefly with myself. At any rate, I left this new teacher after a few months of instruction and was taken to the third trainer recommended to us. He was Dr Mandiczewski. Dr Mandiczewski was a great, a wonderful man. He was in charge of the archives at the Society of the Friends of Music. It was not a municipal or imperial school, but was subsidized. Mandiczewski was the amanuensis of Brahms, so I was very lucky. I studied with him for years, and he was always very nice to me. I had to go a fairly long way from my family's apartment to the one room in which he lived. (At that time most musicians lived rather modestly: I have also seen Brahms's rooms—only two rooms—very different from the mansions our present-day stars live in.) I had to be at Mandiczewski's at eight o'clock in the morning—he had no time to give me lessons at any other hour, for at 9.15 or so he had to be in the archives. I was then eleven or twelve. He allowed me to accompany him to his archives, and stay there as long as I wished. He never paid much attention to my presence, and I could acquaint myself with all the treasures there in perfect leisure. A few simple rooms—I think not even fireproof—filled with the most precious musical documents—numerous manuscripts of the greatest composers and a great collection of works presenting the history of music. While I with awe was idling in this shrine, Mandiczewski went on with his work.

It was the habit of Brahms every Sunday morning of the spring and autumn season to make an excursion (if the weather permitted) into the lovely hilly woods surrounding Vienna. He was accompanied by a few friends, chiefly musicians. When I

15

was twelve to thirteen, Mandiczewski thought me old enough to join them once in a while. I thus enjoyed the unique privilege of spending several Sundays as a boy with Brahms and his companions. One gathered for these excursions at eight in the morning, at a tram-stop opposite the Vienna Opera, took a tram, drawn by one horse, drove through suburbs to the terminal and continued then on foot. On all these occasions Brahms treated me in the same manner: before a meal he would ask me whether I was hungry; after one, whether I had had enough. That was all he ever said to me. Why, after all, should he talk to a child?

I also often saw Brahms indoors. Mandiczewski knew most of those Viennese families to whom good music, in their homes, was an inner necessity. As amanauensis of Brahms he went where his master went. And as my teacher he helped me upwards not only by admitting me to these Sunday walks, but also by introducing me to some of the music lovers whose intimacy with Brahms seemed their greatest pride. In one of these families a private choir gathered once or twice a week, conducted by Dr Mandiczewski and led by the hostess, who in her youth had had a high reputation as a singer. I was asked to accompany this choir, sometimes four-hand with one of the sons of the family, approximately my age. He, Erich von Hornbostel, later a well-known physiologist, died much too young some years ago, in New York. Brahms came occasionally to these meetings. In his last years, he spent much time at the home of a music lover by the name of Conrad. Mr Conrad had three daughters, near my age. Mandiczewski introduced me also to the Conrads, not only as a young musician, but also as a possible playmate or companion for the girls. During the winter chiefly, the Sunday afternoons at the Conrads were devoted to chamber music performances. They had, of course, some music every weekday as well in such a milieu, but the Sunday was for all concerned (the head of the family, a merchant, and most of the professionals, or amateurs, who played the chamber music or listened) the time for leisure and pleasure—not to forget the girls who had no school. I was often allowed to participate actively. My never weakened love of chamber music is certainly rooted in this early chance to hear and to perform it.

Brahms was often present on these occasions. He mostly sat reading in the library, which was several rooms distant from the music room. All doors in the flight of rooms used to be wide open, and, if interested, Brahms might have heard the music very well. Whether he did or not I could not tell. Thirty or forty years later I read to my astonishment that he had. That moreover he had praised what I did at the piano. This story is still circulated. I do not know its origin, and I wish you to know that it was not I who told it. The reliability of many such stories (not only in my case) is questionable. I myself do not compile or supply them (I never have) for advertising or other purposes. This is for other people to attend to. Asked for it by concert managements I advise them to gather the desired data from books of reference and other sources and to select and present what and as they like. I admit that this procedure involves certain risks. After playing somewhere last year, on my return home I found the programme in my pocket. Interested to see whether the annotations in it corresponded to my conception of the works I had performed, I began to read. That the correspondence was not complete did not surprise me. I had experienced that before. What surprised me was the little sketch of my career. It said among other things that Brahms had heard me play at my first recital and had been so impressed that he had become an intimate friend of mine. Perhaps one day I shall read that I played billiards with Mozart.

The Vienna of my boyhood was still divided into two antagonistic musical camps, the Wagnerians and the Brahmsians, who even now are not yet fully reconciled. Wagner was the more popular hero. His work, consisting chiefly of operas, offered more than mere music can. Opera, as you all know, is visible action clarified by words which (instead of being spoken, as in a play) are sung. Thus the words have not only a purpose but are also music. This music is backed, strengthened, completed and kept coherent by music without words, the function of which is the evocation of any atmosphere demanded by the story. It seems impossible to say in which of the many elements of an opera the average enthusiast is chiefly participating. It is theatre *and* music, or vice versa, if you like, and thus naturally more attractive to many than music alone. The pantomime, and especially the ballet, with their predominantly physical aspects and the great importance of a technique not too difficult to judge, are, naturally, still more attractive to still more people. Music is movement. One may walk, stride, jump, crawl, hop—in one word, 'dance' to any music. Children do, if allowed. The category labelled 'dance music' belongs, admittedly, to the servant type of music. You may, or may not, listen to it, be aware of it as mere noise—or even unaware of that.

Operas are not suited for home consumption. They are a public institution. Brahms wrote only 'self-contained' music, including songs and choral works, but none associated with visible action. Most of the works by Brahms are therefore well suited to the home and he was accordingly the hero of the more exclusive, the more refined and individualized group. Wagner provided the sensations needed by those who desired to escape 'simplicity'. His world of gods and legends, of stylized *noblesse* and stylized meanness, carried them above their drab daily existence. At that time I thought that Brahms and Wagner had musically not much more in common than all musicians have. Today, they appear to me musically almost like brothers. I think Wagner to be the greater genius. He tried to solve new problems, to express grandiose visions. Yet, Brahms's untheatrical and less pretentious work is closer to me. What they have in common is romantic pessimism, romantic sensuousness and sentimentality. Also some similar elements in their procedure in composition. What may be the essential difference between their works is a fascinating question. I can here only indicate in a few words what *I* think to be this difference. Both were dedicated to overcoming pessimism and the disintegrating tendency of the nineteenth century (in Europe); to arriving at positive, transcendental, all-inclusive results—like their 'happier' predecessors, living in an age when creative forces were still unified.

Wagner approached the task via symbolism and mysticism, exemplified by conflicts in remote regions. Each of his heroes evades the deed. Even in his only realistic work—*Die Meistersinger*—Hans Sachs resigns, and Walther von Stolzing changes from troubadour to husband. Wagner's work is the glorification of renunciation. No growth follows. Music, to be true, can never be descriptive, nor purposive, nor negative; it is a miracle to what a degree Wagner has helped the illusion that it *can* be all that. Brahms, younger by twenty years, was more modest, turned to nature, to the people, to workmanship. With as much ease as care he produced music directly; he needed neither a programme nor a *Weltanschauung*. He was fed by

18

what will *always* flow. The glow and exuberance of his early works and the marvellous equilibrium of his late ones never want to be more than music. In appearance his music was often like Wagner's; in expression too; in intention hardly ever. As you see, it is quite possible to be aware of, and to appreciate greatness, and yet to like what is not so great much more. There are also other criteria for evaluation and participation than liking.

I was not too attracted to the theatre. I went very often to the opera in Vienna. In my childhood I had very little contact with other children. I seldom played children's games, and I do not remember ever having possessed any toys. Such a child, they say, will soon, much too soon, be an old person. Whether true or not, I think this pessimistic forecast has not worked in my own case. I did not start having real contact with people of my own age before I was thirty. And if as a youngster I was attracted to people above my age, now at sixty-three I turn to the youngsters. Unfortunately they are, nowadays, not too keen on joining with older people. I remember the time when young people still wanted to be with older ones. Maybe it is this change of attitude that has driven older people to their frantic efforts to appear much younger than they are.

I have here a small list, very incomplete, of things which did not exist, or were just introduced, when I was a boy. This list seems to me very impressive, in spite of its incompleteness.

Electricity—very rare.

Telephone—very rare.

Lifts—hardly.

Gas—even gas was very rare.

Refrigerators—not divined.

Immovable bath tubs—practically unknown.

Central heating—none.

Vacuum cleaners—none.

Safety razors—none.

Aluminium—none.

Canned food—only home-canned, in glasses. No tins, except for sardines.

Factory-made bread—just coming.

X-ray—none.

Ready-made clothes—none.

Artificial silk—none.

Paper napkins—none.

Cars—none.
Gramophones—none.
Radios—none.
Typewriters—none.
Underground railways—none.
Department stores—just beginning.
No Films,
Skyscrapers,
Pictures in the Press,
Airplanes,
Submarines.
No Athletics—to the extent that they are known now.
No Payments by Cheque, etc.

Even some of the diseases didn't exist (or had different names then). I remember when 'influenza' appeared for the first time. It was very exciting—and shockingly severe. Technology and science were not yet as popular and worshipped as they are now. They were not yet the topic of most conversations. Great men in these fields were active but only a few of the 'public' knew about and discussed these matters. Unknown were psycho-analysis, the theory of relativity, atom-splitting, and so on. All that might have been in the air already, and perhaps contributing to the Viennese defeatism which I have mentioned several times.

If you were to ask me whether I think that human society, without all these commodities and services, progress and discoveries, was happier at that time than it is now, I would not know the answer. It may well be, I submit, that the more one is inclined, or seduced, to possess, conserve and enjoy material things, the less one may have to give in the personal exchange of souls, minds and brains. By machines man's toil has been eased. He has, theoretically, more time—free time—than before. The trouble seems to be that he has to devote this free time to what the machines produce. Otherwise the machines might rest. Is it to serve the machines well that he prefers acceleration to leisure, for which he now has time? You see how confused I am by the turbulent relation between man and machines—created by him. Maybe it is their revenge, as our 'hard-working employees', to keep us busy when we are lazy.

Real happiness will perhaps then only be established in human beings when much will be expected from their inner

20

qualities and higher potentialities, and less from their excellence as customers for quantities of entirely unnecessary, undesired things and alleged pleasures—time- and thought-killers. Most pleasures in my youth were still connected with active participation in things. There were not as many theatres as nowadays and neither a radio nor a gramophone to sit before. One stayed at home and did something. The change, however, was approaching rapidly. I have never forgotten one of my first impressions of it. In the year 1894 I accompanied my mother to the shopping centre of Vienna to see—with almost everyone else living in the city, or not too far from it—in a window the first factory-made shoes ever shown in the Monarchy. They came from the States. The crowd, to be true, impressed me more than the shoes. They looked just like other shoes, or perhaps not even as fine as those hand-made ones shown in the windows of good shoemakers. The price, to my astonishment, was actually the same for both kinds. Perhaps a year later, I saw the delivery van of a 'Bread Factory'. These two words were in large letters painted on it. That made a much deeper impression—perhaps because I did not see the reason why bread should not be produced in the customary way. I had never heard of anyone experiencing difficulty in getting as much bread as he liked. In the year 2000, maybe, the shoemakers and the bakers will be back. Don't you think so? I believe it. There will probably be only this solution—and human beings could happily be out of *some* of their self-imposed troubles.

Living in Vienna at this late hour of home culture were Brahms, Bruckner, Hugo Wolf and the young Gustav Mahler. It was the last flowering. By the way, Vienna does not quite deserve her reputation as the shrine, the Mecca of music. Vienna was simply for 150 years (or not even as long as that) the most attractive market for musical artists. Aristocracy was not yet disturbed, or checked, in its traditional functions. They had security (in contrast to moneymakers) and therefore no difficulty in observing the obligations of *noblesse*. These included, as you know, the support of art—though not necessarily the understanding or love of it. An obligation to love, or to understand, is, unfortunately, beyond conventions. Vienna as a city—Prague too, later also Budapest—had for her approximately 150 years of good fortune no serious competition. Within this term fall the three (or so) decades of

21

comparative dullness following the Napoleonic excitements. Paris, London and the larger cities in Germany were, compared with Vienna, without musical glamour, though certainly not without vitality.

This is not a course in history. My obviously inexact descriptions are meant only to show that it was neither the soil nor the soul of Austria which gave her a temporarily outstanding position in the musical world. It was also no merit, just a lucky constellation. This has in the meantime wandered to Berlin, London, New York. It might in the future emerge in quite unexpected places, or, better, be everywhere and permanent. Musicians could then stay where they are, or go anywhere. As it was, a young man like Beethoven had, in order to make a career, to leave his home town. Persons recognizing his power, as for instance Count Waldstein, advised him: 'You will not spend your life in this horrible provincial place, where you can have no chance. Come to Vienna. There you will also be stimulated by the variety of folklore: Hungarian, Bohemian, Polish, Italian, and so on. If those people cannot address each other in words—music they know, all of them.' Yet, Mozart, Beethoven and Schubert, to name only the giants, were very badly treated in Vienna. They were, so to say, the first freelance composers. Their creations, daring and transcendental, profound and exacting, met the same inimical reaction from the majority of their contemporaries, colleagues as well as patrons, which since music became autonomous seems invariably to be its fate in such cases. The exceptional, in this field, was and is inconvenient. Mozart was buried in a pauper's grave; Beethoven, though 'internationally' acknowledged as the greatest composer, was at times neglected, almost ignored; Schubert, considered a promising talent, died in poverty. Inertia, jealousy and vested interests continued in this campaign against the superior.

You have certainly all read biographies of these great men. I shall nevertheless give a few more piquant details of musical appreciation in Vienna. Because of a Rossini boom, Beethoven was nearly forgotten. He fell ill and the Royal Philharmonic Society in London had to send him money to buy medicine and pay a doctor. The difficulties involved in arranging for the first performance of the Ninth Symphony were almost insuperable. The first performance of the *Missa*

22

Solemnis was, I think, given in the year 1824 in St. Petersburg, by the private choir and orchestra of Prince Galitzin, in his house, and only much later in Germany and in Vienna. When Schubert died, all his belongings, including his manuscripts, were taxed by the authorities for, let me say, a few pounds— *all* his belongings, including manuscripts. Nobody, apparently, cared. I heard stories in Vienna (I am sure they are true) that grocers were wrapping up cheese in Schubert manuscripts. That reminds me that the manuscript of Bach's Six Brandenburg Concertos was sold, from a cart, for little more than a shilling, but that was not in Vienna. In the thirties Robert Schumann went to Vienna to search there for a posthumous great symphony by Schubert. He had heard rumours about its existence. He found it, fortunately. It is the C major Symphony. Well, all that, horrible as it is, might yet please us, who are always criticized for being, in matters of art, so far inferior to the past! Yet, we should not think that our undeniable improvement in some respects has made us superior. Our age has created new, probably more serious, conflicts.

To get a good picture of Vienna which, as I told you, administrated the riches made by the toiling of the people in the provinces, which were almost colonies, you should read some of the early nineteenth-century writers, for instance the remarkable poet Grillparzer, contemporary of Schubert and Beethoven. He spoke at the funeral of Beethoven—moving lines, on a very high level. Grillparzer had a position in the civil service in Austria; he was a bureaucrat. The civil servants in Austria seemed altogether dissatisfied people, probably because they had not enough work. It was the practice to divide one job among four men, representing the four most influential national groups of the fourteen included in the Empire. Thus the amount of complaints and opposition became easily reduced. Of course, there was not enough work for the four. Even in comparatively modern times, typewriters were not permitted in Austrian government offices—the work might have been done too fast. If one intended to open a store one had to get a licence. The licence was given, if evidence of the demand were shown. Who knows whether we shall not be forced one day to return to this patriarchal restriction of competition? The slow decline of Austria probably began around the year 1700, when Prussia entered the race for power. What is called Austria now is just a region, a name, by comparison with what it was. It is not really Austria. Austria was the Austrian-Hungarian monarchy. What remained after the First World War was a crippled being which could neither die nor live.

I have tried to communicate some of my recollections of the elegant, charming, luxurious Vienna of my boyhood, of the rather frivolous talkative defeatism and the great musicians living in the midst of this atmosphere of decay. I repeat, that I didn't feel too happy—even as a boy, though I had a very good time. I was extremely lucky not only in having the support of those three families I mentioned earlier (whom I have never seen and who have never heard me) but also because, being a pupil of Leschetizky and Mandiczewski, I became associated with two different musical departments. Through Leschetizky I was connected with the virtuoso tradition and introduced to Anton Rubinstein. Through Mandiczewski I made contact with the Brahms circle.

Anton Rubinstein, whose impressive appearance I well remember, was not as simple as Brahms seemed to be. Rubinstein looked and behaved like an international celebrity, though he was not at all showy. He was sweet to me. In the home of Albert Gutmann, the music seller, publisher and concert agent, and in Leschetizky's as well, Rubinstein asked me to sit on his knee while he was playing a game of cards. I heard him play only once, his own compositions. The impression was probably not overwhelming, for it never came back to my memory. I also heard Brahms play, the piano part of his G minor quartet. This impressed me immensely and is still in my memory. It was, naturally, the great music which held and shook me, but also the creative vitality and wonderful carefreeness with which he played. This was to me the real grand style.

In the year 1893, when I was eleven years old, Brahms's Opus 119 was published: three intermezzi and one rhapsody for piano. Since Leschetizky permitted me to choose the music I would bring to a lesson, I got hold of these brand new Brahms pieces, prepared them, and went to my lesson. They were still wet from the printing press, so to say. Leschetizky was furious with me. I shall never forget this, for it hurt me deeply. He made a parody of the first piece—cheapened and vulgarized it. Then, getting more and more angry, he must have worked himself into the ridiculous obsession that I, a child of eleven, had chosen this music with the malicious intent to criticize, to deride him—him, my revered and feared master. You can imagine how frightened and depressed I must have felt by this outburst. Finally, he told me to go and only after three months was I admitted again. Someone convinced him eventually of the absurdity of his suspicion and the indubitableness of my innocence. After that he encouraged me to play as much Brahms as I wanted, and though often rather strict, never again was hard with me. By the way, it might interest you that never did any of my music teachers ask me to pay for my lessons. They all taught me gratis. It was just taken for granted. It was, to my memory, never mentioned.

When I came to Vienna, I had a tutor for general education. I don't remember him, or what he taught me, or any book I had to learn from. When I was ten, someone advised my mother that I might get into difficulties if I was not sent to a public, ordinary school. Intimidated, she put me into a school. I registered at a high school. I passed somehow and was in. I remember only the building and classroom and one of the teachers—even his name. He was a very kind person. I stayed in that school for four or five months. The report I got was not bad. Only in mathematics I seemed to have failed completely. I studied some Latin, much too little to be of any use or value. I was taken out of this school again: it was the first and last I have ever attended. The authorities did not notice my absenteeism and never bothered me. My memories of this experience of normal education are utterly vague, nebulous, neither pleasant nor unpleasant. I had no contact with other boys. I had no friends there because my friends were the Leschetizky pupils, all much older. The only friend my age was another Leschetizky pupil, an extremely charming and talented little girl, who came to America after Hitler marched into Vienna. She was not Jewish, but she could not bear the change. She came here, not in good health, and died in Boston a few years ago. She was a most delicate artist. Her public career was only a local one. Her music was tender, pure, intimate.

My rival at Leschetizky's was a youth three or four years older than I. To him Leschetizky could have said: 'You will never be a musician; you are a pianist.' His name was Mark Hambourg. He really had elemental qualities. His thunderous octaves, incomparable ones, had real fire, were not mechanical. He made a big career, was a very popular virtuoso. He retired many years ago. His style fitted a young man. If, getting older, one remains as one has been as a youth, the effect will not be to appear young but out of date—which sounds like a paradox.

Ossip Gabrilowitsch and Ignaz Friedman were co-students of mine at Leschetizky's, though they came to him several years later than I. I was also acquainted with Samuel Clemens's (Mark Twain's) daughters, Clara and her sister. Clara later married Gabrilowitsch. I remember very distinctly several tea parties at Mark Twain's apartment in the Hotel Metropole in Vienna. His appearance was unforgettably striking. I don't remember that he ever spoke to me.

I began composing at the same time I started playing the piano. My studies with Mandiczewski did not go further than the first elements of counterpoint. I never worked with a teacher on form or orchestration. The only thing which I really have 'learned' in my life was piano-playing. After my one year with Madame Essipoff, I occasionally had instruction from other Leschetizky assistants—five or six of them. They differed in pianistic functions as much as one can differ, and were also not at all unanimous in their approach to music. Each, of course, called his conception the true Leschetizky method. Several published books on it. If a student were to read all these books he would get a considerable demonstration of confusion. What I have learned from Leschetizky himself, I am unable to say, to estimate, to appreciate. He succeeded in releasing all the vitality and *élan* and sense of beauty a student had in his nature, and would not tolerate any deviation or violation of what he felt to be truthfulness of expression. As you see, all this devotion, seriousness, care and honesty is compatible with the virtuoso type represented by him. Why we, today, have in general a less flattering opinion of the virtuoso is a problem I recommend you to think about, again and again.

Leschetizky's limitations showed in his comparative indifference to, or even dislike of, the kind of music in which the 'personal' becomes just an ingredient of the universal. He had, for instance, not much use, or love, or curiosity, for the second half of Beethoven's production. The more glory the music itself emanates, the less it leaves for the performer. It was such transcending music which he seemed to evade, by instinct.

During my educational phase in Vienna until 1899, I never heard, in this most musical city on earth, and in the midst of musicians, of the existence of the twenty-eight Concertos by Mozart, or Beethoven's Opus 106 or the Diabelli Variations, or Bach's Goldberg Variations, etc. The G major Concerto by Beethoven was generally labelled, among musicians, as the 'ladies' ' concerto. Hardly any of the great pianists ever played it. The C minor was only played in conservatories by the lower grades and the C major Concerto only by the debutantes. The B flat major Concerto was simply unknown. Many of Schubert's songs and Verdi's operas were considered so trivial that anyone who pretended to have an understanding of music would have degraded himself if he had confessed to enthusiasm and respect for them. Schubert's Impromptus for piano were chiefly the pastime of governesses. Some of his finest songs had been shifted to the suburbs, arranged for male choruses. We, of course, have in the meantime made gigantic progress. The hurdy-gurdy's repertoire of 'classical' bits has reached operettas and films: visible biographies of geniuses, with greater quantities of their creations performed than the barrel organ could manage. And don't forget the juke boxes.

3

MY mother and sisters left Vienna in '92 or '93 (I am not quite sure which) and went back to the cleaner of the twin cities near my birthplace. They went to join my father whose business kept him there. I was handed over to some strangers and became a kind of lodger. After three years, my entire family came back to Vienna. My father died there in 1927, and in 1942 my mother, at the age of eighty-four, was taken away by the Nazis and never heard of again. My sisters escaped to the United States.

During the three years of my family's absence from Vienna, I had two sets of lodgings. The first was solid and unattractive, the second noisy and exciting. In the second there were three sons older than I and one daughter who was younger. The three sons went to the university. In their free time they either practised sabre duels in the hallway or gobble-competition exercises in the dining-room. The object of the latter was to empty a big jug of beer in one quick gulp. This was my first introduction to academic life.

In my first lodgings, with the comparatively dull people, I had a tutor I did not like very much. Perhaps because he was untidy. He was a medical student, very learned and scholarly, and also deeply interested in music. When decades later I met him again he was a prominent functionary in the administration of the City of Vienna, in charge of art supply to labour. My next tutor—the last in my life, because after I was fourteen I did not have any more instruction—was one of the three militant students in my second lodgings. He too was a medical student. I don't remember having learned much either from the scholar or the fighter. They probably taught me a lot, and if I did not learn much it was my own fault.

Until my thirteenth year I had, as I have already mentioned, lessons not only with Leschetizky, but also with an assistant of his. I was expected to be at the piano for at least three hours every day. That was, I see now, a moderate demand. Now-

28

adays, students are asked to spend at least six hours at their instrument. I, more often than not, did less than my three. What did I do the rest of the time? I had four teachers—the two piano teachers, my tutor, and the teacher in theory. I used to walk to my music lessons. I didn't like the tram and it was cheaper to walk; I was also fond, and still am, of walking. Thus I walked even if it took hours. That is the way I spent much time.

Occasionally, I went to the Imperial Opera or to the Imperial Playhouse. That normally took eight hours. I used to be there at three o'clock and queue up until seven, when the gates were opened; then I rushed up four flights of stairs in a wild race to be one of the first to secure a seat in the gallery. One had a very good time during these queueing hours. Everyone had sandwiches in his pocket, and lively conversations ranging from gossip and jokes to opinions and theories went on as uninterruptedly as water flows in a river. There were, of course, many, mostly young, musicians. Among them often Arnold Schönberg, he, too, racing up the stairs. The older people, naturally, could not always keep pace. One did not see or hear too well, in the gallery. Yet I have rarely enjoyed theatrical performances as much as then. That is another way I spent my time.

I said I had no contact with other children. I hardly ever received any presents, but please don't pity me. It was an extremely happy youth. I was contented, rather fat—I still am —and working leisurely. I think I belong to the lazy type of man. I am still lazy. I have often struggled to overcome my laziness: at times I hated to be lazy, but eventually I accepted this innate defect, comforting myself with the illusion, or belief, that it enabled me to be more alert in the intervals between the spells of, let me call it euphemistically, meditation. Without a regular occupation, with no talent for systematic work, but fairly quick perceptions and a curious mind, a person might easily indulge in the virtues of inertia—which reminds me of Nietzsche's comforting aphorism: 'Idleness is the beginning of all philosophy; why, is it conceivable that philosophy could be a vice?' This, you understand, refers ironically to the proverb: 'Idleness is the beginning of all vices.' Neither the aphorism nor the proverb seem to me the full truth. Yet, as I am, I prefer the Nietzsche version. It is more flattering. And, in this connection, I suggest one admit the term 'alertia' to the vocabulary.

Vienna's last performance of brilliance and charm presented, on the surface, very lively activities in the intellectual sphere as well as in other rather more exacting fields. These activities were, however, lacking in real strength, seriousness and sincerity. At their best they revealed lucidly the many facets of the cherished decadence of the Viennese. It was a fate, not a fault. They sensed that fate, as I have said already.

Just at the door of the *fin de siècle* the City of Vienna was ruled for several years by an officially anti-Semetic régime. Her mayor, the well-known Dr Karl Lueger, was the undisputed leader, or better, misleader, against the poor Jews. Compared with recent events, the Lueger brand of anti-Semitism was very, very mild, although at that time it seemed very wild. I personally did not suffer or notice much of that ugly régime, except that for a long time I retained a certain uneasiness in lonely streets after dark. Encouraged by Lueger, it was a favourite sport of patriotic male adolescents to bully and beat, with a jolly brutality, children whom they thought to be Jewish. I was molested only once, and I am not sure whether the motive for the attack was Austrianism or mere drunkenness on the part of a few lads. Though a very happy child in general those days, I learned the meaning of fear.

I was entirely independent, never regimented. Since I did not go to school, it was of no consequence if I failed in my work. With the one exception I mentioned, I was never examined, and thus I was spared the stigma of not having passed. I was, to be true, also deprived of being praised officially. I did not have to live to a schedule. Even my music lessons were not regular. Arriving at a given hour at Leschetizky's, I had generally to wait two hours before my lesson began. The lesson always lasted at least another two hours—thus some more of my time was consumed. There was still a surplus for which I really cannot account.

By and by I became acquainted with more and more people —very dear people, the same type of persons, or families, whom I have met or established contact with all my life. It must have been my destiny which directed me to such relationships. These people were usually moderately wealthy, always very cultured and interested in all spiritual movements and values, but hardly ever mentioned in newspapers. They were not in the 'public eye'. There were, needless to say, a few exceptions to this. Whether I have evaded the publicized ones, or they me, is an open question.

These friends of mine treated me as a member of their families and always made me participate in the gatherings of the grown-ups. Some of them had children of my age. These children obviously hated me, for good reasons. When I arrived for a dinner party given by their parents it was already their bedtime, or else they had to learn what they were expected to know in school the next morning. No wonder they were jealous, but how could I help them? I remember an extremely embarrassing scene illustrating this bitterness. A boy of my own age who had to go to school the next morning was presented before dinner to his parents' guests. He was allowed to shake hands. He did this perfectly politely. Then he was given some ice-cream to eat, the only part he was allowed, so far as I know, of the excellent menu of many courses that afterwards we were offered. After he had spoken to everybody but me, he suddenly jumped at my throat, a second before the door to the dining-room opened, slapped my face with a smack and great *bravura* and disappeared rapidly. He must have had this prank planned for some time. I, of course, appeared as blasé and as composed as I could afford to be, and tried to take it with a smile. I have not forgotten it. This boy who took his revenge on me approached me, after his parents had died, many years later, in the friendliest manner. Now we were both eligible for the same festivities. The old reason for his enmity was no more.

I also had the good luck to meet the most promising young poets, writers and painters, and some of the already established ones. Violent arguments were fashionable at that time between the conservatives and the progressives, although the violence was not too convincing, maybe not even genuine. It seemed rather affected. The Viennese did not catch fire from the subjects of the controversies: they caught it from their own enthusiasm. They were afraid of even a small amount of sobriety.

I remember two architects, then famous and vehemently criticized for their war on beauty, who were pioneers in the creation and development of much that is now commonplace. I remember also a number of painters and sculptors and designers who deserted the camp of the traditionalists and organized a progressive group which they named the 'Vienna

Secession'. The poster of their first exhibition, a very pleasant and harmless one, aroused a storm of indignation. The whole town acted as if insulted. The same wild despair was noisily expressed when a very noble and well-proportioned edifice was finished—built by one of these revolutionary architects. The general cry was for tearing it down at once. Twenty years later it was shown with pride as evidence of the spirit of Vienna.

Karl Kraus—a sharp-tongued pamphletist in a weekly called *The Torch*, for which only he himself wrote—exposed in Savonarolesque sermons what he thought to be the moral and spiritual debasement of Vienna. He had a strong influence on gifted young people, but none on the conditions he wanted to crush by his words. The feeling of decadence was so strong that the best intellects began to distrust the honesty of their own impulses and the validity of the values they believed in. They tried several escapes. Primitivity was the salvation. Since it was denied to themselves to be primitive and simple, they turned to the child and the so-called savage. With them at least the honesty was not in doubt. This is my own interpretation of the rather sudden infatuation with the exotic after the esoteric, and with purity after the *raffinement*. Maybe this phase was just the transition from decadence via nature to Hollywood. The worship of the child was the transition to its new economic position as an important customer. Babies are, of course, the ideal customers: they want everything they see.

Young and old, just before the turn to primitivity, discussed endlessly contemporaries like Tolstoy, Nietzsche, Dostoevsky, Ibsen and others. Their works were then best-sellers. I saw the Vienna début of Eleonora Duse. I was present at the Vienna début of Yvette Guilbert, the famous French *diseuse,* although I, as a boy of fifteen, had no business to be there. With no school in the morning I could stay at nightly debates as long as they lasted. They ranged from positivism to occultism—with everything in between. The flavour of decadence was never missing. This explains my impulse (enhanced by the advice of some friends) to go westwards, to Germany. The Germans were immensely, though rather secretly, respected and admired by the Viennese, with a kind of condescending awe. They considered them barbaric and boorish in comparison with the beauty, elegance and culture of the Viennese, with their charming (though empty) politeness—in the upper classes—and their soft speech. Nevertheless, a niggling inferiority complex slightly disturbed their self-esteem.

Let me, for a moment return to my own contributions to Viennese culture, before I left for Berlin. I had much contact with Leschetizky pupils coming from all corners of the earth. I had almost no competition, not because of my qualifications, but because there was simply no boy of my age engaged in the same work. Even with the rival I mentioned earlier there was no real competition, for he was primarily a pianist, and I a musician. We played a different type of repertoire. The two prodigies I spoke of at the beginning no longer had any publicity.

In the meantime, my parents came back to Vienna. I stayed with them for my last three or four years there. I also started teaching and earned a little money to supplement the still-continued support of my patrons. My pupils were all older than I. Even Leschetizky, when I was fourteen, occasionally sent me some of his pupils, for consultation, not for lessons. He said: 'Go to Schnabel, and look through this piece with him,' which honoured and flattered me very much and, very welcome, improved my financial status as well.

One of the families in Vienna whom I knew well had relatives in Berlin who were much interested in art. One day they surprised me with the announcement that their brother had suggested I should come to Berlin and stay with him as long as I liked. I accepted this invitation with great satisfaction, curiosity and hopes. My only regret was to be separated, and at such a distance, from a girl-friend—as they are named here.

One day in the spring of 1898—I think it was May—I took a train for Berlin. I must have travelled for sixteen hours. When I arrived, there was no one at the station to meet me. I took, as advised, an open horse-drawn coach and told the driver to take me to the address I had been given. The streets in Berlin were very pretty at that time of the year; the chestnut trees were in bloom along the canal. I was strongly impressed. After Vienna, the distances seemed immense. (The horse didn't move very fast either.) Two things struck me before I had spoken to any German, except the porter and cab driver. First, I saw signs on all apartment houses: *Aufgang nur für Herrschaften*. This is almost untranslatable. The closest would be: 'Entrance [actually 'ascent'] for Masters only.' Later on I found out—what goes without saying—that the quarters of the lower classes posted no such warnings. It was, however, not the *fact* of having two staircases in a house, it was the way in which this practical device was indicated, which was so new and startling to me. This seemed so very different from easy-going, leisurely, aristocratic, democratic Vienna. There is such a thing as a democracy of aristocracy, and in Vienna, if a man did not talk too much about his rights, he had quite a good life. The second shock I received from another sign, this on restaurants. It said: *Weinzwang,* which means: 'Wine compulsory.' These were two ineradicable impressions.

I approached my address, but the street to which I was going was under repair and closed to all vehicles. I did not know what to do. I had several bags. I thought, 'This is horrible. They should have done something about it.' Just then I saw a very nicely dressed chambermaid approaching me to ask whether I was Mr Schnabel. She had been sent to the corner where they thought I would stop. She helped me with the bags and led me to my destination. The name of my host was Cassirer. They were very prosperous, in the lumber business, I think, although they never mentioned that. All their children and grandchildren later played more or less important parts in German intellectual life. One son, Ernst, became a highly reputed philosopher. He died in New York not long ago. From Hamburg University, where because of Hitler he could not stay, he went to Gothenburg, in Sweden, then to Oxford, finally to Yale and Columbia. His cousin was an internationally known art dealer and one of the first and most efficient promoters of the French Impressionists and the generation of artists following them. A man who helped launch Manet, Cézanne, Van Gogh, Picasso, and so on.

It was very good for me to come into such a family. There were five brothers with lots of children and I had a splendid time. They rarely asked me to play for them. I had no work to do at all, but apparently my host, Mr Eduard Cassirer, did not quite approve of my conduct. I was sixteen then, grown-up—by my own judgement. I stayed up late and slept until noon. Perhaps I even started to flirt with his daughter. Anyway, one day I received a note from him saying that my room was needed for a relative who had just announced that he was coming to Berlin. In other words, I was given notice. However, one of my host's brothers was so indignant at this lack of understanding for a young man of talent that he decided to make it up to me. He said: 'Now Schnabel, don't worry. Go to any hotel you want and I will pay for everything.' So I chose a hotel where a close friend of mine, a young lady from Vienna, had just arrived, and I still don't know whether Mr Cassirer ever guessed the reason for my choice.

My first stay in Berlin was, you can easily understand, a thoroughly pleasant experience and also gave my career a promising push. I had been introduced to several persons familiar with the musical world. They encouraged me to come back to Berlin the following winter for a début recital.

When I returned to Vienna, they greeted me as if I had travelled around the world. I went to see Leschetizky. He also treated me now as one who was fully fledged. I was no longer the pupil but a guest and friend; he asked me to play *for* his pupils. This was, in reality, no change of practice, for during the whole time I was with him as a pupil I used to play in every 'class', as the weekly gatherings of all his pupils were called. The only difference between my role as a guest and my function as a student was that now the master did not interrupt and criticize me—though there was certainly sufficient reason to do so.

Among my friends in Vienna were some who used to invite me to spend the summer with them—mostly in the mountains. I was thus early acquainted with the Alps. Every Viennese is —the mountains (not very high ones) look into Vienna. Leschetizky and many of my friends lived in suburbs close to these mountains. My lifelong passion for mountaineering and hiking dates from pre-Vienna days, for my birthplace was also surrounded by hills not unlike those adorning Vienna. It is not too easy in America to satisfy this passion. Of all human beings the most ignored in the States seems to be he who walks out of love, just for the joy in walking. I nevertheless tried. The four summers I spent in New Mexico were most enjoyable though very different from my European experiences. Cattle, horses and wood-cutters were responsible for trails which took weeks to discover. And in four summers of walking in the woods there, every day for at least eight miles, I never met a single soul. True, it was a remote and unknown place, and no sightseers, motorists or tourists ever approached it. Yet, there were villages and one city close to them. I went another summer to Colorado's very, very beautiful mountains, woods and lakes. There were many people around but the majority of them were on horseback—a great disadvantage to a wanderer. The smell, the dust, the stopping to let the riders pass—I did not go back. I am too old and too lazy for adjustment of this kind.

I have now come to the end of the Austrian, the first section of this report. My thirty-three years' stay in Germany will form the second. During all these thirty-three years I retained, by the way, my Austrian citizenship.

After my début recital in Berlin I went once more, for the summer, back to Vienna. In the autumn of the same year I returned to Germany, this time for good. For my second visit to Berlin, that which included my début recital, I arrived equipped with several letters of introduction to a few more individuals interested in art and to a few others active in promoting it. With most of these people, the contacts then established lasted as long as permitted by life—or until forced by Hitler to be interrupted. Each of them was kind and generous. Even Mr Cassirer who once, in fully justified indignation, had asked me to leave.

My début recital in Berlin was of course given in the smallest hall. It was under the management of Hermann Wolff, at that time the ruling impresario in Germany, especially in the realm of concerts. He was not the type of manager we know now in the States. He was, before turning to music, professionally successful in some other business. A passionate music fan and quite remarkable in his own domestic music supply, he desired to become an insider, to devote himself entirely to music and musicians. He preferred the company of musicians to any other company and found that the best chance to establish closer and permanent contact with them was to become their representative in business matters. He abandoned his uninteresting branch of business and approached his favourite musicians: Liszt, Wagner, Brahms, Tchaikovsky, Joachim, Hans von Bülow, Anton Rubinstein, Sarasate, Patti, etc.—composers, teachers, performers (not yet lecturers), offered them his services, and started. He died years before the First World War. His wish for association with music and musicians had, for decades, been fulfilled. His widow continued in his spirit, which with the enormous expansion of the music market was no easy task. Intimacy and *noblesse* in public life were—I have already pointed several times to their fate—reduced to inconspicuousness—though, by no means, killed. Hitler also stopped the Wolff agency. Wolff's son, Werner, formerly successful conductor of the Opera in Hamburg, lives now, with his wife, an opera-singer, in Chattanooga, Tennessee. They try, and I hear with astonishing results, to give music there a 'lift'. Pioneer work. His precious collection of letters written to his father by practically all the great musicians of half a century is a treasure to be envied.

Hermann Wolff was somewhat curt, even sour, in his attitude towards me, the young man from Vienna. Yet, he was never unkind or unjust. The main thing was that without any words or fuss he started to help my public career. Maybe his severity had an educational purpose. He did not ask me to provide photos, or to see the Press. Nothing of that kind. Our present standard of publicity was still far away, at least in Germany. I had to play; that was all.

At my first recital I played a Schubert sonata. This was hardly ever done at that time, or before. I did not do it to be different, but simply because I loved it—I had my best success with it. It was not at all as boring as its reputation made one expect it to be. Some reviews were very favourable. Others advised me to change my occupation. One recommended I should apply for a teacher's position at the Institute for African drum languages (*Trommelsprache*). I did not change my occupation; I even got engagements (through Hermann Wolff, and without publicity). From the day of my recital on, I earned my living, quite alone. It was not exactly opulent. In the first years of my career, when autumn arrived, I had not a penny left. I had eaten up everything, and if no new engagements were in sight, I naturally felt uneasy, impatient, pessimistic even. I had, however, always access to the help of some friends. One of my first engagements was at Potsdam. I played a concert with a military band. It was horrible. My fee was thirty shillings. You see, I really started at the bottom. Nowadays cadets are presented in generals' uniforms, novices urged to appear, as Venus appeared, perfect and immortal—'stars' at first appearance! This does much harm.

4

BEFORE I went to Germany for good I had composed a few pieces, some of which were performed in Vienna. One day Leschetizky invited his pupils to participate in a composer's contest, for piano pieces. As was usual, every contestant had to post his composition to the jury in an envelope inscribed with a motto, enclosing another envelope containing his name and inscribed with the same motto. Only when a composition was admitted to the final test (a performance by the respective authors, at which all Leschetizky's pupils and several guests of rank would by vote choose the three winners) was the envelope containing the composer's name opened. One of the judges told me—much later—of the surprise and amusement he and his colleagues felt when of the small number of accepted pieces *three* (all I had sent in) turned out to be mine. They were also startled by the selection of my mottos. For a youth of my age—fourteen—they seemed very unusual. One I remember—it was set to the piece which won the first prize: four lines by Richard Dehmel, a young poet then considered a most promising genius. They said—in verse and rhyme, of course—that only when man has been weaned from all that is purposeful, and does not know anything but his impulses, will the divine essence of enraptured folly and great love be revealed to him.

One of the judges was a Viennese composer, internationally known for his piquant, unpretentious and carefully written salon music. He gave me an introduction to Mr Simrock, his publisher in Berlin. The Simrock publishing firm was established in the eighteenth century and its noble record belongs to the history of music. One of my first acts in Berlin was to see Mr Simrock, a man with a long white beard. He was fairly courteous, but rather cool and I felt a bit nervous. None of my music had been printed before. He said: 'Mr S. has told me about your work. Now let me see the pieces of which he speaks.' I handed him the music and after a glance at the pieces he asked me to come back in a week. I came back, to learn that they had been accepted for publication. But their original title was not acceptable. Instead of 'Three piano pieces' as I had (arrogantly) called them, they were named:

(1) *Douce tristesse, Reverie.*
(2) *Diabolique, Scherzo.*
(3) *Valse mignonne.*

I did not protest. After all, what's in a name? If you are interested, perhaps you can find these pieces in some library or the basement of a music store. They would surely be more popular than most of the works I produced later on, for they have a certain similarity to one successful type of contemporary music.

In Berlin, my manager, Hermann Wolff, quickly got engagements for me. One of them was a tour in Norway. I had to play at fifteen concerts there. It was the first time I had either seen or crossed the sea—and it was quite an experience, what with the winter, a small freighter and high seas. The star on this tour was a then already famous violin virtuoso (I was merely the accompanist). We played sonatas, I also played some solos—Mr Wolff had insisted on this—and at the end the star performed musical fireworks, with the piano as background. I had also one performance with an orchestra, playing Beethoven's Fourth Concerto. I remember this occasion chiefly because in one paper I was criticized for having reduced a lion to a well-trimmed poodle.

When I first met the great star, I did not believe my eyes. He did not look like an artist: his appearance was indicative rather of a circus director or an animal trainer. He was very fashionably dressed, with the underlined elegance displayed in shop windows.

Norway—to which later I often returned and always with enthusiasm—did not impress me on this first acquaintance. It seemed to me much more provincial even than Austria, compared with Germany, my latest yardstick. One feature of this tour had, however, a lasting effect on me. My violin virtuoso taught me to play poker, two-handed. I learned it quickly—it does not take long. After my short apprenticeship we devoted ourselves to this noble pastime during all the many hours we spent in trains, going from concert to concert. Experts told me later that two-handed poker counts among the surest and lowest ways of catching a mug. No wonder, then, that I lost almost my entire fee. It was undoubtedly not very chivalrous of a man near his forties to teach a seventeen-year-old comrade such a game. Yet, I have to be grateful to him: by initiating it, he also ended my connection with poker, which, by the way, even at the outset I thought silly and boring. The star proved a good teacher and was probably very amused. I returned to Berlin, saw Mr Wolff and reported my mishap and the empty state of my pockets. He got terribly angry with me, a poor simpleton. He was perhaps disappointed in my talent for card-playing.

Then I had some more concerts in Germany—several with orchestras. The only orchestra I had heard before I went to Germany was the Vienna Opera Orchestra, identical with the Vienna Philharmonic. The Vienna Orchestra of the Imperial Opera, as well as all the big Royal, Ducal, State or municipal Opera Houses in Germany, employed a double set of players, up to perhaps two hundred pieces, engaged in operatic and symphonic work. Afternoon performances were unknown. Since orchestras were not overworked, high quality was guaranteed on all occasions.

The musicians in Vienna and Germany were, so to say, court —state—or city owned. Their contracts ran for life. Would you say they were slaves? With short contracts, competition, union rules, dependence on private sponsors, in one word: insecurity, orchestral performances become alarmingly expensive. Art must suffer if it is too deeply involved in financial difficulties. It might interest you to know that the Vienna Orchestra in the 'nineties gave only ten regular subscription concerts and one pension fund concert in a season. The regular concerts were on Sunday mornings.

The clientele for symphonic music was very limited, comprising at the most a few thousand people. As everywhere, this number increased steadily during the following decades. In the 1790s even a few thousand would have seemed Utopian. Jean Paul, a German writer, reported on his first visit to Leipzig attending a concert there, which had attracted an 'enormous crowd, perhaps a hundred people'. The Berlin audience, when I arrived there, was probably twice as large as that in Vienna (though in relation to the population practically the same).

The orchestras in the smaller German cities where I had my

40

first engagements naturally sounded different from the Vienna Philharmonic. Subtlety, inspiration and brilliance were not the outstanding features of these bodies. The conductors were, like their orchestras, in most cases serving both opera and concert. They also had, as a rule, a life job, employed by kings, dukes, princes, states, cities (until 1918 Germany continued to have many courts). It was usually an association of music lovers who were in charge of concert work, hiring the orchestras from their respective bosses.

The Berlin Philharmonic did no opera work. It was exclusively a concert-performing body—as American orchestras are. London and Paris each had several concert orchestras. All these organizations were self-contained, operated on a cooperative basis. In Berlin a subsidy was eventually granted by the city, on condition that special concerts were presented to labour and student groups. London and Paris orchestras adhered—Paris still does—to the so-called Deputy system. By this system each member is allowed to send to rehearsals and performances a substitute. Whether the chosen substitute also has the right, having attended one rehearsal, to send another substitute to the next—and so on—I don't know. You can easily imagine the consequences of so much *laissez faire*. Instead of an ensemble one might get just an assembly. I myself was once involved in troubles caused by these practices. It was in London. The 'incident' got publicized and helped to accelerate the elimination of this anomaly. I was sorry to hear that it has been revived recently, economic conditions being responsible, as they were before.

In contrast to the modest quality of the German provincial orchestras and their conductors of whom many, especially the older ones, were either *routiniers* or pathetic—or even *routiniers and* pathetic—the audiences were of the highest quality, better than in Vienna, with her talented Philistines—an unhealthy amalgam—and their preconceived, pretentious value-judgements, their worship of traditions simply because they were traditions, their enthusiasm for fashions simply because they were fashions—in one phrase, their lazy superiority complex.

The German audiences in the medium-sized towns were composed of people who loved music unselfishly. They knew most of the music they went to hear at concerts. They knew it very well. There was probably not one in these audiences who was not involved, actively or passively, in home-made music—and without any fuss made about it. It was part of family life, old and young co-operating. The children were present and listened. Public concerts especially for children did not yet exist: youngsters deeply attracted to music simply attended some concerts. Last winter, when I was playing at one of the largest American colleges, a girl student asked me how the young people's attitude to art music in her country compared with that of a corresponding group in pre-Hitler Germany. I said that it did not compare at all. Schools, colleges and universities in Germany did not present 'star courses' to their students. Musical performances at public, elementary schools had just been initiated and the children's reactions, written down or expressed in drawings, were put on file. I saw some very interesting examples of these, gathered chiefly from proletarian districts, where, naturally, home-music was not practised. The relation to music by children of the middle and upper classes was established by home culture and traditions. And, as I said before, those to whom music meant most became the future audience. They were then already familiar with much of the concert repertoire, or even with operas, and particularly interested in all that was new to them. They were not disappointed by mediocre performances, for, after all, mass production of the supreme achievements is still denied by Providence, the so far only known supplier of genius, and mechanical reproduction had not yet reached all corners of the globe.

Germany had an astonishing number of theatres, many of them offering plays and operas. The orchestras employed there, as I have already told you, also played at concerts. Each of the towns thus equipped had an amateur mixed chorus. And, I have to bore you with repeating this all-important fact, home-music had not yet completely surrendered to modern trends. The theatres, with a season lasting nine or ten months were, because of the small number of their potential patrons, compelled to have a very comprehensive repertoire. Seventy different works each season were, I estimate, not unusual. (Here we may see a parallel to the present-day cinemas.) And it was still a time when the 'what' came before the 'how' and 'who' and 'how much'. I, by the way, cannot ascribe to the conception of the 'better' being the enemy of the 'good'. The imagined 'best' is, I think, the greatest incentive of any effort towards it. Humility is more productive than conceit, be it in the giver or the taker.

My short description of the normal musical situation in Germany in the first decades of our century is intended to point to the important fact that when audiences are superior to performers it is by no means harmful to art. On the other hand the cry for 'first class' services only may contain some dangers for it.

At my début recitals in Munich and Leipzig I played the same programme, including works by Brahms and Schubert. The morning after, I was naturally impatient to learn from the papers whether I was good, mediocre, bad, or all three by turns. By the way, it was not until the second half of my career that my interest in the printed reaction subsided. It was then clear to me that reviews are addressed to the customer, not the salesman, that I have only exceptionally learned anything by reading them, and that their stock exchange quotation function did not affect me any longer, for I had, in the meantime, made a name, been accepted as a trade-mark. Some technical, concrete criticism has, I repeat, helped me occasionally. If, for instance, I was told of my inclination to hesitate before first beats, to rush and blur figurations, to pound the bass, etc., I knew what to try to avoid. If, however, I was blamed for not having grasped the spirit of a work or a period, for having sinned against this or that style, for having failed to create the atmosphere of a moonlight night, or a lover's despair, of innocence and drama, for being hot, cold or tepid, I was always at a loss what to do.

My Leipzig début brought me Press approval of my Brahms and disapproval of my Schubert interpretation. For the 'austere, nordic bleakness and heavy seriousness' of Brahms's music (this was the official stigma fixed on his work) I was said to be naturally equipped, chiefly by my firm and rigid rhythm. To Schubert's colourful, lilting, charming, sweet and open music I was said to have no access. Three days later in Munich I read the exact opposite of the Leipzig verdict. There I was entirely the Viennese, southern type, gaily or sentimentally wandering in the woods, along brooks, with the birds singing. In both cities I retained these initial labels: cerebral for Leipzig, sensuous for Munich—until Hitler's advent in 1933. I wonder whether they would still react the same way if I were to go there now.

Shortly after I arrived in Berlin, one of the leading critics there invited me to see him. He was, by the way, a brother-in-law of Gerhart Hauptmann, then the most celebrated young playwright in Germany. At our first meeting I learned that this critic had two other activities in addition to his journalism: vocal teaching the one, advising a music publisher the other. He told me all this very modestly, almost shyly. The publishing firm he worked for had just been established, under the name of The Three Lilies. He knew, probably through the three piano pieces published by Simrock, of my attempts in composition and offered me a contract. His firm printed a score of songs of mine and another set of three piano pieces. The title pages were, on his suggestion, designed by a young and very successful Hungarian architect. I was happy and grateful. The Three Lilies were not, however, fitted for commercial competition and died, after a few years of tender life, in their sleep. I have no idea, for I never investigated, where the 'stock' of this delicate enterprise was buried. There must have been a good number of unsold copies of my opuses, hidden somewhere. By now they are presumably ashes.

Only two or three years after I took up residence in Berlin I started a chamber music ensemble—a trio. The violinist was at that time Joachim's best pupil; the 'cellist, a Dutchman, concert-master with Nikisch's Berlin Philharmonic Orchestra, was considerably older than we two.

The Berlin *Philharmonie*, an adapted roller-skating rink, comprised at that time three halls. Our chamber music concerts were given in the so-called Oberlicht Hall—originally meant to be just a foyer. The prices of admission were low—what one internationally terms 'popular prices'—yet the audiences were composed of music lovers able and used to paying also 'unpopular' ones. They sat at tables and were allowed to order beer or mineral water, but not food. There was, nevertheless, no disturbance or noise, but always perfect silence and attention during the performances. Actually, only very few of our listeners took the chance of satisfying physical and spiritual thirst simultaneously. This fact soon led to the abandonment of the pessimistic belief that beer might enhance the attractiveness of music. The tables were removed, the seats multiplied, the takings improved. Manager and music-lover were equally benefited by separating beer from art.

Our concerts, given on subscription under the auspices,

naturally, of Hermann Wolff, were from the outset a genuine success. We presented a wide repertoire of chamber music works with piano, in all combinations of instruments; we had singers as guest performers; we very often played contemporary works. With my career as a 'roving mount-a-platform' developing rapidly, I had, after, I think, three seasons, to give up this dear enterprise. Yet, my apparently innate attachment to ensemble playing made me soon return to it. Carl Flesch became and remained for two decades my partner. Shortly after we started playing sonatas together, the young Belgian 'cellist, Jean Gérardy, joined us. We became a trio—travelled together and had a good time. The outbreak of the First World War stopped our happy co-operation. Gérardy, the Belgian, of course, did not stay in Germany. He stayed on Belgian soil, died there much too early, still a very young man. Flesch and I asked Hugo Becker, a famous German 'cellist, to take Gérardy's place in our trio. He accepted, and our collaboration lasted for many years.

5

In my last talk I told you about the first period of my time in Germany. It was as if I had left not only Vienna, but the nineteenth century behind me as well when I came to Berlin. It was very, very different from Vienna.

I have talked a lot about the atmosphere in Vienna, of jesting defeatism and precious, playful morbidity in the 'nineties, of her gradual decay. Now, Berlin seemed quite the opposite. There was the atmosphere of energy, of growing confidence, activity, alertness, and while in Vienna the character of public life was still dominated by a rather effete aristocracy, in Berlin the self-made man marked the character of his city.

Anyhow, Vienna and Berlin should not be compared. Vienna was historically a centre. The aristocracy, the big landowners in Bohemia, Hungary, Croatia, Poland and so on, lived in Vienna and only rested on their estates. Some had palatial residences also in Prague, Budapest and Cracow, but they didn't spend much time in them: they preferred Vienna.

Germany was still decentralized. There was not only one state or one court. There was Bavaria with Munich, Saxony with Dresden, there were the large free towns of older days like Hamburg, Frankfurt—to give only a few examples—to which no parallel existed in Austria.

Berlin, an upstart compared with other German towns, was not the same attraction in Germany as Vienna had been in the Austrian Empire. Germany had, moreover, considerably more cities of over a hundred thousand inhabitants than any other state in Europe. Most of these cities had traditions and prestige—and ambitions to excel each other. Prussia, younger and of somewhat colonial origin, was only by and by considered and admitted as a peer. Yet, Prussia proved to be the most efficient and thus Berlin developed at an amazing tempo. Still, the aristocracy of Bavaria, Rhineland and Saxony did not like to come to Berlin: they rather snubbed her—probably with a kind of envy dressed as discrimination.

Compared to Vienna, Berlin was definitely not attractive, at least not to the eye. It had neither the fine architecture nor the lovely surroundings, nor the 'patina'. The Berliners were also not as polite, as pleasant, as superficially amiable as the Viennese. Yet the much-maligned German virtue of obedience (as long as it was not abused) had a certain value. The Viennese were not obedient but servile, which to me seems worse.

Now to my own experiences. Personally I enjoyed immensely my first ten years in Germany. I was received in a new way. I saw some hope for myself and yet, no longer having teachers, I was even lazier than before. I did not have to prepare anything for lessons, so I really wasted an enormous amount of time just idling. In Vienna, where almost the entire population loves to spend its time in coffee houses, I had not taken up this national vice—maybe I was too young; but I made up for this in Berlin, though only at night. I would play billiards and cards and then sleep until two o'clock the next day. I had at first very little work and with the intoxication of my first total 'independence' probably no urgent drive towards self-imposed tasks.

This was the first year, a not too easy one, in spite of my idling and my carefree behaviour. I lived in a rather poor neighbourhood, with a Viennese friend of mine who was two years older than I and an apprentice in a bank. He went to Berlin a year before I did and his greater familiarity with the city was naturally an advantage to me. We were lodgers in a cobbler's flat. It was shabby, noisy, somehow frightening.

I got a Bechstein piano, a grand. Bechsteins did not charge me for it. They were, in Germany, what Steinway is in the States and Bösendorfer in Vienna. The Bechstein piano was for certain musical purposes an ideal instrument. Why the best pianos made in Germany, in Austria, in France and the United States differ so conspicuously, is a fascinating question.

I have thought a lot about the cause of these differences and I have come to the conclusion that it must have been the personality of the locally most successful, most respected, most influential pianist of an earlier generation which decided the character of the instruments. His style, his repertoire, his ambitions presented a model, created a fashion, acquired validity. I estimate that three-quarters of the piano music publicly performed in Germany before 1900 belonged to the pre-Wagnerian epoch. Pianos were built in accordance with the sonority requirements of that music (as understood by the pianistic 'commander-in-chief'). Three-quarters of the music performed in the States belonged to the post-Wagnerian epoch, demanding more 'extrovert' qualities of key- and sound-boards. It is desirable and, I think, also feasible gradually to abandon these provincial distinctions of pianos and to provide a type good for any musical climate.

Accustomed first to Bösendorfer, then to Bechstein, finally to Steinway (I never came into close contact with French pianos), I needed for each of these transitions quite a time before feeling at home and happy with the new tool. Bösendorfer, Bechstein, Steinway are, however, all at the highest level of piano-making.

Through my Vienna letters of introduction I met three ladies, all in their early thirties or thereabouts and married respectively to a big publisher, a big steel manufacturer and a big banker. They studied music very seriously, had studied it since early childhood and were accordingly very advanced players. All three asked me to give them lessons. I was then eighteen and new in Germany and it was really a marvellous chance to have these three pupils. I also remember a young man who was always ailing and had to stay at home. He asked me to play for him twice a week. Each time he paid me something like three pounds. So, you see, I was soon standing on my own feet.

Yet, occasionally I had not enough to live on. Fortunately, some of my friends, guessing this, helped me with lunch and dinner invitations. Besides, at that time in Berlin you could go to a kind of cafeteria and, if you paid sixpence for a glass of beer, you were entitled (for an unlimited time, as nobody supervised you) to eat an unlimited amount of very good rolls with mustard—for nothing. So in an emergency I would do that.

My life during this first year in Germany was fortunately not *only* leisure. In addition to the work with my lady pupils I had also quite a number of concert engagements. Actually, I made a rather rapid start to my career. I have already told you about Potsdam and Norway. I also went on a concert tour through East Prussia. These concerts—especially in towns which seemed rather expanded villages, with a population often below ten thousand—were sponsored by the big landowners of the region but organized and also subsidized by the state. It was always the highest ranking representative of the state—sometimes a civilian, sometimes an army man—who was in charge of these concerts. In the towns honoured and trimmed with garrisons you would see an audience made up of the garrison commander, his wife and all his officers with their wives, followed by judges, doctors, civil officials, a few business men, and crowned by the sponsoring magnates and families. Sometimes the garrison also furnished the ushers, with an officer's orderly or some retired sergeant directing their functions. I remember one place where I played Beethoven's Sonata Opus 101 as the first item. As you know, it opens with a very delicate movement. The retired sergeant who had been selling programmes and tickets at a table behind the last row counted his takings during that delicate movement, throwing copper and silver coins on to a china plate which he had ready on his table. I remember this episode as one of the most successful frustrations of an atmosphere in my rich collection of such events. It was so successful that it stopped my performance after I had fought my way to, perhaps, the middle of my sensitive piece. That was done to music by a German sergeant who only did his duty. He knew no better—his superiors had forgotten to warn him.

One of my first concerts was in the small East Prussian town of Rastenburg. To get there I travelled all night, with a Belgian violinist, who was to perform in the same concert. We were very curious to meet a singer who was also engaged for our joint recital of three, she as the 'star'. Her name was Therese Behr and she had been enormously successful in the two or three years since her public career had started. She had arrived the night before at the inn at which our manager had booked all of us. It was a very primitive place but not without a certain cosiness. When we arrived, there was still the smell of stale beer and chicken *bouillon* from an all-night wedding celebration. The porter took us up to our rooms and, in passing by a door, I saw a lady's skirt and jacket hanging on a hook (no hangers yet in Europe at that time). In all hotels (and also in homes employing servants) clothes were hung before the door to be brushed or cleaned and shoes put out to be shined. The porter informed us that the dress and shoes outside this door belonged to the singing concert star. I made a joke about the size of her boots—they were snow boots as it was winter-time. As it was six o'clock in the morning I was certain she was still asleep and I did not lower my voice in making my joke. Some hours later, at breakfast, I met the lady, in the not yet smell-free 'restaurant'. She laughed and said: 'I heard you talking about my big feet.' This, you will understand, greatly embarrassed me. We ought to have rehearsed then but the weather was so fine and the countryside so inviting with all the deep snow that I suggested: 'Shouldn't we go for a sleigh ride? It would surely be a real treat and we can rehearse just before the concert.' She and my Belgian colleague agreed, so we enjoyed a long excursion in a troika (three horses, Russian style) and came back just in time for a cup of tea. Then we went to the hall to rehearse (I had rehearsed with the violinist in Berlin). Much later Miss Behr told me that it had been a strange rehearsal because I had insisted on playing my own compositions for her instead of rehearsing her songs. She naturally got a little nervous and impatient, but later I sight-read her programme quite to her satisfaction and the concert went very well. A year later we were engaged and five years later we married.

We appeared from then on—for three decades—in countless *Lieder* recitals together. My association with the art of *Lieder*-singing is thus a close one and allows me to speak with some authority about this delicate and very exacting branch of musical expression. Its public career was short—it lasted hardly a full century. Its decline was, obviously, a consequence of the gradual, automatic adjustment of men to mechanization, mass production and commercialization. The *Lied* has actually its most adequate place in the cultured home—and we all know that the mass production of cultured homes has not yet come very far. We also know that the endless offer and supply of not-home-made pleasures cannot be resisted, especially not by the young ones. In public performances *Lieder* should be presented in intimate halls. Which successful musical performer would relinquish the biggest halls if he can fill them, and obey artistic demands if they involve sacrifices? Opera singers are rarely able to do justice to the *Lied*. The 'real' *Lieder* singer is, vice versa, not usable for operas.

The real art *Lied* is a German creation. Folklore, songs, chansons, madrigals, arias, etc. were known and popular before the *Lied* appeared, were most likely the steps leading to

50

it—the latest, tenderest and most individualized example of the forms found by music.

Franz Schubert's *Lieder,* seen as a whole *œuvre,* have so far not been equalled. Schumann, Brahms, Hugo Wolf, Moussorgsky, Richard Strauss, Gustav Mahler, Debussy, Fauré have contributed precious creations to the *Lied* literature. And there, thinned out in its last phases, it stays. A few contemporary composers have written interesting *Lieder.* They are not performed. How can they expect performances when the best of the past are not in great demand? Programmes of song recitals today are, as a rule, an astonishing juxtaposition of disparate items.

How can you compensate for the loss of the exaltation experienced by a close association with the unique treasure of *Lied* literature? I see only one way: all who are drawn to it, who play the piano and can read music (many 'music lovers' nowadays confess proudly that they cannot—even if they play the piano) ought to get Schubert's (and other) songs and devote some of their free time every day to communion with them.

In Berlin I was soon introduced to several musicians, among them the celebrated conductor Artur Nikisch. I played for him, amongst other things, my own piano concerto—I had just composed it. Nikisch was extremely kind to me and decided to help my career.

When I was twenty I was engaged as soloist with the Berlin Philharmonic Orchestra in concerts at Berlin and Hamburg, and in Leipzig with the Gewandhaus Orchestra. Nikisch was the conductor on all three occasions. Touring orchestras were not yet in vogue. The Hamburg subscription concerts of the Berlin Philharmonic were more an extension—or excursion—than a tour.

At my three débuts with these wonderful orchestras I played the Second Concerto by Brahms and was from that day on for a long time labelled a Brahms specialist. (Not in Munich, however. You remember?) I was the first to play the B flat major Concerto in several cities—Brussels for instance (at least I was told so).

In those days house concerts were also still customary and I was engaged to perform on some such occasions. I remember a very unusual one at the house of Count Hochberg, intendant of the Royal Opera in Berlin. He asked me to play, among other pieces, Mozart's D major Sonata for two pianos. The other pianist, he told me, would be Dr Karl Muck, a name hardly ever mentioned in my Vienna days. He was then first conductor at the Berlin opera. To co-operate with him thus was a privilege; it was also a great pleasure.

Another time I was invited to play at a house concert (a soirée) in the palace of Prince Henckell-Donnersmarck, but was warned beforehand that the Princess occasionally behaved in a rather peculiar way. I was summoned to her a few days before the event. She wanted to know what my repertoire was. Then, before I had a chance to give the information, she told me that under no circumstances would she allow me to play Chopin—that her guests were accustomed to the best only and therefore might not like my Chopin interpretations. Since she had never heard me, I could not discover the reason, or any reason, for such astonishing treatment. Later on, someone provided a clue: she was Polish. At this soirée the artists were separated from the guests by a red rope and forbidden to mix. After the performance some of the people on the spectators' side of the rope dared to begin conversations with me—and no one got hurt. The whole affair was not at all to my liking and made me avoid house concerts of this type, the society type, in future—where most of the audience have just a superficial—if any—connection with music, but all of them a place in high-life.

Long after this conflict with noble manners I learned from my manager, Mr Wolff, that the Princess had cut my fee. Asked whether it was by mistake she replied: 'Oh, no! It happened on purpose. First I did not like his music much and, secondly, I hated his hair tonic.' Wolff waited years before telling me of that trick of how to save money: he thought it might depress a young man—particularly the reference to the hair tonic. He had sent me the full fee, the difference coming out of his own pocket.

I have mentioned my shameful laziness in those days. I prepared my concert repertoire at the eleventh hour, so to say. But even on concert days I used to play billiards all afternoon. As soon as the game was over, I rushed home, dressed in a hurry, consumed quantities of strong black coffee, arrived at the hall a bit later—more often than not—than the audience, ran to the platform and dived into music. It was inexcusable nonchalance and I think of it only with repentance—and a shiver.

Among my friends in Berlin were a widow and her son, a young professor of chemistry. Her father had gone to the United States between 1840 and 1850, I think, but she had returned to Germany after her marriage. These two became my dearest friends. My entry to their home caused a kind of revolution in their mode of existence. When I first went there, their style of living was almost isolation, voluntary of course, compared with the style by and by developed after I intruded.

I brought to them a letter of introduction from Vienna and was the first professional musician with whom they established a personal contact. After only a few years, every Sunday evening their house was full of young musicians from all parts of the world. They were soon joined by older and old musicians (also of all races, colours and creeds), for the reputation of this unusual home was spreading rapidly and every musician seemed to be lured there. Until the First World War and even afterwards, up to the middle 'twenties, these most stimulating gatherings went on—every Sunday. The great majority of the Sunday-nighters were professional musicians; a small minority of excellent amateurs and an *élite* of music lovers were also admitted. The presence of twenty to forty musicians at each gathering was quite usual. Some of them performed what they liked—chamber music, vocal music, solos—and the audience, as you can imagine, was all participation and naturally critical, though never prejudiced or jealous.

I spent many of my summer vacations with the young professor and his incomparably enthusiastic mother, visited them in Berlin also on week-days (without music and musicians) and once every week they took me to a play or an opera. They suggested to me a performance of my piano concerto, at their expense. I was overjoyed, and one Sunday morning in the winter of 1901–02 I played it with the Philharmonic Orchestra before an audience of invited listeners. An exemplary present to a young artist!

This Berlin Philharmonic Orchestra was, I think, the only self-supporting orchestra in Germany at that time. Later on, the City of Berlin subsidized them. They were engaged by the manager, Hermann Wolff, for a series of subscription concerts every season, each programme being performed twice: a so-called 'public rehearsal' on Sunday morning, the 'concert' on

Monday night. On two other evenings of the week they gave 'popular' concerts. On the remaining days any conductor who wanted their co-operation could engage them.

On the occasion of the performance of my own concerto I also gave what I believe to have been the first performance in Berlin of Paderewski's only piano concerto.

6

I THINK that outside Germany one has a rather mistaken idea about the role of regimentation there at the beginning of this century. Any notions derived from National Socialism's later actions give an absolutely false picture. For instance, in the ré-gime of the young Kaiser, a pompous, bombastic, moody, capricious fool (that is how the Germans regarded him—not my judgement), the Imperial Court was frequently criticized or ridiculed. The Press quite fearlessly poked fun at some of the very odd statements which the Kaiser so often made. Once after the opening of a state-sponsored exhibition of modern art he commanded a group of painters, sculptors and architects to the palace and regaled them with an 'educational' address, ending with the proud sentence: 'Art which exceeds the limits I have drawn is no art.' You must not think that anyone in Germany took that seriously.

The Prussian nobility had its faults but also its great virtues, and the bureaucracy was neither slovenly nor corrupt. The bureaucrats were a rather colourless group, not exactly lively, but very reliable, absolutely reliable. This reliability might also have been a reason why the business leaders, working as they did from morning until night in the rapidly expanding pros-perity, left politics and government to the trusted old guard. So did the scholars, professors and teachers, who did not par-ticipate in public life either. If they had, events might have taken a different turn.

It was a very animated period. During this time—up to 1914—I performed chiefly in Germany. Unfortunately I did not speak any language but German. I had learned some French, but not enough to make me risk going to a country where they spoke only French. Of English I had then no knowledge whatsoever. So I travelled mostly in Germany, a market which anyhow could easily absorb a musician's total capacity. I think there could have been only a few concert-consuming places in Germany where I did not perform at least once.

Occasionally I played also in other countries—two or three times in Spain. The first time was with the Bohemian String Quartet. They were four fascinating men, a wonderful blend of great simplicity and great vitality, and they were also superb players. The second violin, Josef Suk, was Anton Dvořák's son-in-law. After a few years the viola player, Oskar Nedbal, changed to conducting and composing. Suk, too, was composing—quite remarkable music. We had a splendid time together playing quintets and quartets in Madrid and other Spanish cities.

The next time I went there was with my wife, giving joint recitals. I played the piano parts, of course, for her *Lieder* selections. She had been asked to sing exclusively in German. The Spanish concert societies had rules more rigid than those in any other country. The audiences in most cities were composed entirely of members of the concert societies. And these societies were not of the usual type—committees which open, after reserving seats for themselves, a subscription to the general public. To be a member was a social distinction. The membership was accordingly much greater than the number of available seats in the halls or theatres where their concerts were given. Hosts of applicants for membership were kept on waiting lists, with, however, small chances, for when a member died his children had a priority. Yet, the concerts were often very poorly attended: the members paid but did not go. The non-occupied seats were not allowed to be sold to persons who were keen to go: I could not get tickets for friends of mine, though the houses were by no means full. Then, at these concerts the audience was expressly requested, in print, not to talk: talkers during this type of Spanish entertainment were threatened with exclusion; their membership was in danger. But the admonitions seemed to be only slightly successful. Members were also forbidden to leave before the end of the programme. Encores were banned, too. In this respect they were safe with me! The programmes were decided by a committee of a few gentlemen, who often chose what were considered the very inaccessible works of musical literature. It was all so exclusive and tied to etiquette that neither the performer nor the audience felt too happy at these Spanish musical celebrations.

56

It was very striking that during my several visits to Spain I was never introduced to a woman; except one, and she was English—the Queen. We had been asked to give her a private concert at the palace. Only once was I invited to a Spanish home: it occurred in Valencia and my host was a small *bourgeois* whose daughter tried piano playing. Much later, coming for the first time to the United States—directly after another tour in Spain—I was compensated, for here I was introduced chiefly to women.

In 1904 I went to England and had the great honour of playing at the Royal Philharmonic Society with Hans Richter conducting. Richter started as a horn player, became in his youth an intimate friend of Richard Wagner, later on conductor of the Vienna Opera for many years and still later conductor of the Hallé Orchestra in Manchester. He was a great man. I saw him often in Vienna, for his house was just opposite Leschetizky's. I had, however, no personal contact with him.

I again played the B flat major Concerto by Brahms and had a real success. But, as I have said, being somehow self-conscious about my monoglot state and having enough concerts in Germany, I did not exploit this success in London. What I remember best of this first acquaintance with London —best, because it was so terrifying—was my ride from my hotel to the Queen's Hall, where the concert was given. Not used to traffic of London proportions (Berlin could not compare), I took a hansom cab much too late; at each busy corner one had to wait and wait and wait—what cumulatively and in contrast to my feverishly quickened pulse seemed eternities. I just made it—and what a relief that was.

In 1905 I went once more to London for a very short stay, and after that not until 1925. In the meantime I had acquired some knowledge of English, had been in the States twice and was thus less timid in this respect. Occasionally I went to Italy and France, rarely to Scandinavia, but fairly often to Austria, chiefly to Vienna, and to Prague and Budapest. I never enjoyed playing in Vienna. I cannot say whether it was resentment or prejudice or inhibition, but I never felt really happy with the Viennese audience. It contained—I have said this before—too many talented Philistines. Perhaps I am being unjust towards them. Perhaps I am subjective in this respect. I believe this lack of affinity has been mutual.

Then I went three times to Russia—Czarist Russia. These trips were among my strongest impressions. The preliminaries were unpleasant because Jews, as a rule, were not at that time admitted to Russia and I had to stand around in the Russian Embassy's ante-chamber with letters of recommendation. I did not like that at all. I did not see why a musician, or anyone, should be excluded because of his being a Jew. That was actually the only time I really felt humiliated in this regard. But then the religious curtain was lifted and I received permission for a stay in Russia.

First I went to the Baltic provinces. The City of Riga made an indelible impression on me: it was the most cosmopolitan, international, vivacious place I had so far seen. There were the Latvian natives, the majority of peasant stock; then the Russian administrators and garrison; the German merchants, here from the old Hansa times on; many German nobles living on large estates, and finally a flourishing Jewish population of doctors, lawyers, teachers and merchants. This blending of traits gave the city a special, almost unique, diversity and fascination.

I played there with orchestra. This, too, was unforgettable. The symphony concerts were played by the opera orchestra and took place in the Riga Municipal Opera House where as a young man Richard Wagner had conducted. Many decades later Bruno Walter held the same job. The operas were sung in German.

When I had to play there, the Opera administration had been quarrelling for months with the German musicians' union which, strangely enough, also ruled the Riga Orchestra. It was late in March and the union had been notified that the orchestra's contracts, expiring on 1 May, would not be renewed. The musicians answered this lockout with secret sabotage and 'passive resistance' pinpricks. For each rehearsal and each performance some important players were absent, because of illness; substitutes were unavailable because the Institute was already under union boycott.

Once more I had to play Brahms's B flat major Concerto. It was the first French horn's turn to be sick—and the situation looked hopeless. A young coach and assistant conductor offered to help. He said he had learned at the conservatorium in Cologne to play the French horn and would be willing to try. We accepted with gratitude and he played the exacting horn part at the rehearsal in the morning quite well. We admired him greatly, for, as you know, the French horn is one of the most difficult instruments to play. Wanting to do an even better job in the evening, he went on practising—instrument and part. By mid-afternoon—no wonder—his lips became swollen from such abnormal demands on them. Yet he was determined to go through with the chivalrous adventure, in spite of his considerable pain and corresponding nervousness. His bravery was, in general, rewarded by an astonishing performance when, suddenly and of course in the most noticeable place, he got lost, meandering alone for a few seconds through the score. It was a bizarre moment.

I report this event in such detail because the hero of the horn was Fritz Busch, the now world-famous conductor. And I have still to add that during the rehearsal and the concert I saw—and could not resist looking at him whenever I had a chance—among the violinists in the orchestra a blonde boy, touchingly different from the rest by his face, his devotion, his independence. He was, I learned, a non-unionized guest, sixteen years old, visiting his brother in Riga, and welcoming any opportunity to make music. His name—Adolf Busch.

After Riga I went to Moscow and St Petersburg. There I became acquainted with Koussevitzky, an unsurpassed double bass virtuoso who had already deserted his big instrument to play on a still bigger one, the orchestra. He was in the infancy of his conductor's career, which everyone expected—and rightly so as we know now—to become a glorious one. In Moscow I played—don't be shocked!—Liszt's E flat major Concerto, Mr Mengelberg from Amsterdam conducting.

Meanwhile I remained very active in Germany, played with Nikisch every year in Berlin, almost every year in Leipzig, but rarely in Hamburg where the Berlin orchestra went only for six performances a year, usually without a soloist. In Hamburg, however, a local symphony orchestra engaged me regularly.

I saw Nikisch often, at rehearsals, concerts and those memorable Sunday dinner parties given by Hermann Wolff, the manager, at his home after each of the Sunday morning 'public rehearsals' for the Monday concerts. These parties were a delight for body and soul: exquisite food and wines and a brilliant, stimulating and amusing group of people.

Nikisch, as I knew him, was rather taciturn. He seemed

59

more amiable than warm and always somewhat detached. I never saw him angry. He was an addict to poker playing. I did not play poker for, quite apart from my Norwegian mishap, it really bores me. I simply have no gambling instinct. As a spectator I was occasionally present when Nikisch played it. It was very instructive. The atmosphere of a rite— silence for hours, complete solemnity, maximum concentration, hardly any movements (facial ones are, I hear, suicidal) —not my idea of pleasure!

This description ought to have revealed that I had not much personal contact, nor even conversation with Nikisch, to whom nevertheless I felt so attached. It was not the same with Richard Strauss, with whom I played first in 1905, also in Berlin and with the Philharmonic Orchestra, at the concert which was to decide whether he was good enough to become permanent conductor of the series of symphony concerts given every season at the Royal Opera House in Berlin. Felix von Weingartner was the other choice. Strauss had been invited by Hermann Wolff, who apparently in his heart preferred him to the other contestant. So he arranged this special concert and I was honoured to be the soloist. It was an all Beethoven programme; Strauss conducted an overture and the Fifth Symphony, I played the Fifth Concerto. His performance of the symphony was fulfilment. No performance I have heard since, even by him, has reached such heights. It was inspired, overwhelming—fire and firmness. He received one of the greatest ovations I have ever witnessed. He was no 'star'—only a candidate—before this concert. After it he was one—and, naturally, he also got the job.

Later on he did not always make the same efforts in his conducting. From time to time he did the wonders of which he was capable, but more often, particularly in operas, he was just enjoying himself. I heard operatic performances during which he behaved as if he were quite alone. He would enjoy certain parts and caress them but would just pass over other less challenging or moving ones.

Strauss was almost the opposite of Nikisch: a bit haughty, sometimes brusque or sardonic. He, too, loved the daily card game—but not poker. He liked vivacious pastimes, noise not excluded. I remember one gathering where the system of voting then valid in Prussia was discussed. It had three classes of voters, of which the highest had, I think, four votes *per capita*, the middle class perhaps two, the lowest, at most, one vote. At our gathering almost everyone present agreed that this obsolete distribution of civil rights had lasted long enough and should be abolished. Richard Strauss did not agree, becoming very excited and red in the face—I had never before seen him, this rather cool man, so aroused—and shouted, accompanied by bangs on a table, that this three-class voting system contained at least some justice. He thought it absurd that his vote should not count more than that of his baker's. He maintained passionately that if the nobility class abdicated, culture would abdicate too.

The card game Strauss played was called Skat, which was very popular in Germany before Bridge dethroned it (Bridge was still unknown then, at least in its present 'scientific' form). I played Skat and also Tarock, the favourite game in Austria.

I was naturally very eager to meet Strauss as often as possible. The easiest way was via Skat. A number of rich but—in Berlin at least—definitely not aristocratic people always gave opulent dinner-and-Skat parties for him—this was generally the only bait which made him come to their houses. It was a fair bargain. He got luxurious meals, played for high stakes, always won, stayed late and did not pay much attention to the people entertaining him. They were rewarded with the right to boast that this famous man was their friend.

I managed to be invited. After such parties, Strauss occasionally walked home and allowed me to accompany him. And here my pleasure began. In order to enjoy these fairly long walks and talks, I participated also in the high-stake Skat. One day, however, I lost so much on such an occasion that I tried to discover a less expensive way of meeting him. I was not very successful. I did not play Skat again and only rarely met Richard Strauss.

At the turn of the century an organization called 'The People's Stage'—*Volksbühne*—was established in Berlin. It was inspired and built up by a small group of writers with the intention of acquainting the working class with such products of the spirit which so far had been out of their reach or never addressed to them. They started with a handful of members, all workmen—or women. I had not been in Berlin long when the *Volksbühne* invited me to co-operate with them. I did, and from that day on played for them several times every year. They quickly gained a very large membership and in a short time became an exemplary institute. Their programme included by and by all kinds of presentations from the very exacting to the honestly lighthearted.

When I arrived in Berlin there was only one opera house, perhaps three playhouses, three concert halls, one variety show and one house where light opera was given. The last one had only a short season. In the playhouses as well as the opera, concert halls and even the two remaining places all presentations seemed addressed to one and the same group of persons, numbering ten thousand, I estimate. When I left Berlin in 1933 the number of people out every evening had multiplied; there were now three (at times four) opera houses, six concert halls, countless theatres and variety shows, in addition to the mushroom-like growth of eating, drinking and dancing places, crowned by the cinema, the greatest consumer of consumers.

The *Volksbühne* existed long before this multitude of joys and choices. First an agreement was made with the few theatres and the Philharmonic Orchestra: every week one or two of their performances were sold to the *Volksbühne* as closed performances for their members. Then, not yet twenty-five years old, the *Volksbühne* built their own theatre—one of the finest modern theatrical buildings in the world with, fortunately, ideal acoustics. It was built by Oskar Kaufmann, the architect who had designed the title pages of some of my early compositions. In 1927 I played all thirty-two Beethoven sonatas there—for the first time in my career. For that series, half of the spacious house was reserved for members, the other half was open to the general public. All seats were drawn by lots.

Austria had compulsory military training, starting at the age of eighteen. I had thus to appear, once every year from 1900 to 1914, at the Austrian Consulate where a doctor, in the presence of one army and one civilian functionary, would decide about my qualifications as a warrior. The Consul-General was fond of my music and kind to me. He told the doctor not to rush my mobilization—there was no urgent need to have me in the army. The doctor noticed a slight irregularity on one of my toes, thought my compulsory service to music more promising and each time set me free for it.

7

AMONG my acquaintances in Berlin there was the Mendelssohn family. It had been a century-old tradition with this family to have music in their homes almost every day. There were two brothers, Robert and Franz (it was the latter's house with which I had the closer contact); Robert played the 'cello and Franz the violin. They had the finest existing Stradivarius instruments. The sounds they produced on them were not absolutely the finest and I have heard finer sounds on inferior instruments; but they were very good amateurs.

The number of musicians gathering in their home was in most cases not larger than was necessary to perform what was desired, in contrast to the other home of which I told you earlier, where so many young and old musicians came as audience—and as a stimulus to those who were physically active. The Mendelssohns were rather conservative in their attitude to music. In this they were guided by Joseph Joachim, who in his later years became quite aloof from contemporary music of an untraditional type. It was not welcome at the Mendelssohns'; at the other home, however, one was asked for it. The level was very high in both homes, perhaps somewhat higher at the Mendelssohns', because there also amateurs participated in the performances. I think house-music is at its highest conceivable level when amateurs mix with professionals, all doing it for love.

I had the honour of playing several times with Joachim. I was much too young fully to appreciate this, even to enjoy it. You see, I rebelled somewhat against accepting long-established authority and heroes among contemporaries; so I was probably prejudiced and thought his style out of date. Only thirty years later it dawned on me that of course he was right.

I also played occasionally with Ysaÿe, who was considerably younger than Joachim and of a different school. To him, playing chamber music was an excursion into almost unknown territory; Joachim, on the other hand, was officially the highest authority on chamber-music playing.

A friend of mine in Frankfurt-am-Main was the famous Louis Koch. I mention him because he had one of the finest collections of musical and other precious manuscripts. Each time I went to Frankfurt he invited me to spend hours in his house, alone. His housekeeper had instructions to open to me whatever I was interested in. So in that house, quite by myself, I read or played from manuscript works like some of the last Beethoven sonatas and the last three Schubert sonatas. It was an inestimable experience.

I want also to tell you about the institution of music festivals in Germany at that time. Cities in all regions held regular festivals, some annually, some less frequently. There were regular Bach Festivals at Leipzig, Regensburg, Breslau and Königsberg; there was the Silesian, Schleswig-Holstein and Rhenish Festival and every year that of the *Allgemeine Deutsche Musikverein*—the national association of German Musicians—founded by Franz Liszt at the time of his activities in Weimar. The function of this last-mentioned festival was to present contemporary music, first performances of works by German as well as non-German composers. It is in the nature of such organizations that they become reactionary when they get too old; so after the First World War the International Society of Contemporary Music was founded, because this National Association of German Musicians had become very eclectic and neglected the best contemporary music.

At one of the festivals I met Prince Friedrich Wilhelm of Prussia, a young, very learned man, passionately fond of music, who lived there in a medieval fortified castle. He owned one of the finest violins existing and was able to produce amazingly scratchy and ugly tones on it. To a musician it was —in a way—a satisfaction to hear such ugly tones on such a good instrument, for it proved that it is not the instrument which makes the sound.

I was occasionally 'commanded' to play chamber music before this Prince. He also came to my house. I could not have said no, for he was a very autocratic man and could be rather angry if you did not agree with him, even in matters as far removed from art as refusing to drink more wine as a guest in his house (he was one of the finest vine-growers in the Rhineland). At one festival he gave a luncheon party just before an afternoon concert at which I had to perform at three o'clock. I sat next to him. Several kinds of wine were served; he drank to me and I had to drink, but when I politely and carefully declined the third glass he turned his back on me and did not speak to me again for the rest of the meal.

Among the musicians who have impressed me most in my life—not including my childhood—were Busoni, Schönberg, who were both older than I, and, later on, Křenek, who is eighteen years younger than I. Hindemith also impressed me although I differ from him on many non-essential questions, mainly those concerning the approach to music.

Busoni was the greatest figure—there is nobody like him. He was fascinating both as performer and composer and also as a personality. Unfortunately I could not see him as often as I wished because he was nearly always surrounded by a group of people who were a bit too expensive—I would say—for me to take into the bargain. He had a great affection for freakish people; he felt a kind of sympathy for them. Every day after lunch he had this group for two to three hours—a strange collection, not very gifted either. He was very good to them. Yet, with a kind of devilish glee he would tell them the most absurd things about music which he simply invented. They accepted blindly all these fantasies and would afterwards spread them as the last word on music. When I once had a chance to see him alone, I said: 'Your young friend So-and-so tells me you say this-and-this.' He began to grin and called him an insect. There was this somewhat impish trait in his make-up; otherwise he was a marvellous man, incomparable in vitality. If he and Eugen d'Albert, who also had a most fascinating personality, had been combined in one, the result would have been one of the greatest musicians of all times, for d'Albert had all the raw material and Busoni all the refinement. About each other they spoke rather ironically and were mutually somewhat irritated.

Both after their fortieth year began to neglect their piano playing—it meant less and less to them; they preferred to compose. D'Albert, with his elemental qualities, had been labelled the 'Beethoven player', then Frederic Lamond became his competitor and eventually successor. Finally, much later, I had the honour to receive this 'heavyweight title'. We three are more different than you can conceive, but Beethoven embraces us all.

Neither d'Albert nor Busoni was ever really happy in the United States. This was probably the time of Paderewski's greatest triumphs here. Perhaps they felt inhibited because of their awareness of being so different from his type. There are some very interesting letters by Busoni, who enjoyed writing, about his experiences in America.

I shall never forget the last time that I saw him. It was after the First World War, shortly before he died and when he was very ill. I saw him alone. When I entered the room he looked at me for a while and then said: 'Schnabel, you are acquiring a face.' It impressed me deeply—a great compliment. It meant that I had none until then, of course. I was then forty. . . .

As my career had developed so quickly in Germany, when I was still quite young I had already attained a position which enabled me occasionally to try to help other musicians. Once in Lübeck I attended a concert conducted by a young man named Furtwängler, who fascinated me very much. On another occasion, in Strasburg, I met a young conductor by the name of Klemperer; he also fascinated me greatly. On both occasions I wrote immediately to my manager, Wolff, telling him how impressed I was and recommending these young men as strongly as I could. I cannot say it was due to my influence, but by the time I returned to Berlin both of these men had already been invited by my manager to come and display their gifts there. Both made great careers very quickly. During the next years Furtwängler became an intimate friend of mine —at times I received several letters a week from him, as he liked to discuss every detail with me.

Around 1910 there was great excitement about a prodigy in composition—comparisons were made to the young Mozart. His name was Erich Wolfgang Korngold. His father was music critic for the most important newspaper in Vienna, successor to Eduard Hanslick, who was generally considered the leader of musical criticism in the German language in the nineteenth century. I gave the first performance of a sonata of Korngold's which he wrote when he was twelve. The work was really amazing; of course, this is a relative judgement, for you cannot help but automatically judge a work by a twelve-year-old boy differently from that of a sixty-year-old. Yet I think even today, if one can see it in this perspective, it is still a most amazing piece. Korngold, who became and remained my friend, later went to Hollywood and started to write music for films.

During this time in Berlin I also witnessed, in 1905, the first triumphs of Max Reinhardt. He started with the most delicate and intense performances of plays. I remember all these productions because I went to each of them. He was a great man, but not long afterwards he turned entirely to show business. He also went to Hollywood.

In these years I also did my first editorial work. Together with my friend Carl Flesch, with whom I played so many duo and trio concerts, I edited the Mozart piano and violin sonatas for the firm of Peters—the Peters edition. I shall not defend this first edition of mine. It does not correspond with my later ideas about editions; but I do not think it is worse than most of the other—according to my later conceptions—'bad' editions.

My first son was born in 1909 and my second in 1912, so when the war broke out they were little children. In the second, third and fourth years of the war, living conditions became rather unusual in Germany. For instance, of the many foods which are here considered absolutely indispensable for one's health—or even to survive—we had none. There was practically no milk, butter, sugar, oil, chocolate, meat—and many other things were missing. I do not know how one went on. I do know that after eating the incredible war-time bread for three years, one morning my jaws went on strike—they would not work any more; they refused to move.

And we were in a privileged position. I had been rejected for military service, for the same reason as before. I was travelling a great deal to all those countries which were not at war with Germany and could be reached without having to pass through countries which were at war with Germany. I played in Holland, Switzerland and Scandinavia, and each time I was there friends offered to send me parcels of food. So we were a little better off. About twice a year my boys got some bars of chocolate. Yet they became quite strong.

I remember that in April 1915 I gave a concert in Milan. That was very unpleasant, because at that time Italy had just decided to declare war on Germany. As I came from Germany, in the neutral countries, too, I was always attacked by pro-Allied newspapers as a 'representative of Prussian militarism in music'. The reviews I got in such papers are simply not quotable. In Sweden and in Holland I received the finest bouquets. One critic in Amsterdam started his forty lines of insults by saying that coming to hear me was not worth using up the soles of his shoes, added that the doll in *The Tales of Hoffmann* had more soul and animation than I had, asked why I was not a sergeant at the German front and stated as the climax that I played 'like a convict counting peas'.

Lacking the right food and having no fuel to heat my apartment, in the third and fourth year of the war I acquired very serious neuritis in my shoulders and arms, supposedly caused by trying to stretch my hands, which were always contracted by the cold. I had seven more attacks in the following years; then, fortunately, it went completely.

In the third year of the war the German military authorities became suspicious because the Austrian military authorities did not pursue the war with the same energy and zest as they did, particularly not in what is called 'combing all men available for service into the army'. I was called again and the doctor who examined me—the old doctor—said: 'I know you have been here several times before and we have always rejected you because of something on your foot that prevents you marching for long stretches.' I replied: 'Oh no, I am a passionate mountaineer. I have done all kinds of climbing in the Alps.' I shall never know what made me say that. Instantly I realized that it was fatal. The doctor now had no other choice but to say 'accepted'. How I still escaped the service is hardly conceivable. I was then thirty-four. The German Foreign Office, wanting to help, requisitioned me for propaganda in foreign countries. But that meant playing also in countries occupied by Germany. I was asked to go with the Berlin Philharmonic Orchestra to Brussels, Weingartner conducting. I had to accept, of course. I cannot know whether I would have done it voluntarily—I do not wish to appear in a better light than I deserve. But as it was, I could not refuse. I played before an audience made up exclusively of German uniforms.

For a while the German Military Authorities recognized this activity. Then I was called for an examination again, this time by a German officer, not a doctor, and he told me that 'to wear the Emperor's uniform is a higher honour and more important than any art or spiritual value could be'. Now the Austrian Foreign Office was kind enough, when the Germans asked them to send my files, as always to answer that they could not find them—each time after several months, of course —and so the war ended before I was drafted.

But I had other difficulties. For instance, one day Her Royal Highness the Crown Princess was the patroness of the two-thousandth performance of *Lilac Time* and some lieutenant in charge of this charity performance had the splendid idea of making me appear in the dress and costume of Schubert, to play one or two pieces. When I was asked to do that, I really felt, blasphemously, that I would have preferred the war. However, I had a friend, a most remarkable man, holding a very high position in the German Foreign Office. I hastened to him, pleading for his assistance, telling him that I would gladly play for the Crown Princess as many Schubert sonatas as she liked, but I simply could not appear in *Lilac Time*. He helped me and it seems he even admonished the lieutenant who had conceived the idea. Then I remember he wrote me a charming letter saying: 'Is it not as well that higher intelligence goes always with the higher office too?'

8

TWICE in my life there have been long periods during which I did not compose. The first lasted from 1905 until 1914. Before 1905 I wrote works which would not have annoyed even the most reactionary schoolmaster. My first composition after the interval was a piece for contralto and piano, called *Notturno*—to a text by Richard Dehmel. Nowadays it would be considered rather conservative, but up to 1922 it was criticized or entirely rejected as a product of insanity and impudent violation of good taste, with no trace of music, honesty or talent. From then until 1925, when I again stopped composing, I wrote four string quartets, a quintet for piano and strings, a string trio, one sonata for violin solo, one for 'cello and one for the piano. I think that is all.

Only one of these pieces, the first quartet, has been published, but several have been performed. In these works it can be seen how the basis from which I proceeded changed from a harmonic one to a more exclusively melodic, rhythmical and formal one.

Meanwhile, during the First World War I had some contact with a German major, the son of the director of the Prussian Academy of Music. His father had obtained this position through his influential connections—a position which otherwise, as a Jew, he could never have held. The same connections also made it possible for the son to choose his career as a professional soldier.

I knew the Major as a very nice man. He was married to a French violinist and I was a guest at his house a number of times. I was invited to several meetings, or rather, seances. These meetings were held in the Major's home apparently to please his superiors of the German General Staff who were very much attracted to occultism.

Count von Moltke, the head of the German Staff, was one of the disciples of Dr Rudolf Steiner and I met Dr Steiner in the Major's house. I did not feel too easy at these seances, but nevertheless it interested me to see the Prussian Military Chiefs attending these mystical rites and I felt that it revealed something about the very strange make-up of the upper-class Germans, who in many respects were at the same time methodical, aggressive and mystical.

In 1914 in an address to the people the Kaiser made his amazing statement: 'Now I know no longer any parties, now I know only Germans.' This made it possible for an association by the name of Deutsche Gesellschaft—'German Association'—to be formed, being representative of all interests and views. Even Communists were admitted. But the majority of those in charge were Social Democrats.

The association was guided chiefly by Walther Rathenau, whom I knew quite well. He was a big industrialist and statesman; an idealist and a liberal, who had great integrity and a brilliant intellect. The members were from all branches of activities. They used to gather to discuss subjects pertaining to conditions in general and they also occasionally discussed music. I joined the Deutsche Gesellschaft and remember with much pleasure and gratitude the evenings I spent there. We had very scintillating times and the meetings were productive of mutual contacts.

I was also a member of the German Alpine Association. I have told you already that all my life I have loved mountain climbing. In 1924—I had already been a member for twenty-five years—the German Alpine Association gathered in Berlin to decide that the number of Jews admitted as members would from that time on be limited. That was the second occasion on which I felt very much ashamed of my generation, for the mountains did not make this kind of distinction. The first occasion was when I was present in 1917 at the inaugural meeting of the Fatherland Party, which I did *not* join. The United States had come into the war, confidence in winning was rapidly weakened in Germany, and the worst kind of diehards and demagogues came to the fore. I remember the terrific shouting (public-address systems did not yet exist at that time). The speakers were prominent people from all walks of life. One man, I remember, the mayor of one of the largest cities in Germany said, 'Germany will lose the war if we don't follow the example of our enemies who have no scruples at all and don't hesitate to tell any lies. We Germans are much too honest in our propaganda and our only chance to improve our situation would be to surpass our enemies in telling lies.' I cannot remember ever having felt as ashamed and disgusted as I was that night.

In September 1918 I had to go to Belgium—to play in Brussels and Antwerp on 28, 29 and 30 September. On my way from Cologne to Brussels I was on a train with a great many old German soldiers who had been called to Belgium to guard railway stations or for some similar purpose for which one could employ old soldiers—men over fifty.

They were absolutely frank in expressing their views on the situation. They told me how a few days before the Kaiser had addressed the workmen in the Krupp plant at Essen and they ridiculed the Kaiser and openly discussed his address in the most drastic terms. I could not repeat the words—they were beyond anything you could conceive—but they impressed me with the feeling that the end was coming. They expressed defeatism and the utmost dissatisfaction with the régime.

When I arrived in Brussels I was guest of the Federal High Commissioner for the State of Belgium. He was a foul man, and a fool as well, but fascinating, nevertheless. Twenty years before he had had a few piano lessons with me. Since then he had tried everything—become a writer, and also edited a rather fashionable magazine in Germany. He was unbelievably insolent and nothing could stop him. I was surprised to see his utter cynicism and, in fact, the cynicism of all the German officers and officials I met at that time in Brussels.

After one of my concerts there was a supper party, where the Major was also present—in whose house the seances had taken place. I have not forgotten this occasion. We talked all through the night, the Major, a professor and I, mainly on matters which had nothing whatsoever to do with politics or the war. But also during this night the Major told us, without having been asked, that all files of the German Administration in Belgium had already been transported to Germany.

Now I was sure the end was coming and was very happy. On the way back from Brussels to Cologne I travelled alone in a compartment with one of the German officers I had met in Brussels. He was an artist, rather a young man, intelligent— and just as cynical as all the others. He was married to the daughter of one of the biggest industrialists in Europe—a German industrialist connected with I. G. Farben. This man told me that in four to six weeks there would be a revolution in Germany—just that. I thought he was very well informed and kept silent about it.

Before we came into the station at Cologne the lights went out, the compartments were pitch dark and the train stopped for a full hour. We saw tremendous fireworks in the sky. The officer thought it was an air-attack on the station, but apparently nothing happened and afterwards he said it was only some sort of practice, or rehearsal for the Germans.

On 5 October 1918 I was in Munich. At six o'clock on that day, evening 'extras' were circulated in the streets reporting that Germany had asked for an armistice. That very night I decided to go and hear a lecture by a man named Maximilian Harden, who was one of the best-known commentators and publicists. For years he had edited a magazine called *The Future*. He was very boastful and conceited. (Maximilian Harden was a pseudonym, not his real name.) I went there out of sheer curiosity—generally I liked his antics, but today the whole concept of his lecture had been changed by the report in the 'extras'. At seven o'clock he had to start the lecture and at six-thirty he had heard such news that none of what he had intended to say would hold any longer. He was as white as chalk and trembling. His talk was a blend of defeatism, whining, accusations and speculations. There was an unbelievable atmosphere among the thousands of people present, as for all of them also much had changed since the report had come out. An explosion was never far off; however, it did not come.

On 6 November—these are the only dates I remember of my musical activities during those last days of the world war —I played a trio recital with my colleagues Flesch and Becker in Bonn. It was a very pleasant concert and we had an even more pleasant supper in a charming hotel where they served very good wine.

At midnight the head waiter came to our table and said there was a telephone call from Cologne to say that a revolution had broken out. Just that. You see, that is the way it may go if you ever experience the outbreak of a revolution—some head waiter may come and tell you about a telephone call.

I became, of course, very nervous as to whether I would get home to my family in Berlin and how I could get there. Also, I had a recital scheduled in Kassel on 8 November. It was not very far from Bonn to Kassel, but a revolution had just started and I did not know how to proceed. So I asked this head waiter, 'What would you advise me to do?' He said, 'I would, in any case, take the first train to Cologne tomorrow morning, if there will be any going.'

I did this. When I arrived in Cologne there were thousands of people, with their luggage, standing around in the station— sheer chaos. I could not carry all my luggage alone, being a pianist and always careful not to overstrain my hands, as all pianists are. So I stood there with thousands of others and watched what was happening.

What was happening was that young soldiers, some only sixteen years old, and old soldiers, absolutely quiet and silent, without saying a word, would approach generals and colonels and cut off their epaulets and take their sabres from them. The generals did not say a word either. It all happened smoothly, silently—as if it had been ordered and was being carried out correctly and obediently.

Finally an old railway employee felt some sympathy for me and said, 'Do you want a porter? Do you want to deposit your luggage?'

I said that that would be wonderful. So he said, 'Now, I shall take care of it. You come here every hour and ask whether a train is leaving Cologne.'

I said, 'All right, I shall do that.'

'However,' he said, 'as far as we know, no train is leaving Cologne.'

I went to the ticket hall and there I saw triangles erected of broken rifles and carbines. The rifles had been broken into two and were piled up very neatly. Then they were loaded on trucks and thrown into the Rhine, which was very near. That is how a revolution went. It was most impressive.

I went out of the station and looked at the beautiful cathedral just opposite. To the left was the new and large Rhine bridge and there I saw that everything was being directed by five or six wild-looking sailors with red carnations; they came from Kiel, the naval base.

I thought, 'What shall I do?' then walked around and watched the revolution. I did not see much revolt but there was an atmospheric vibration everywhere. Every hour I went to the station and tried to find my old man, my friend, but no train was leaving.

Then I went to the Hotel Excelsior and had a very good lunch. Other people were lunching there peacefully, unaffected by the revolution. Finally when I went back to the station in the afternoon, my friend said, 'There is a train leaving at four o'clock.' He also said that the train went through Kassel. I said, 'That is really a miracle because that is the city where I have to go.'

However, this train would be very full—or rather, as we discovered, it *was* already full. You could not enter via the steps and doors any more; so my friend lifted me through a window into a compartment. I had a first-class ticket which normally would have entitled me to sit in a compartment where only three other people were admitted. There were only four seats, but when I entered through the window ten or eleven soldiers were already sitting there. So we squeezed together good-naturedly and with good humour and then began the very long and slow journey.

I started discussions with the soldiers. All ten or eleven of them had, when they heard there was a revolution, left the hospitals or jails in which they had been. Some of them were prisoners, some hospital patients, and I got a little nervous because the two men between whom I sat took quinine pills continuously and told me that they had malaria. I did not feel too comfortable on that account. Then I noticed that all these soldiers were equipped with many new things and had an enormous amount of new luggage. I said, 'I am interested and curious. Are you bringing this to your wives and families?'

'Well,' they said, 'there was a revolution, so we went to the department stores and took these things.' They said that very naïvely and innocently. And so it goes.

At one o'clock at night I arrived in Kassel. I went to the hotel where I had a room reserved. Everything was in order. It was very quiet in Kassel; the revolution had not yet arrived there.

The next morning I contacted the hotel manager to ask him whether my recital would take place or not. He said, 'Nobody can tell. Nobody knows anything.'

It was drizzling, I remember. I went out, wanting to see how Kassel reacted to the revolution and to the end of the war. It was very dreary, dull and sleepy, but then, coming to the main street, I was given a handbill, to be at the biggest square of the city at twelve o'clock.

I went there and found twenty or thirty thousand people gathered waiting for something. Amongst them I saw children

75

playing and having a good time. A few minutes after twelve a car rushed into the square at high speed. In the car were five sailors; they looked very similar to the sailors I had seen in Cologne—perhaps they were the same ones. There was also one civilian in the car. He stood up and said: 'The Kaiser has abdicated.' Then something quite indescribable happened, for these thirty thousand people reacted as if now there could only be a rosy future for all mankind. There was immediate relief in their faces and they seemed to believe they would have a happy life from now on and no trouble need ever be expected any more.

This was 8 November. My recital was given and was sold out. It was very nice. The next morning I left by train for Göttingen where I played a matinée recital and the following day, 10 November, I finally arrived in Berlin.

In the meantime, from Göttingen I had telephoned my family and my wife had told me that the revolution in Berlin had also started on 8 November. On this day, which was a Saturday, she had promised our two little boys that they would see *Hänsel and Gretel* in the afternoon at the opera house. Then she was warned not to go out but to stay at home; but when she saw how unhappy the children were she did not have the heart to deprive them of the expected pleasure; so they went and saw *Hänsel and Gretel* on the day of the revolution. Many other children were there and they enjoyed it just as much as they could.

After the first days of the revolution the army came back, a new government was put into power and already the old rulers secretly began to prepare for a return to the old glory of the country.

I was travelling a lot but it was very difficult to travel in Germany then. There were marauding troops—so-called volunteers—and you never knew when you came to a town whether you would be suddenly in the midst of shooting. The trains were never heated and always overcrowded. You could not find a porter anywhere and if you sent your luggage in advance it did not arrive. So I used to travel with as little luggage as possible. I wore heavy tweeds and sportswear because it was so terribly cold.

I remember a recital in Kiel in February 1919. I had sent on some luggage of mine, which was very unwise—but I simply could not carry it and there were no porters. This luggage did

76

not arrive and I had nothing but a kind of little music case in which I had also a brush and comb. So I could not dress for the concert. Anyhow, when I arrived in Kiel that was not the only trouble. I was told there was a general strike in the city and since most people were living in the suburbs it was very improbable that there would be a concert. Also they had no lights.

I said, 'All right.' I was at that time ready for anything, you see. Then the president of the concert-society, whose guest I was, came and said, 'You won't believe it, but the concert will be held. All these people will walk miles in the dark streets with torches.'

Next to the hall, which was, by the way, the building of the German Trade Unions and the best hall in the city, where all concerts were given, there was some fighting with revolutionary groups and thus the roof of the building opposite the hall was manned with machine-guns and at any moment they were prepared to fire upon the building in which I gave the concert.

Well, we all behaved rather courageously and in a carefree manner, so I went there with a torch. Somebody came with me and there I was in my tweeds to play the recital. When I came to the corner of the street where the hall was situated, I was stopped by a soldier, a boy of fifteen or sixteen. He asked for my passport. I produced it—I always carried a passport in those days. Then I asked him, 'In whose name, if you will be so kind as to tell me, do you ask me for my passport?'

He said, 'In the name of the Red Soldiers Bund.'

I was glad to give this recital. A few candles were lit and simply as a spectacle it was very impressive.

I had similar, if not such poignant, experiences playing in Breslau, Bremen and other places. There was always shooting somewhere around the corner or in the parks. It was very dangerous to move about in the streets after nightfall. Maybe you would call it adventurous, or romantic.

At this time I was given the title of Honorary Professor. I was the last one to receive this title in Prussia. The Minister of Education thought that I deserved it, so I received the title from the new government just before it was decreed that the Professor title would be granted only in connection with an office, but not as an honorary one any longer.

Many things were changed with the coming of this new German government. There was a very noticeable and

77

considerable change of atmosphere, I would say. In the Ministry of Education a new man by the name of Kestenberg—a pupil of Busoni—made reforms immediately, particularly in school music. He was also the man who later introduced the licence for all music teaching. Musicians had to obtain this licence—by passing an examination—before they were allowed to teach.

In musical matters there came, from 1919 on, a wonderful upswing among young people that lasted about a decade. In 1920, a new director was named for the State Academy of Music in Berlin. He was an opera composer who was hailed by the Press and particularly by one very influential man as the new Richard Wagner—or equal to Wagner. His name was Franz Schreker. He had an enormous success, too big a success, perhaps, in proportion to his merits as an opera composer. He was a very good musician, a charming and rather naïve man. When he became the head of the State Academy he had as his assistant Professor Schünemann, an excellent musicologist.

Professor Schreker brought with him a few pupils from Vienna, among them Ernst Křenek who at that time was only nineteen. When he first came to my house he played his First Symphony for us on the piano, which was really an overwhelming and impressive piece. We established a friendship which fortunately is still continuing.

There was also a young man from the Baltic, Eduard Erdmann, a Latvian of German extraction, a pianist and composer—a man of great genius. And then there was Alois Hába, the young composer from Czechoslovakia who introduced the quarter-tone scale and created quite a stir with it. Yet, that was certainly not his purpose; he is a man of absolute integrity. And his compositions in quarter tones are most interesting.

9

THE years from 1919 to 1924 in Berlin were, musically, the most stimulating and perhaps the happiest I ever experienced. I was approaching my fortieth year and there was a change in my life—in this respect: until then my contacts had always been with people older than I, while from 1919 on I was very much attracted by young musicians—I mentioned some of them yesterday—and they responded very willingly.

These were very lively and productive contacts. The young musicians came at least once a week, and either played their compositions or listened to me playing something for them; then we talked and discussed the works until three or four o'clock in the morning and had a good time. Some of them developed into very remarkable men; some also became internationally famous.

Two young composers of this group, Ernst Křenek and Eduard Erdmann, told me one day that they were going to write light opera, to make quicker money than with the heavier type of music they usually composed. I advised them against it, feeling certain that it would be a failure, for I am convinced that in order to produce a successful light opera it has to be the best work of the composer. If he does it only as an act of condescension, he will not succeed. But they insisted, telling me that they had studied all the most popular and effective work in the field and would simply imitate it—on purpose— and probably do it better.

So they went ahead with their attempts. Often they played for me what they had just composed. Erdmann had great fun with it, but gave it up very soon, while Křenek was tougher and completed his light opera. His publisher wanted to provide for performance, so he asked Křenek to come and play his work for some people competent to judge its value. As Křenek told me afterwards, after he had played the first page of his score the expert got up and said, 'Mr Křenek, much too good!'

79

This is a very instructive story, you see. If the light opera composer, born and gifted to write that type of music, were to compose an oratorio and play it for an expert, he would say, 'Much too bad!'

During this period I also gave, together with six other musicians, a performance of Schönberg's *Pierrot lunaire* in Berlin, conducted by Fritz Stiedry. We had twenty rehearsals without being paid. Instrumentalists who were members of the Berlin Philharmonic Orchestra took part. I remember that the viola player in this ensemble was Boris Kroyt, a very young man, who later became the violist of the Budapest String Quartet.

Kroyt had told us he knew of a young Russian 'cellist who had just come to Berlin; he was absolutely unknown, was living in an unheated attic in the cold winter, and was undernourished. He said, 'He is a very remarkable artist, most promising,' and recommended him as 'cellist for our ensemble. So this tall young man, Gregor Piatigorsky, was brought to my house. He played one solo piece for us and we were all very much impressed by his music as well as by his charming personality.

The flute in this ensemble was played by the first flautist of the Berlin Philharmonic, who was also manager of the orchestra—and, as it happened, just then the position of first solo 'cellist was vacant. He was so impressed with Piatigorsky that he engaged him directly from these rehearsals to become solo 'cellist of the Berlin Philharmonic. Quite an amazing story, which Piatigorsky himself, as I have read and heard, told often in interviews, adding some amusing details to it.

He said that each time we had a rehearsal, there were some sandwiches prepared for an interval, but since Piatigorsky was the hungriest of all and there were several pieces in which he did not participate, he went to the room where the sandwiches were kept—so he says, if you can believe him—and ate them all, so that when the others came none were left.

In 1925 Eduard Erdmann performed a piano sonata of mine at the festival of the International Society of Contemporary Music in Venice. This piece was not very popular with the greater part of the audience, and there were two musicians who seemed particularly annoyed, so that when the piece went on and on—endlessly, as it seemed to them—one of them shouted very loudly, *'Allora basta!'* ('That's enough!') But Erdmann continued playing.

The inscription reads "In kind memory and with thanks for the many dinners from your jester. Artur Schnabel 14/III/. . ."

Theodor Leschetizky, Artur Schnabel's piano teacher, with dedication ". . . in memory of hard and happy hours (lessons)." (The German word *Stunden* means *hours* as well as *lessons*.) The musical quotation is from Schumann's "Papillons".

CONCERT-DIRECTION HERMANN WOLFF, BERLIN W.

Freitag, den 31. October 1902
Abends 7½ Uhr

im Oberlichtsaal der Philharmonie

III. Populärer Musik-Abend

veranstaltet von

Anton Hekking, Artur Schnabel
(Violoncell)   und   (Klavier)

Alfred Wittenberg
(Violine)

unter gefälliger Mitwirkung von

Ferruccio Busoni.

PROGRAMM.

1. Trio F-dur, op. 18, für Pianoforte, Violine und Violoncello   *C. Saint-Saëns*
   Allegro vivace — Andante.
   Scherzo, Presto — Allegro.

2. Zweite Sonate für Pianoforte und Violine . . . . *F. Busoni.*
   Langsam — Presto — Andante più tosto grave*) — Andante
   con moto, variazioni e Coda.
   *) Choralgesang von J. S. Bach: „Wie wohl ist mir, o Freund der Seelen, wenn ich in deiner Liebe ruh."

3. Noveletten, op. 29, für Pianoforte, Violine und Violoncello . . *N. W. Gade.*
   Allegro scherzando.
   Andantino con moto — Moderato.
   Larghetto con moto.
   Finale. Allegro.

4. Variationen für Pianoforte und Cello über ein finnisches Thema
   »Kultaselle« . . . . *F. Busoni.*

Concertflügel: **BECHSTEIN.**

Während der Vorträge bleiben die Saalthüren geschlossen.

Eintrittskarten à 1 Mark
sind in der Hofmusikalienhandlung von Ed. Bote & G. Bock, Leipzigerstr. 37,
sowie Abends an der Kasse zu haben.

IV. Populärer Musik-Abend: Freitag, 14. November 1902, Abends 7½ Uhr
im Oberlichtsaal der Philharmonie
unter gefälliger Mitwirkung von Frl. **Elisabeth Saatz.**
PROGRAMM: **Schumann**, Trio A-moll. — Gesang. — **Tschaikowsky**, Trio A-moll. — Gesang.

Programme of an early concert at which the author performed.

A photograph taken probably in 1904.

The Artur Schnabel Trio, left to right A. S., Jean Gérardy,
Professor Carl Flesch.

Berlin, 1932. Taken while the author was teaching. Photo: Paul Snyder.

Photograph taken at Manchester 1933 when receiving his Hon. Doctorate of Music from the University, after reading "Reflections on Music".

A. S. with his two sons. New York 1938. Photo: Blackstone Studios.
Inc.

Tremezzo, Lake Como, Summer 1938. Among those with Artur Schnabel are his wife, Therese, his son Stefan, his daughter-in-law Helen, his daughter Elizabeth M. Rostra and her son Jean Christophe Herold, soprano Maria Stader, conductor Fabian Sevitzky, violinist Szymon Goldberg, pianists Leon Fleisher and Noel Mewton Wood, and Peter Diamand, now Director of the Edinburgh Festival. Photo: K. U. Schnabel.

Taken near Los Angeles in 1939. Left to right: Mr. Nierendorf (art dealer), Otto Klemperer, A. S., Richard Buhlig (piano teacher) and Mrs. Klemperer.

George Szell and the author at a concert in Australia in 1939.

At rehearsal, about 1943.

Artur Schnabel with his wife Therese, and son Karl Ulrich, about 1946. Photo: O. E. Nelson.

Taken at Edinburgh in 1947 or 1948.

Rehearsal for the Edinburgh Festival (1947). Left to right: Joseph Szigeti, William Primrose, Artur Schnabel and Pierre Fournier, Photo: Gerti Deutsch.

On hilltop overlooking Lake Como, 14.9.1950. Left to right: A. S. Mrs. Sampson, Helen Schnabel his daughter-in-law, Therese Schnabel and Sir Robert Mayer. Below granddaughter Ann Schnabel. Photo: K. U. Schnabel

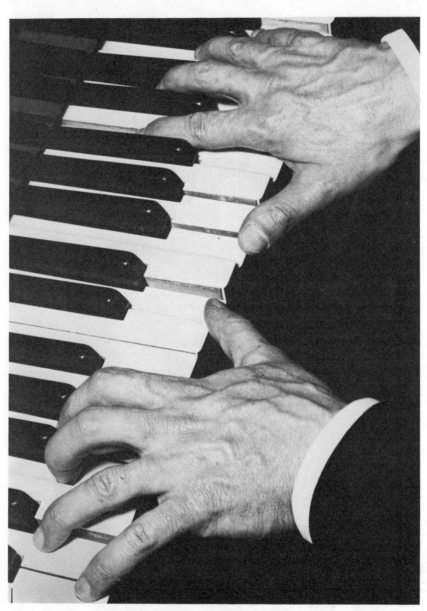

Artur Schnabel's hands.

Lady Mayer holding the bronze cast of Artur Schnabel's hand which was made by Eric Gill. The original plaster cast was given to Clifford Curzon on the occasion of Sir Robert Mayer's ninetieth birthday.

Artur Schnabel's grave in Schwyz, with the Mythenstock mountain in the background. Photo: K. U. Schnabel.

Toscanini was also present at this performance and even ten years later he said to me, 'Are you really the same Schnabel who wrote that horrible music I heard ten years ago in Venice?' So I had to assure him it was the same man. He seemed still to suffer remembering it.

This was my musical life. In other respects the life in Berlin in those years was not always so pleasant. The relief after the Kaiser's abdication did not last and was very soon followed by terrible irritation and nervousness and more difficulties than I had witnessed or experienced before. Friends separated over their differences of opinion in politics, and there was much fear and confusion.

Here also, I remember a symptomatic story. One night Rathenau gave me a private lecture in the house of friends. With a sheet of paper and a pencil and with very many figures, he demonstrated at length to prove that Bolshevism must be the economic and spiritual ruin of human society. The next day I left for Vienna, and there at luncheon I sat next to a Hungarian nobleman whom I had never met before. He was very much interested to hear from someone who had just come from Berlin what was going on there. One of his many questions was: 'What is that Bolshevist Rathenau doing there now?'

There were other signs that public life had changed considerably. It was noticeable, for instance, when the wedding presents given to girls in *bourgeois* families suddenly changed conspicuously. Instead of the piano, which for a century they had received when they were married, they now got a car.

This had further consequences. Before the time of the car, at the beginning of the twentieth century, it was part of the social prestige of the upper classes to join the choral societies of the city, simply to belong to them. All winter they rehearsed for one of the works to be performed in the spring. Now such choral societies had to be dissolved and it became difficult to hold them together, even if one was ready to pay the singers. On the other hand, some workers' social societies were established now, and several of them were really most remarkable in their accomplishments. Only very few of their members were able to read music. The others simply sang the very difficult music by ear.

In December 1921 I went for the first time to the United States. I was then thirty-nine and had never been to America before. I was somehow afraid to go and try it. Colleagues of mine who were celebrities in the United States had already given me much good advice. One told me, for instance, never to be arrogant in the United States and never to discuss certain subjects. He also advised me not to play certain works; for example, he said, 'You cannot play all twenty-four preludes by Chopin in America. The greatest number possible there would be eight, a selection of eight.' I would not know how such a selection can be made. But then I found that six years later he himself played all twenty-four.

Another colleague told me, 'You cannot play the C minor Variations by Beethoven,' because Mr Hall, who at this time was apparently 'the voice' in musical circles, had published a story about Beethoven entering the house of his friend, Johann Streicher, the piano maker, and hearing Miss Streicher play something on the piano. He was rather bewildered by the music he heard, and said, 'What *are* you playing there?'

'But Mr Beethoven, I am playing your C minor Variations.'

I refuse to believe this story—I am convinced it is simply invented—but even supposing Beethoven did make that remark, it would obviously have been one of his jokes. He was fond of them. However, Mr Hall concluded that Beethoven had repudiated the piece and so my colleague said, 'You must not play it in the United States.'

One of my most famous colleagues advised me that I should never leave the stage during the first hour of my programme. 'Because, you see, the first hour is the unimportant part of the programme; it is the "duty part" and most of the people hardly listen to it. Only when the "family part" comes, the people participate.' Well, I did not believe this either. Yet I noticed later that it was really the practice of some virtuosi in the 1920s to play the first half of the programme straight through. I myself heard Paderewski play—the only occasion on which I heard him—Beethoven's Opus 111, and it is true that in this first hour the audience was not very appreciative, did not participate as much as in the second hour.

My début at Carnegie Hall was on Christmas Day, 1921. There was a blizzard blowing. I don't say it was a great success. The Press was not bad. But some people immediately tried to initiate me in the tricks of changing from the type of musician I consider myself to be into some popular type.

I remember that the manager of my piano company said to

me, 'Now listen, Mr Schnabel, you have to be sensible when you come here. Let me say you have ten qualities. It would be sufficient if you used only five of those. Then we'll make a lot of money. We'll store the other five qualities and when you come again you can take out those other five qualities and again use ten.'

I took these things very seriously at that time, and replied, 'You are mistaken. If I really have ten qualities, as you describe them to me, I am attracted only by tasks requiring fifteen qualities.' But he looked blank.

Then I remember an editorial in the *Musical Courier,* which I used to read then, but have not since. This editorial was called 'Salesmanship.' It said, 'Now here's a very good artist and musician, Mr Schnabel. Why is he not sensible? Why does he insist upon playing this repertoire? He could make plenty of money if only he had a little more flexibility and elasticity. He came here to sell his wares, and if he wants to sell his wares, he must also take into account the demands on the market.'

I knew who the writer was; we had a friend in common. I think the man was absolutely right. So I asked my friend to tell the writer of this editorial that I agreed with him. 'He is only erring in one respect. It is true that I came here to sell my wares, but he confuses me with a warehouse.'

Mr Hurok was my manager at that time (apparently he was content with minor celebrities in those days). He arranged that on my first tour I should use the Knabe piano, and he sent me a list of famous musicians who had used it before. The Knabe piano is a very good piano, but it did not satisfy me very much. As a whole I am quite readily pleased and content if I succeed in realizing, let me say, 50 to 60 per cent of what I set out to do. It did not come to such high percentages on the Knabe piano.

When I made my début with the Chicago Symphony Orchestra at the beginning of 1922, playing Brahms's D minor Concerto, a rather unpleasant happening occurred with this piano. In the middle of the concerto one tone suddenly refused to sound. I tried and tried, and finally hit the key with my fist to demonstrate to the audience that by no means would this key produce a sound. The hammer simply did not go up—I don't know what the reason was. So the piano had to be removed from the platform. There was a lift, and another piano was brought up from the basement, a piano which was not intended for concert use and had not been tuned for a long time. And I had to continue my début in Chicago on that.

I was not too happy with such conditions. Yet I tried the Knabe piano for a second season, 1922–3. Steinway refused to let me use their pianos unless I would give up playing the Bechstein piano—which I had used for so many years—in Europe. They insisted that I play on Steinway exclusively, everywhere in the world, otherwise they would not give me their pianos in the United States. That is the reason why from 1923 until 1930 I did not return to America.

After my Chicago début I went to several small cities in the Middle West and everything was so new to me that sometimes I had to go back to the station to discover the name of the town in which I was playing, for at first they all seemed to look alike.

On this first American tour I was, of course, interviewed. I was not accustomed to that and probably did not say the right things. In Europe the people say there are more views than interviews. Though after the First World War, this custom became more and more popular even in Europe, particularly in the form of questionnaires addressed to a number of persons known to the public. I can remember some of these questionnaires perfectly—I always answered them in a manner which I hoped would be very different from all the other answers, simply for the sake of fun. I wanted to see my answer among the other answers.

One very ridiculous question was, 'How do you spend your week-ends?' I said, 'It is the lot of an artist not to know week days. He knows only holidays. So I cannot answer this question.' Of course I was satisfied when I saw how most of the other answers read, some reporting how they jumped into their Rolls Royces to reach the seashore, others protesting: 'How can I have a week-end with my amount of work?'

Another question was: 'Who was your best pupil?' I enjoyed that one as it gave me a chance to limit my answer to one single word in German. I said: *'Jeder,'* which means 'Each one.'

In 1923, the year of Hitler's Beer Hall Putsch, I went for the first time to Soviet Russia. All foreign artists who were invited there were invited by the government. In Germany the noisy, ostentatious and rather repellent behaviour of war profiteers perhaps gave me, who reacted in a correspondingly ostentatious form, the reputation of being a Bolshevik. I received a good many anonymous letters threatening me at that time. So it may be that this reputation of mine was the cause of my being invited to Russia.

I think that probably in every artist you will find both: the anarchist and the aristocrat, and wherever he sees an extreme or perversion of the one side, he will turn to the other. Thus, in Germany, provoked by the behaviour of these war profiteers, my anarchistic side was aroused. But when I came to Russia, where it seems they were waiting to receive me with open arms to embrace a *tovarisch,* I did not react as they apparently expected, because my aristocratic side came out.

Of course, it was absolutely different now from the Russia I had known in Czarist times. Then, the wealthy classes were amiable, gay, very elegant and attractive. Now, you did not see anybody any more who was elegant or amiable. Before, I had seen only samples of misery in the lower classes, but now they all seemed much happier, while my friends from the old times lived in misery.

A man had been delegated to keep me company and be the master of ceremonies. He told me that my first concert would not be held on the date set for it, but that it would be held four days later. So I asked—it was in Moscow—'What about my concert on Saturday in Leningrad?'

'Oh, we'll fix that too.' You see, this was organized from one place, one central management. So I had four days to wait before I played and I spent the four days not understanding one word of Russian. I sat every day for hours in the office of the man in charge of musical affairs. I think he had been a dental worker before, and did not know the difference between the piano and other instruments, but he was a very nice man. My presence in his office was not noticed by anybody. I sat for four days in the corner on a sofa and watched these happy people who, apparently for the first time, were allowed to use telephones. There were always some thirty people around smoking cigarettes and soup was brought and they talked and talked. I enjoyed it immensely—there was real vitality, child-like joy.

The evenings I spent in the theatre. It was a most fascinating theatre—not because of what happened on the stage; but because of what happened in the auditorium, for the audience acted too. They participated to such an extent in the happenings on the stage that it was very exciting to watch. By the way, all the modern innovations in production and stage technique I saw there first. That also was very interesting. And so was opera, where all operatic techniques were adjusted or altered in order to become propaganda.

Finally I gave my recital in this big theatre, for five thousand people. It was packed. People were silent. But then—the last chord of Beethoven's Opus 111, the final piece on my programme, had not yet died when someone from the gallery shouted: 'La Campanella!' Others repeated 'La Campanella! La Campanella!' I thought it was rather strange. I got an explanation for it afterwards. The one foreign pianist who had given concerts before I went there and had become very popular, played Liszt's Campanella after the last item of each programme, so they seemed to believe that this was part of the concert, absolutely inseparable from any recital. I think they did not particularly want to hear 'La Campanella', but from sheer politeness, or habit, they asked for it.

The morning after my recital somebody translated the Press review of the leading paper to me. In the meantime it had become clear to them that I was not the Bolshevist they had expected, so the reviewer said that for the *bourgeois* world my interpretations might have been successful, but there was no doubt that the revolution had not had the slightest influence on my conception of Beethoven!

Two days later I played the same programme in Leningrad, where the rumour of my not being a Bolshevist had not yet spread. There I got a review in which it said that my rhythm was expressive of the labour battalions marching against the bulwark of capitalism.

A young Russian pianist who was very successful there at this time was Vladimir Horowitz, then nineteen years old. He played for me privately and I was very impressed. I was, later, instrumental in getting him out of Russia.

10

A MUSICAL event of importance in 1920 was the Mahler Festival in Amsterdam. As far as I know, it was the only Mahler Festival which ever took place. There was, of course, in 1907 or 1908 the special performance of his Eighth Symphony in Munich, called by the management the Symphony of a Thousand, but at this Festival in Amsterdam all Mahler's symphonic works were performed. It lasted ten days and was accompanied, as a kind of sideshow, by a series of concerts at which only contemporary music was played. Among this music there was a composition of mine.

One of the characteristics of this Festival in Amsterdam was the presence of hundreds of musicians from foreign countries—musicians as well as writers on music and people connected with music—all as guests of the City of Amsterdam from the moment they reached the Dutch soil to the moment they left it. Now, all those guests who came from countries east of Holland had been going comparatively hungry for years, during and after the war. Here they had a marvellous chance to make up for their deprivations—and they took advantage of this chance. Some stayed with Dutch families who offered them hospitality; others received coupons which were accepted in all restaurants and hotels—and everyone had a glorious time.

The very famous violinists and 'cellists who were invited were also asked to play as concert masters in the orchestral performances, and they did it with great enthusiasm.

I must admit that not all the foreigners who enjoyed this rare occasion to eat enough—and the food was superb—behaved very well. When they came to the concerts they could hardly breathe—they had eaten so much—and then they slept during them because they were so worn out from eating. Yet, as I have said, it was a remarkable occasion for music as well.

During the 1922-3 season I made my second tour in the United States. This time it was a coast-to-coast tour. It was rather uneventful and I was very unhappy. Whether I was unhappy because the tour was uneventful or whether the tour was uneventful because I was unhappy, is an open question. In any case, I had only a very moderate success and certainly did not deserve more; so you see that the American people had good judgement at that time.

It may be that inhibitions and prejudices prevented me from doing as well as circumstances would have permitted. I disliked and still dislike the star system, and I believed and still believe that I belong to a department of music to which the performers who in this period were most popular in America did not belong. Thus, it may be that my approach to the public musical life in the United States was a wrong one and consequently I felt somehow frustrated and did not do so well. My recollections are therefore rather scant, and not very important.

I was intoxicated by the sonorities of the Philadelphia and Boston Symphony Orchestras and their perfection of execution such as I had never heard before—which does not mean that I had not heard interpretations equal to theirs, or even surpassing them, because perfection of execution and interpretation are, it is hardly necessary to say, not identical. The first time I played with the Boston Symphony Bruno Walter was conducting. It was his début in the United States.

Apart from that, I was very much impressed on my way to the west by the scenery: here was a spaciousness of nature unknown in Central or Western Europe. But my personal experiences were all of a minor kind: for instance, I remember how when I went to Colorado Springs I found that one of the waiters at my hotel came from Vienna. He invited me to go for an excursion in his car and took me up to a mountain peak.

Arriving at a town in Montana I found a telegram from the place where I was booked to perform next, not far from there, saying that the concert would not take place, as the night before, in a meeting of the committee, it had been decided to dissolve the concert society because of lack of funds. Since I had accepted the engagement in Germany a year before, I thought it was rather late to accept a cancellation—two days before the concert was to be held. As the town was in any case on my way to the next concert, I decided therefore that I would at least put the wind up these people and have some fun. So I telegraphed: *I don't accept cancellation, am coming.*

88

They wired back: *But we have no hall. We have no piano.* And I wired back again: *Insist fulfil contract, am coming.*

Finally, I arrived. At that time a tuner always travelled with me, and by our combined efforts we located three ladies of the society: the treasurer, the chairwoman and another committee member whose function I could not identify. They came, rather excited, to the hotel, and said, 'We are awfully sorry, but we have no funds—we have absolutely no funds left. You see, this was the first year of our concert series. This society was formed only last year, and we invited artists for ten subscription concerts, the seventh of which your recital would have been. But we have spent all our money on the six preceding concerts.' I said, 'I have come all the way from Berlin, Germany. Our contract was concluded a whole year ago. Do you expect me simply to give up this concert?' They replied, 'We can't help it. We have no funds.'

Next I went to a notary public to get him to confirm that I was present, and then I went to the hall, together with my tuner and another witness. Of course, I could not get in: the hall was closed and there were no lights. After that I left and did not pursue the matter any further. I had at least had my fun.

There were heavy snowstorms at that time. I went to Salt Lake City, where I saw the big Tabernacle and was told that it has a ceiling of cow-hide and such unique acoustics that one can hear even the echo of a whisper. That is not especially good for music, of course. I remember that I arrived in Salt Lake City after dinner and had hardly entered my hotel room when the newspaper office telephoned me and said that their reporter and photographer must see me immediately. I agreed to see them and was told, 'They are already on their way.' A few minutes later there was a knock at the door; the reporter came in and asked, 'What is your name, please?' That was rather surprising. I told him, and he asked me other questions.

Then I went on for my first concert in California. I have forgotten the name of the town; it was somewhere inland from Sacramento. My wife was with me on this second tour of America. We had to take a coach, or 'stage' from Sacramento which was crowded and had a distinct smell of garlic, but we arrived in good time for the concert. As usual, I went to the concert hall to see the piano—I always went with my tuner.

In the meantime, my wife was unpacking our luggage at the hotel. On my way to the concert hall I passed a newspaper office and saw my name in the window. I stopped and read that 'Mr Schnabel, because of the heavy snowstorms, cannot arrive in time for the concert and therefore it will be held five days later.' That was quite surprising again, you see. I entered the newspaper office and said, 'Here I am.' 'Well, we can't do anything,' they replied. Then they telephoned their three ladies: the treasurer, the chairwoman, and that third one, informing them that I was in town. I was called to the telephone and told, 'We are awfully sorry, but your local manager at San Francisco told us that it was impossible, or at least uncertain, whether you could come; so he postponed the concert for five days. He also wishes you to take the next stage to San Francisco, at eight o'clock. It is an express stage, and it is the best connection you can get.'

So I rushed back to my poor wife and told her, 'You must pack again at once—we haven't even time to have something to eat.' We took the 'stage'. It was dark—pitch dark—and while we were not allowed to leave the coach, the driver made at least three stops for himself to have a drink, or a chat, or something. But we had to sit in the dark coach all the time until after midnight, when we arrived in a place which was not San Francisco, but Oakland. How was I to know? Nobody told me. I had rooms reserved somewhere in San Francisco and here I had arrived at the bus depot in Oakland. We had a great deal of luggage and there was no porter. Somebody shouted, 'Hurry, hurry. The last trolley to the last ferry is going in three minutes.' Nobody had informed me of all these things, but somehow we managed to get all our luggage into this last trolley and on to the last ferry and at two-thirty in the morning we arrived in San Francisco. By the time we got to our hotel it was three o'clock. I did not feel like a human being, but like a parcel, and it took me some time to recover from the effects of being shipped around in this way.

Our hotel rooms were unusually large and I remember there was a door—a very large and wide door with mirrors: when you opened it, three extra beds came out.

In Los Angeles I met an old friend of mine, a Viennese, whom I had not seen for more than fifteen years. When I had last seen her, in Berlin—it must have been about 1905—I had given her a somewhat unusual photograph of myself—not one of those publicity pictures of which numerous copies are made, but rather a portrait. Only two copies existed of this photograph—one which still remained with my family, and this. My friend contacted me in Los Angeles and invited me for a meal. When I arrived the first thing she showed me was an old, discoloured newspaper page displaying the picture I had given to her. It was unmistakably the same picture, even every detail of the clothing, every fold in my jacket was identical. She had found this paper about five years before, lying in the street. Seeing the picture, she had picked it up as she was sure it was an announcement of my coming to America. But to her great amazement a different name appeared below the picture and the text said that this was the man who had been murdered in the park the day before. Looking further she discovered that it was a paper from a different town and that its date was long past.

She gave the paper to me and I still have it. It was some comfort to me that at least I was pictured not as the murderer but as the victim! The matter has never been explained. Perhaps photographers sometimes sell their stocks of very old pictures to newspaper offices who use them whenever a needed photograph is unobtainable, with hardly any risk, being so remote in time and place from the originals. Yet even then it remains inexplicable why the one person owning the only copy of the picture in America should find this paper, long after it was issued, in a street of another town.

Back in New York I had a real experience—my friendship with Mrs Harriet Lanier, a woman with a splendid personality, character, and mind. She was the founder of the Friends of Music, an organization which performed rarely heard choral and orchestral works under the direction of Artur Bodansky. I was in touch with Mrs Lanier until her death in 1932. She came to Europe every summer, and in 1931 we stayed with her for three weeks in a fourteenth-century Gothic palace in Venice, where we had a wonderful time. We ought to have stayed longer, but my nostalgia for grass, trees and animals— all absent in Venice—became so great that I was compelled to leave.

Before I left the United States in 1923 I had a conversation with the manager of the Knabe piano company which I have not forgotten. He told me that it was impossible to co-operate with me, because I lacked understanding of the situation. He said that in order to please the 'man in the street' and the 'tired business man'—two mythical beings, of course—one must behave musically quite differently from the way I did. 'Your famous colleagues all want to please and serve the man in the street. Why not you?' he asked. I remember that I answered, 'I don't want to bother him,' and left. Still, he sent me a box of very good cigars to my boat. Nevertheless, I did not come back. Not until 1930, for the reasons I explained earlier.

When I returned to Germany inflation was well on its way there. You cannot imagine what that means. It was the maddest episode I experienced in all my life. The disunity of the Germans after the First World War had completely disappeared and this inflation established perfect unity. Everybody was gay and alert, in the best of spirits. Nobody had anything else in mind but how to get rid of his money as quickly as possible for whatever he could get or do with it, because the value of money was decreasing every hour and a few hours later he might get only half as much for it as before. Everybody ran around with brief-cases full of notes. Finally, towards the end of this period of inflation, a ride on the bus cost several billion marks. I received my fees in packages of notes and once, after I had played with the Philharmonic Orchestra in Berlin, I had to ask a man to help me carry my fee home. On my way I passed a delicatessen store and to relieve my helper I spent half of my fee on a couple of sausages. The next morning I saw in the paper that by now I could not even get one sausage for the other half of my fee. So I laughed heartily—like all the others.

It was really amazing. Everybody rushed to the country to get whatever the farmers would give him. He would pay the highest prices, because half an hour later they would be still higher. The farmers sold all the beautiful things they had made in their best, century-old traditions—furniture, tapestry and decorative items—to city people, then they rushed to the city to buy whatever they could in department stores. Foreigners came and bought big blocks of flats for a few pounds.

But music went on absolutely undisturbed during this period, animated and stimulated as never before. The three, sometimes four, opera houses playing simultaneously in Berlin gave, in addition to the classical and romantic repertoire, operas by Richard Strauss, Pfitzner, Stravinsky, Schönberg, Hindemith, de Falla, Křenek, Schreker, Rathaus, Korngold, d'Albert and many others. The majority of these works have never been heard in this country.

As a result of the German inflation, I lost, for the second time within a few years, all my savings. It seemed rather irrelevant then, as it appeared to happen in a cycle; I was beginning to get used to it.

In each of the following years I played in Russia again, so that I went there for four consecutive seasons, in 1923, 1924, 1925 and 1926. After that, I stopped going because I thought it unsuitable for foreigners to witness the way in which things were developing there. Some of our old friends suffered so much that I could no longer stand it.

While in Russia I met the composer Alexander Glazunov. He was the kindest and most polite elderly man I have ever met, very formal and punctilious, and still behaving as if he were living in the same circumstances as before the revolution. He had a very large apartment, but it was never heated and they lived only in one room where they had a stove. Even in that room, however, it was so cold that I always had to keep my overcoat on when I visited him, and even his vodka, which he always offered to me, did not help much. Anyhow, I could never quite keep pace with him, of course. He was unhappy because some of his musical colleagues whom he appreciated very much did not agree with him that certain tones in classical works, like the C major Symphony by Schubert, or in Beethoven, must have been mistakes because they were too unusual, too unexpected. He really suffered when I and other musicians told him that we were convinced those tones were absolutely right, just because they were so unexpected and unusual. In my opinion, in a work of a genius the unexpected is more probable than the common.

I hesitate to tell this story, but it is so sweet and characteristic that I will try to overcome my hesitation. Glazunov loved to play some of his compositions for me. One night his adopted daughter, a very charming girl, played a newly composed small piano piece of his for me and I sat with him, two rooms away, in the warmer room, to listen to this piece. She had a very sonorous tone, fortunately. She played this rather inconspicuous work and suddenly he grasped my arm and said, 'Did you hear it? A dissonance.' But I had not even heard it.

It was very moving, because he was disturbed and hurt by the fact that a man like Stravinsky should have success. He said, 'Of all the two thousand pupils I taught at the conservatory in St Petersburg, he had the worst ear.'

In 1926 I was in Russia during Easter Week. I had heard so much about the persecution of religious worship that I decided to go to all churches which were open. With a Russian friend I went during the night of Saturday to Easter Sunday to twenty-six churches. All these churches were crowded and there were many soldiers in uniform, soldiers of the Red Army who were—so it seems—not forbidden to go. I am bound to say that I did not see many signs of any particular ecstasy of participation. But the people were present, and it was my impression that the same people had been in the churches the week before.

Meanwhile, in 1925, I went to England, for the first time after an interval of twenty years. My concerts were arranged by the piano firm of Bechstein. They were very anxious that I should play in England: their pianos were highly appreciated and widely used there and they even had some workshops in England where they were finished and repaired. I played two recitals in a small hall in London and had considerable success. From then on until the outbreak of the Second World War I returned every year for a great many concerts in England, as well as in Scotland and Ireland. I was very happy there. I established contact with people who became intimate friends of mine, among them Mr and Mrs Samuel Courtauld. I stayed with them in their beautiful house with its wonderful collection of paintings.

One day Mrs Courtauld told me that she was a little tired of supporting Covent Garden Opera, which she had done continuously since the First World War, and asked me whether I knew of something else they could do on behalf of music. So I devised the plan of the Courtauld-Sargent concerts, which soon became a regular institution, were extremely successful and should be imitated everywhere. I am convinced they would be a success wherever tried. To describe the idea in a few words: it was a plan of presenting a series of symphony concerts to those music lovers who were not in a position to pay the high prices for tickets to the regular symphony concerts. It was named the Courtauld-Sargent Club because Sir Malcolm Sargent became the regular conductor of the series. Membership was restricted to employees of department stores, smaller stores, shops, banks and other firms. Each of these firms had to take at least six subscriptions. They would find out how many and which of their employees were interested in music, and make a decision accordingly. The series consisted of six concerts per year, each concert given twice. The concerts were always fully subscribed and the quality of the audience was wonderful.

There was a deficit every year, but it was not more than about two thousand pounds, and the main reason for this deficit was that Mr Courtauld was so generous in granting rehearsals. Five to six rehearsals were often allowed for one concert, and when Hindemith and Stravinsky were asked to conduct one of their newest works they could even have seven or eight rehearsals. And you know how expensive rehearsals with a full symphony orchestra are.

Yet, I imagine that even with fewer rehearsals an organization like this would probably have a small yearly deficit and would therefore have to be subsidized. Applied to chamber music, however, such an organization would surely pay for itself. I have very often suggested trying it in the United States and I am absolutely convinced it would be a great success. But nobody has wanted it, so far. I do not know what the reasons have been.

In England I also established a lasting friendship with Walter J. Turner, the writer and poet, and with Sir Robert Mayer, who was born in Germany but had lived in England since his boyhood. He organized, for the first time, concerts for children and by 1939 his organization was so successful that these children's concerts were given in twenty-eight English towns. The children who participated were selected by their schoolteachers. They were always prepared for the programme by the teachers, who also went with a group of them to the concerts. It was a really exemplary organization, a model of how it should be done.

In 1924, a German newspaper publisher who had already expanded the range of his enterprise to include the publication of magazines and books, decided to enlarge his activities still further by adding music. The name of the publisher was Ullstein and his music publications were called the *Tonmeister* edition. Only works for piano, from Bach to Brahms, were included in this edition. Ullstein approached me, asking whether I would edit Beethoven's piano works for him. I agreed, but in the end I edited only the thirty-two sonatas and the Diabelli Variations.

At this time, as I have already told you, I stopped composing and the next ten years of my life were dedicated chiefly to editing, touring, beginning to make recordings, and to my work at the State Academy in Berlin—for also in 1924 this institution asked me whether I would take on a class. I had really ideal conditions; whatever I requested, was granted. For instance, the minimum number of students in other classes was eighteen, but I was permitted to limit my class to seven pupils. I have never had more than seven—and all seven had to be present at all lessons. I discovered that this is a rather productive way to teach—provided you don't have hundreds of pupils. Also I requested that, in case the schedule of teaching should interfere with my travels, I be allowed to give the lessons even late in summer, when the academy was closed, at my home. That was granted, too. They also allowed me to give my lessons at the academy at night, from nine o'clock until midnight or even later. Then the caretaker, my students and I, were the only people in the building.

I was intensely grateful for so much co-operation. Yet, in 1930 I resigned, chiefly because there was a kind of nationalistic German spirit among the majority of the other teachers which made me finally dislike the whole organization. I was considered very foolish to give up such an ideal position— with very good pay, and all the freedom I wanted—but you see, each time I came to the faculty room I was exposed to this constant friction and conflict, to differences of opinion leading to a rather aggressive, violent tone. I preferred to leave.

11

In addition to the thirty-two Beethoven sonatas which I edited in the late 'twenties, I did some other editorial work. Together with Carl Flesch I edited for Peters the three sonatas for piano and violin by Brahms, and I made a new piano score for Brahms's violin concerto and Brahms's double concerto for violin and 'cello. Ullstein published the thirty-two sonatas singly, but when nine years later Simon & Schuster, the American book publishers, made an excursion into the field of music publishing—one of the very few they made—they decided not to follow the German example but to publish the thirty-two sonatas in two volumes. Thus while in the German edition each sonata began on page 1, in the American edition each volume has between 400 and 500 pages and the pages are numbered straight through from 1 to nearly 900. However, unfortunately Simon & Schuster forgot also to change the references to page numbers in the footnotes. And so someone using this edition may find in one of the late sonatas of Volume Two that he is told in a footnote on page 812, say, to look for a parallel passage on page 7; looking for this, he finds that page 7 is part of the first sonata in Volume One and gets terribly puzzled as he sees, of course, no sense in it. Yet I trust that after a while every musician will be able to figure out what happened.

In 1927 I played the thirty-two sonatas for the first time in a series of seven matinée recitals at the beautiful theatre of the *Volksbühne*—the 'People's Stage'—in Berlin. In 1928 my wife and I gave six joint Schubert recitals, performing the great cycles, many *Lieder,* sonatas and other piano solo compositions.

Berlin was becoming more and more unpleasant in those years. Every day you could watch elderly, bald-headed, fat men goosestepping through the streets in uniform and brown shirts with swastikas, roaring their gruesome songs, dreams of the glorious days when the world would be theirs and Jewish blood would splash from their knives. This is a literal quotation.

In 1929 I was asked once again whether I would not agree to make records. Until then I had consistently refused to do so. One of the chief reasons for my refusal was that I did not like the idea of having no control over the behaviour of the people who listened to music which I performed—not knowing how they would be dressed, what else they would be doing at the same time, how much they would listen. Also I felt that recordings are against the very nature of performance, for the nature of performance is to happen but once, to be absolutely ephemeral and unrepeatable. I do not think there could ever have been two performances of the same piece by the same person which were absolutely alike. That is inconceivable.

Nevertheless, I eventually became convinced that in spite of all defects the value of recordings would still be great enough to justify them. Then I was very flattered at being asked—it was the first experiment along this line—to record all the works that Beethoven had written for the piano.

These recordings would be available only to subscribers. That was an experiment, too, and I think it worked out very well. The company was surprised by the great number of subscribers in England, the British Commonwealth and on the continent of Europe. In the United States the records were not released until much later, and even then only some of them. I don't know what the reason was.

Memories of my first year of making records in London belong to the most painful recollections of my life. I suffered agonies and was in a state of despair each time I recorded. I felt as if I were harried to death—and most unhappy. Everything was artificial—the light, the air, the sound—and it took me quite a long time to get the company to adjust some of their equipment to music, and even longer to adjust myself to the equipment, however much improved it was. Then perhaps I became more indulgent—I no longer expected and demanded so much. Even so, one day after I had worked with this company for seven years, they told me that my nickname among the employees and engineers was still 'The Changer'.

For ten years, from 1929 to 1939, I made all my recordings with the same engineer, so in the end the two of us did the work quite alone. There was no interference and I was, by then, very pleased with the spirit of the thing. In the meantime, everything had been changed. Acoustic conditions had become better and there were also certain improvements in the technique of recording.

In 1930 Dr Koussevitzky invited me, without an intermediary and without employment of a manager, to come and play at the Brahms Festival at Boston. I accepted with great pleasure; but there was the question of the piano. Steinway still refused to give me pianos in the United States unless I would play on Steinway also in Europe. The solution found was that Bechstein decided to send two pianos for me from Germany to America, at their expense, since they were trying at that time to establish branches in the United States. In this they were not successful, since the depression came just then.

In American books of reference I always find that this Brahms Festival in Boston is quoted as having been held in 1933, the year of Brahms's hundredth anniversary; but it really took place in 1930. It does not matter, of course. The dates don't make any difference.

I played eight times with the Boston Symphony, which was a fascinating experience. I had a very good time, too. It was the month of May and I almost became a favourite of Boston Society in these weeks. That did not last very long, unfortunately. It must be that I am not suited for that kind of role. For instance, I have never in my life received fan mail. I do not say that I miss it; but I did not get it, you see.

In reviews I have often even been referred to as 'an artist for men'. Now, I don't know whether this is meant as a compliment to me or as a compliment to women. Whatever it means, it is nonsense, of course. But it recalls another epithet with which the Press has labelled me throughout my career. From my youth on, whenever I played somewhere for the first time, I read the next morning that 'this young man'—or later, 'this Mr Schnabel'—'is a serious artist'. I never ceased to be startled and surprised by that, for I am still absolutely convinced that all performers are serious artists. There are no artists and no performers other than serious ones.

I would say that Mr Jack Hylton or Mr Kostelanetz, for instance, are for my state much too serious, almost deadly serious. I would name them as typical representatives, prototypes, of what I call 'highbrows'. That is absolutely so, because Mr Kostelanetz, for one, takes the greatest pains to conceal simplicity with sophistication. And that is exactly my definition of a 'highbrow'; someone who, with the greatest effort of sophistication, tries to conceal simplicity. Yet strangely enough it is those who struggle all their lives towards simplicity who are always called highbrows. The confusion is apparently caused by the fact that the sphere in which they find themselves is more elevated and less accessible.

All my life I have also been termed 'austere', 'professorial', 'scholarly', 'ruminative' and so forth—with a few exceptions, which were: 'the tipsy Gypsy', or 'Wagnerian neo-romantic bombastic hyper-expressive', or just an 'amateur'. This last-mentioned bouquet was presented to me in New York City.

Now, what interested me most during my short visit to the United States in 1930 was, apart from the Boston Symphony Orchestra and Boston Society, the situation of Prohibition. The speakeasies and boot-leggers fascinated me—the way in which everyone participated in what were supposed to be dangerous activities. Of course, I also felt how very demoralizing it was. But I have never seen anything like it anywhere in the world.

Then I went back to Germany, but played very little there. In those last three years—I left Germany in 1933—I did, however, a lot of touring. I played in Italy, Spain, Greece, Turkey, Palestine, and gathered new experiences; particularly in Palestine. I shall never forget the shock I felt when, after arriving in Jerusalem, I went to the Church of the Holy Sepulchre and saw there more than a dozen chapels—I don't know the exact number—round the tomb. I was startled and asked the friend who had taken me there, 'Why so many chapels?' He said, 'In order to separate the people who come here to worship, the different sects of Christians who otherwise would start quarrels and fight each other.' I remember how very depressing this was to me; and I heard afterwards that as long as Palestine was under Turkish rule it really often happened at Easter that these worshippers had to be separated by the whip of a Turkish guard, a Moslem. . . .

I was fascinated by the scenery in Palestine and, particularly among the Arabs and Bedouins, to view the scenes of domestic life which apparently were the same as they had been two thousand years before. With amazement I saw the marvellous accomplishments of the young Jewish settlement, especially in agricultural activities.

My concerts, I am bound to tell you, were not too popular.

They were not quite to the people's taste and did not arouse much enthusiasm. But I remember a few things, which I will tell you now.

When I played in the different cities, some employees or custodians in the halls were a bit embarrassed because I was not received with the same enthusiasm as the violin virtuoso who had preceded me on this tour. These men tried then, in a most charming way, to comfort me. One of them came and said: 'Mr Schnabel, you must know, a piano is not a Yiddish instrument. The real Yiddish instrument is the fiddle.'

More sophisticated was a young man whom I suspect not to have been in Palestine much longer than I had been there myself. He approached me with the following pronouncement: 'Mr Schnabel, I cannot express to you how grateful we have to be to you for bringing Beethoven to us. We have been waiting for him for two thousand years.'

Apart from these tours I went every year to England. There is a very special type of experience you have in English concert halls. What is common to most of them is the artificial blizzard arranged on the platform. It is merciless towards the performer. The listeners, quite comfortable in their woollies, jerseys and overcoats, want to combine open-air pleasure with the enjoyment of music.

Once—it was in Bristol—the current of cold air was so powerful that I thought, 'this platform is a death trap'. I had warmed my fingers in the artists' room, but when I began to play my hands got colder and colder, until my fingers were like icicles. And meanwhile the potted palms around me were waving in the wind. I thought, 'I am simply not strong enough for this. I don't have the constitution of a Shetland pony.' Finally I became so tired and desperate that I swore never to come back to the place.

My manager, Mr Tillett, never tried to persuade me. He immediately agreed with me when I told him that I did not want to play under certain circumstances or in certain places. He accepted my reasons and would never recommend me for such places. If they asked for me, he would say, 'Mr Schnabel does not want to accept. He is nervous about his health,' or something similar.

But five years after my experience in Bristol, my manager asked me: 'Would you accept an engagement in Bristol? It is in that hall where you decided not to play again, but in the meantime the hall has been renovated at the expense of £40,000, and is now an ideal place.' So I said: 'If you say so, I shall gladly accept.' I was then on tour with Bronislaw Hubermann and we were giving ten joint sonata recitals in England.

A German tuner, employed by Bechstein's representative in London, always travelled with me in England. He knew my idiosyncrasies and particularly my dislike of gusts of cold air. When we reached Bristol, he went early in the afternoon to the hall to see to the piano. As soon as I arrived, he came and whispered in my ear: 'That draught is still there! I even know where it is coming from. I discovered the hole in the wall.' So I was prepared for the worst.

The hall was marvellous. The artists' room had thick carpets and a whole wall was mirrored, the last word in luxury and opulence. We went to the platform and there was really the same wind which had been sweeping through this hall before the £40,000 were spent. But this time the platform was crowded with people sitting around us; and I, playing from music, had to employ the help of a man who turned pages. Since the pages were constantly flapping about, tossed by the wind, he had to hold his left arm over the music, which did not exactly make it easier to see the notes.

The situation was pathetic. Hubermann and I remarked loudly and frankly that in such conditions the amount of inspiration available could hardly be very considerable. We tried to do our best, but it was quite hopeless. By the time we started the second sonata, we had given up any idea of playing *Con amore*. It was Brahms's G major Sonata, I remember. Somewhere in the first movement there was a mark in my part that my page-turner should go to the violin stand and turn a page for the violinist. He did this. In the meantime, the pages of my music were blown in rapid succession to some place in the last movement. Fortunately, I knew the piece quite well by memory and was able to continue playing. Then the man came back and tried to find the place where I was. It was extremely irritating.

All the people around us were aware of this lamentable situation. When the first movement was ended, a girl who sat in the second row of seats on the platform very shyly got up, approached my chair at the piano, presented me with a hairpin and said, 'This perhaps might help.' She got an ovation from the audience. Hubermann came across to the page-turner and instructed him how to use the hairpin, as a clasp holding the pages together. Then we continued the concert—in somewhat better spirit.

I think that the ratio of the cost of this hairpin to the £40,000 spent on the renovation of the hall gives cause for reflection.

In Oxford the hall was not renovated, so I really never played there again after 1934. I refused, because this hall, also used as a gymnasium, was on the third floor of a very old building built along a narrow cul-de-sac, on the first and second floors of which there was a police station. This position proved unfortunate in various respects.

My first concerts there had taken place on week-day afternoons. I heard some noises from the outside—from people who were singing, walking or talking—because the windows were open, of course, in winter-time. But it was not really bad. For some reason, the puppies in the kennel opposite the hall were quiet; I did not even know that there was a kennel.

Then, however, came the occasion when I had to play there on a Saturday night—when Merry Old England comes out. It is hard to describe all that happened during that concert. First of all, one heard running water all the time, apparently in connection with the gymnasium; also, at irregular intervals, calls to the police station. Telephones ringing, running water —and the acoustic manifestations of a good number of people having a very gay time outside.

When I sat down to play my second group, I heard church bells, chimes. I thought, 'That must be nine o'clock,' and waited, counting quietly, 'one, two, three . . . nine, ten, eleven, twelve, thirteen——'; the audience was chuckling because everybody was initiated except me. I did not know what was going on. By the time I had counted up to seventy-five, I thought, 'Well, this might go on all night,' and started playing. But then something must have happened in the kennel, because now the puppies started barking very loudly—for a while in competition with the chimes—and kept it up for the rest of the programme. All the noises were very clear and strong as the windows were open. So music was, I think, the only thing which was not heard at that concert.

Afterwards, people apologized, in a very charming way. 'We should have told you about Great Tom of Christ Church, which strikes at nine o'clock to signal the closing of the college gates. It strikes 101 times because there were originally 101 students. Also,' they said, 'we should have chloroformed those puppies.'

These were the two most drastic experiences. I had others also, as for instance once when I played in Folkestone. I arrived by train, at three in the afternoon; the concert was to start at five o'clock. It was drizzling English winter rain. There was no taxi-cab. As I had no luggage, except a little handbag, I decided to walk. In summer, Folkestone is a lively seaside resort, but in winter-time there are mainly the thousands of retired people who live there permanently.

I came to the hall which is built into a cliff; one enters from the top downwards. In the hall I saw many ladies eating and drinking tea. They arrive at three o'clock when such a five-o'clock concert is given.

My piano technician sat on the platform, tuning the piano, and the platform was arranged as if for a funeral—so many flowers, and just that type of flowers. I was never fond of that. I asked my tuner to find out whether tea would be served during the concert also. The knitting was noiseless, of course; but the tea service was not. He was assured that this would stop at a quarter to five.

Next to the platform there was a kind of trapdoor leading down to the artists' room. I spent the next two hours in that artists' room, sitting in an uncomfortable chair. What else could I do in Folkestone in drizzling rain? Nobody came to look for me. The window of the room was directly above the beach, facing the Channel—in good weather it would have been a beautiful view.

At ten to five, a man finally came to see me and said: 'I am the manager of this show. Glad to meet you.' He asked: 'How long does your programme last?' I said: 'Approximately two hours.' 'What a nuisance! What a nuisance!' he replied. I never forgot that. He said: 'Well, you can take one piece out of the programme.' 'All right, I shall play one piece less, if you wish.' 'Well, I am only the manager of this show. If the president comes, I shall suggest that to him. You know, our people have a dinner at a certain hour and they would be very disturbed if this routine were changed. They are very orderly people, very orderly people, you know.'

Then came the president, a white-haired clergyman, to whom

the manager simply said: 'That item, Number Two [it was Beethoven's Sonata Opus 110], will not be played by Mr Schnabel. Will you please announce that to the audience?' The president, not asking any questions, went to the platform and said that item Number Two would not be played. No response. It simply would not be played.

'Well,' the manager said, 'you can kick off at five o'clock sharp, if you like.' So I went and 'kicked off'. I played my programme through. The audience remained lifeless and devoid of any vitality. I felt that the music was like a tree in the desert and I went on playing.

By now, my three items having been played, I had finished fourteen minutes before the customary exit of the audience. So the manager said: 'We want to get our money's worth. You can play thirteen more minutes.' 'All right; fine. Very good,' I replied, and then I practised some pieces there which I had to play a few days later in another town. I said to myself, 'What does it matter?' I played some intermezzi by Brahms and then the audience left.

I went back to the artists' room. The two men came, handed me a cheque and left. Then, since my train back to London was not until after eight o'clock, I took my time over changing in the artists' room; and when I left the room, went up those steps, which were more like a ladder than a staircase, and through the 'hatch', I found that the whole building was dark, pitch dark. Fortunately I had some matches with me—I was still smoking at that time.

So I tried to find a way out. There was no light anywhere—in this huge building—it was like a labyrinth in the darkness. For at least half an hour, always carrying my little handbag, I wandered, a lonely wanderer, through this dark building, using up all my matches. Finally, I saw a light and made my way towards it. And there, to my amazement, I met another lonely wanderer. I asked him: 'Can you tell me how to get out of this building?' He said: 'Yes. You have to go up there. You are a lucky fellow,' he continued; 'if I had not been here in the building, you would have been locked in all night.' I said: 'That's wonderful,' and escaped.

In the drizzling rain I walked back to the station. I had still time, so I asked the man at the news-stand whether there was a place where I could get something to eat. He said: 'What a pity you weren't here for lunch. There is a very good place just opposite the station; but it's closed in the evening.'

The fact that it was nearly always draughty in British concert halls and that windows were hardly ever closed, also had the consequence that when there was a dense fog it might come into the hall. I remember that once in Glasgow I actually could not see the audience. There *was* one, however.

I played the complete cycle of the thirty-two Beethoven sonatas (each time in seven recitals) only four times in my life: twice in Berlin, once in London and once in New York. In Berlin I repeated the cycle, this time at the *Philharmonie,* the hall where all the orchestral concerts of the Berlin Philharmonic Orchestra took place, during the winter season of 1932–3. The series started, I think, in November 1932; it ended on 28 April 1933.

In the meantime, the National Socialists came to power. The right to broadcast my seven concerts—the cycle of the thirty-two Beethoven sonatas—had been bought by the state-controlled German Broadcasting Company. Apparently, when Hitler took over they were commanded to stop broadcasting these concerts, for the last three recitals of my series, from February on, were not broadcast. I found out about this only from people who wanted to hear my concerts on the radio (the hall was sold out) because the Broadcasting Company never notified me. They fulfilled all their obligations towards me and never said a word. They just announced to their listeners on the air that the concerts would not be broadcast, without giving any reason.

In fact, when I left a day after the last concert—and I have never been in Germany since—the two directors of the music department of this radio station came to say good-bye to me. They were rather sentimental and embarrassed, but they did not even mention that my last concerts had not been broadcast, which I appreciated very much.

In the autumn of 1932 the City of Berlin had started preparation for a Brahms Festival, for the Brahms anniversary year of 1933. The representative of the city council who was in charge of preparing and arranging this festival was a very charming man. I think he was a Social Democrat and the preparation of this festival was an honorary function of his. He had come in 1932 to discuss the festival with me and we had agreed that all the chamber music works with piano which

106

Brahms had written would be performed in the festival by Hubermann, Hindemith, Piatigorsky and me.

Now, when Hitler came to power, we knew, of course, that the Brahms Festival, if held at all, would certainly not include us as performers. So it was no surprise when, also on my last morning in Germany, this man telephoned me and said: 'Mr Schnabel, I have to tell you that I am no longer in charge of the Brahms Festival and plans have been changed. If you want to negotiate with the new man in charge, it would be——' I interrupted him, saying: 'I expected that.' And I think these were about the last words I spoke in Germany: 'Though I may not be pure-blooded, I am fortunately cold-blooded. Good luck to you.'

12

DURING our summer vacation in 1932, after having spent a few weeks in the Swiss mountains my wife and I went down to Italy to visit friends living on Lake Como. We were so fascinated by the beauty of nature and the way of life there that we asked our friends to see whether they could find a house for us where we could spend our next summer vacation.

In the first months of the following year, 1933, the new régime was inaugurated in Germany and I decided immediately, though a foreigner, to leave Berlin. But I still had to complete my series of thirty-two Beethoven sonatas. The last of these concerts took place on 28 April.

Meanwhile, our friends on Lake Como had found a house for us and we had already arranged to go there earlier for the summer vacation, as originally planned.

My family left Berlin in May. We had bought a car—our first—and my sons had just learned to drive. Their first application of their freshly acquired technique was to take their mother all the way from Berlin, over high mountain passes, to Italy. Somehow they managed to arrive, fortunately.

I was on tour at this time and joined my family somewhat later on Lake Como. We liked it so much there that we soon decided to rent the house on a permanent basis so that we might come back at any time we liked. During the first summer we had none of our belongings there as it was a furnished house. In the autumn, however, we made arrangements for all our possessions which could be removed from Berlin to be shipped to Italy.

We stayed in this house until 1938 and were very happy there. Each summer we taught there for three or four months, my wife and I and also my elder son. My class alone consisted of fifteen or more young pianists. You can imagine how surprised tourists must have been when they passed through this little village and out of nearly every house came sounds of classical piano music, mostly good performances of the most exacting works.

Everyone seemed to have a good time, especially the young students—except that on the way to their lessons they had to climb about two hundred steps. That was not too pleasant, but I had to do the same whenever I came home, since our house was on the hillside and a very long staircase led up to it.

The winters we spent in England. My younger son, who had just finished his studies in a dramatic school in Berlin, came with us and joined the Old Vic and stayed with them for four years; at first he was a student, but quite soon he was given the chance of participating in performances on the stage, beginning with very small parts. This training was inestimably valuable for him.

In May 1933 I played at the Brahms Festival in Vienna. I mentioned that my participation in the Brahms Festival in Berlin had been cancelled. So Vienna, at that time not yet incorporated into Germany but independent, engaged us for their festival instead. We played Brahms's trios and quartets—Hubermann, Hindemith, Casals, and I. I also played the B flat major Concerto, with Furtwängler conducting.

Mr Schuschnigg, then Minister of Justice and Education, made an inaugural speech to greet and welcome the guests, especially the guests from other countries. I remember this speech particularly because three times in his address he said 'Bruckner' instead of 'Brahms', which was very revealing. It did not happen because he was ignorant of music, but simply because he liked Bruckner's music much better. When it happened the second and third time, we all became rather nervous, for we had all come to the *Brahms* Festival.

Performances went very well and we had great fun and pleasure at our rehearsals, with plenty of time. After one of our evening concerts (I tell you this because it is rather interesting and also instructive) we went to a very popular restaurant in the basement of a hotel. There were about fifty people there besides us. Around midnight Furtwängler came, with two friends, and his behaviour seemed planned and prepared. In the presence of these fifty or more people, he addressed Hubermann and me, asking us once more whether we would not change our minds and come back the following winter to play in Berlin with him. We had been asked before and refused, of course, to do so, for reasons which you can easily guess.

Hubermann asked me to answer first. I made it very simple and said that if all the musicians who had been excluded or fired in Germany for political or racial reasons, if all these musicians were called back and reinstated in their former positions, then I would agree to come back. But if they were not called back, I would have to stick to my refusal. To my great amazement Furtwängler replied—and this was obviously not prepared—that I was mixing art and politics. And that was that.

Early in 1933 I had received a letter from the University of Manchester in which they told me that they had decided to grant me an honorary doctor's degree, but would like to know, before making a final decision, whether I would accept it. I had never had contact with anybody at this educational institute, and did not know a single member of the faculty. So I replied that I felt extremely honoured, even surprised, and would accept gratefully. They then asked me to come and receive the degree on the day when all their doctors' degrees would be conferred. Unfortunately, the date coincided with the Brahms Festival in Vienna, so I could not go and told them so.

They then suggested arranging a single ceremony at a date when I could come. In that case, however, since it would take much less time for one man alone to receive the doctor's degree, than for the usual five or six, I would have to speak or play in order to fill in some time so that the ceremony would not be too short. I answered, 'I will try,' and as I did not want to play on this occasion I prepared an address.

When I arrived for the ceremony, the atmosphere in the large auditorium was very solemn and I remember that I had to walk very cautiously because the cap I had to wear was much too small for my head and was always on the verge of falling off. I mounted the platform and there were two professors, one of them proposing me for the degree, and the Chancellor, who conferred it on me.

One of the professors also read a document explaining what had caused the university to offer this honour to me. It was a short document and it mentioned that they had decided to give me the honorary doctor's degree not only for what I did but also for what I omitted to do. It did not go into details about

110

this, and then called me the 'Aristides of music'. My classical education was not sufficiently wide for me to know what this meant. I had to consult the dictionary to find out, but naturally concluded that it was not an insult.

In the same year, 1933, Steinway changed their attitude and agreed to let me use their pianos in the United States, even if I continued elsewhere to play the Bechstein piano which I had played at concerts all my life. Thus, from 1933 on, I went every year to America.

In 1935 I went again to Russia, and was very much surprised by the enormous changes. It was more than eight years since I had been there. During this visit I heard the first performance of Bach's St John Passion in Russia, with the full Gospel text sung by a Russian choir. In a musical and artistic sense the singing was not quite satisfactory—they had never before been exposed to music of this kind and this style—but the devotion and ecstasy with which these Russians sang their parts was very marvellous to see.

When I was in Russia in 1925, Bechstein had sent a piano there for my concerts with the idea that it would be sent back to Berlin when I left Russia. But at the time of my departure, the Philharmonic in Leningrad, a state-run institute, sent a telegram to Bechstein, asking whether the piano could remain in Russia as they had the intention of buying it after a while, and promising that it would not be used in the meantime. Bechstein granted this request and the Leningrad Philharmonic really bought the piano sometime later. But even after they had bought it the piano was very rarely used—only for gala concerts. Otherwise it was kept in a safe place and was cleaned regularly—and caressed by the charwomen. So when I arrived in Leningrad in 1935 I found my old piano, and it was in wonderful shape.

At that time I accepted an invitation to return to Russia in 1937, but I cancelled that tour, because in the meantime a wave of antagonism against foreigners started to rise. This antagonism eventually led to all foreign conductors who for years had been the leaders of Russian orchestras, from Tiflis and Odessa to Moscow and Leningrad, having to leave the country. Some of them were told they could stay on condition that they became Russian citizens. But as far as I know none of them accepted. Most of them were artists who had lost their jobs earlier in Germany when the National Socialists came to

111

power; they were welcomed in Russia, were successful there and did very good work, but then they were fired in Russia too, and had to leave again.

I cancelled in good time, long before the concerts were to be given; but the Russians refused to accept my cancellation and continued to telephone me and send me telegrams wherever I went. How they managed to locate me, I don't know. I had cancelled the tour while I was in the United States, but as soon as I had returned to my home in Tremezzo, on Lake Como, they telephoned me there. I got my secretary to speak to them, telling them that I simply could not come.

Then I went to visit my mother in Vienna. It was the last time I saw her. I had not been in Vienna an hour when to my great amazement the porter at the Hotel Bristol telephoned my room, announcing that Moscow was on the line. I told him: 'Just say I am not here.' This he did.

From Vienna I went to Warsaw, as I had arranged—in connection with the tour I had planned in Russia—to play in Warsaw and Prague. At my hotel in Warsaw a telegram from Moscow had already arrived. It was rather mysterious, how they knew my itinerary so well, but it seems they had a good service.

Meanwhile, in 1934 I had played the thirty-two Beethoven sonatas in London and in 1936 I played them in New York, in a series of recitals at Carnegie Hall.

That was also the year when in New York the New Friends of Music was founded by a pupil of mine and her husband. I think I am allowed to say that I was rather instrumental in helping with the planning and establishment of this organization, which arranged a series of sixteen chamber-music concerts every season.

Another pupil of mine founded and organized, together with her husband, the Pittsburgh New Friends of Music, also a chamber-music series. There, in a much smaller city, it was more difficult, but the organization still continues. Pittsburgh was the only city outside New York where a chamber-music series of this type was then established and managed to survive. Now, in 1945, after consultation with me, the Music Guild of Los Angeles has been founded and might be particularly promising because a department of the Chamber of Commerce is also represented in it.

In 1937—I think it was 1937—I gave a series of seven recitals of works by Mozart, Schubert, and Schumann in London. I have never repeated this anywhere else.

In March 1938 I was touring in the United States and one of my concerts was in St. Louis. I had just dressed for the concert and come to the hotel lobby on my way to the hall, when an 'extra' was handed to me by which I was informed of the invasion of Austria by the German army and the incorporation of Austria into Germany. In other words, I was informed of the loss of my Fatherland. As you know, it had already been mutilated and crippled after the First World War. But now even this Austria ceased to exist.

I was not in the best of spirits that night and really don't know how I performed because my mind was filled only with this event. Upon my return to New York, I immediately took steps to arrange for my immigration to the States, and for my wife's immigration. My sons had come earlier, in 1937, and were by this time already residents of the United States. With the help of my friends and agents who advised me, I arranged to get my American immigration visa in Havana, and come to the United States from there. Although I was born in Austria, my birthplace became part of Poland after the First World War, so that according to the American immigration laws I came under the Polish quota. But I had an Austrian passport. My wife, who was born in Germany, came under the German quota, but also had an Austrian passport. All this seems rather complicated, but at that time it was still really quite easy and could be done in a comparatively short time.

It had been arranged that I should be in Havana on 1 May in order to receive my visa and I had extended my stay in New York to wait for this date. When I arrived in Havana, the American Consul very kindly told me that he was terribly sorry but the Polish quota for May was already filled and closed and that he could include me only in the June quota. He told me that it was very pleasant to stay a whole month in Havana and suggested that I wait. But I had obligations in Europe and asked him whether my documents could not be transferred to Milan. He said that that was possible and he would send them there.

When I saw the American Consul at Milan, he said: 'I am terribly sorry, but only the Consulate in Naples is competent in immigration matters.' So I said: 'All right. If you will be so kind as to transfer my documents to Naples, I shall arrange to be there.' But then I found out that there was a regulation limiting the validity of a visa to three months. Therefore, if I received a visa under the June quota, I would have to arrive in America not later than September, otherwise my visa would become invalid. My professional commitments, however, were such that it was impossible for me to go to America before February. So I had to ask the consul in Naples whether he would give my June quota number to someone else, who might be very happy to get it, and put me on the December quota instead. He was very friendly and did this for me. Then I arranged to give a recital in Naples on 21 December, so that I could go to the American Consulate on 22 December, to be examined and receive my visa.

But by the end of October the Italian government had been induced or persuaded by the Germans to introduce restrictions and discriminatory laws against Jews. Under such circumstances I did not, of course, want to play in Italy, nor did I want to stay there any longer. So I cancelled my concert in Naples and wrote to the American Consul, asking him whether he would kindly transfer my documents to London. He did this and that was the end of their long journey: Havana-Milan-Naples-London.

In London there were still some complications. Our Austrian passports were no longer valid because Austria had ceased to exist, and we did not want German passports. Fortunately we were able to obtain British certificates of identity—a kind of interim passport—which could be used for travelling.

During all these months I continued playing and somehow—in spite of all the complications caused by the rapid changes of circumstances in Europe at that time—I was able to fulfil most of my engagements. At the beginning of 1939, while I was in England for the last time, I met my elder son who had come there from America, on a concert tour of his own.

Finally, in February 1939, I arrived in America, and a month later my wife followed me. As I had accepted a tour in Australia for the summer of 1939—which is winter there—I had to apply, almost immediately after my arrival as an immigrant, for a re-entry permit, the document which enables a resident alien to leave and re-enter America. It was granted to me and I left from Los Angeles for Australia. That was a very happy summer—or winter—whichever you want to call it. All those

114

paradisical islands—Hawaii, Samoa, the Fiji Islands, and then New Zealand, and Australia herself, where one did not see many signs of trouble or dissatisfaction, feuds or rifts. All seemed so happy and beautiful.

Music in Australia has not many traditions and the halls are not too good. But they have an ideal broadcasting system. I was a guest of the Australian Broadcasting Commission. They had at that time 1,100,000 subscribers who each paid £1 annually. Of course, with these £1,100,000 annually, this organization could provide really the best programmes, the best music—independently of any sponsors. Their concerts were given not in studios, but in concert halls.

I always hope that some day this system will be introduced in the States. I think nobody would be unwilling to pay a small sum a month if he could hear musical and other programmes without the interruption by advertisements, and especially without the dependence upon commercial sponsors and advertising agencies and their taste. I have asked many people. Nobody said he would not want to do it.

I had booked my passage back from Australia via the Orient and Suez to England, where I had commitments for the autumn of 1939. But by the end of July the world situation seemed so threatening that I changed my booking, fearing that otherwise, in the event of war, I might suddenly be stranded in Bombay, Calcutta or elsewhere on the way.

Furthermore, I had just received a cable from my younger son in New York, informing me that he had married an American girl whom I had never seen. I was curious to meet her and that was an additional reason why I changed my booking and bought a passage via the Pacific to California and from New York to England. I still have a claim on this latter part of the passage with the Cunard Line.

By the time I arrived in Honolulu, the Second World War was about to break out. It was 2 September. Then I went on to Los Angeles and after September 1939 I did not leave the United States again. In the meantime, we all became American citizens.

In these years since 1939 I have devoted myself to composing, teaching and performing. During the time from 1935 to 1939 I composed several large works, and since 1939 I have written many more. My teaching consisted of private lessons in New York, not to very many pupils, and five courses in five successive years at the University of Michigan in Ann Arbor. These courses were not actually arranged or run by the University, but were inspired and established through the initiative of the piano teachers at the Music School of the University. The University only supplied the premises, the pianos, and all facilities. Otherwise, these were just private courses to which I admitted only six performing students each time. But the number of listeners or 'non-performing students' was unlimited. I gave this course five times and I always enjoyed it very much.

My stay in New York, from 1939 on, had a very different character from the previous times I stayed there; partly because I was a permanent resident now. I moved to an apartment hotel. All our belongings had remained in Italy and during the war they could not be brought over. I had already taken it for granted that I would never see them again, as Italy was an enemy country. But after the war I received the news that miraculously all our belongings were safe—including all my music, my books and the manuscripts of many of my compositions. Friends had hidden them in a farmhouse in the mountains, before it was too late.

In New York, however, what made my life so very different now, was most of all the enormously increased number of people with whom I had contact. These additional people were the refugees. They came from all countries in Europe, from all the cities and towns where during my tours I had accepted their hospitality in the days when they were living in splendid circumstances. Most of them were by no means intimate friends of mine, just people who had invited me whenever I came to their town, be it Budapest, Hamburg, Rome, Prague, Amsterdam or any of the countless smaller places where I had played, years and decades ago. They had been important people in their respective communities. Now, here they were nonentities—and penniless. I could not, and did not want to, refuse to see them. Yet, as you can imagine, it meant a tremendous demand on my time, for there were so very many of them. New York, on the other hand, became fascinating in a new way by their presence.

While I was still in Tremezzo, on Lake Como, I received one day a cable from the University of Chicago. It was such a long cable and the number of words prepaid for an answer was so great that it nearly killed the postmaster with excitement be-

116

cause in that little village he had never seen or even dreamt of such a costly cable from such a great distance. I was asked in this cable whether I would, in principle, be willing to accept some activity here—to talk or lecture or co-operate in some other way. It also announced that Mr and Mrs Swift, of this hall, would come and see me in Tremezzo, to discuss this with me. They came one afternoon and the result was that in 1940 I gave three lectures here in Mandel Hall, which later on, in 1942, were published by the Princeton University Press. That was my first co-operation with this university.

In 1943 I dispensed with managerial services for my pianistic performances. My relations with American managers were never too fortunate or warm, I would say. You see, they are rather different from Hermann Wolff, whom I have mentioned so often here. These men had little interest in music, not much of a feeling for it, and no respect for quality. At least, that is what I think. They seemed rather to be salesmen of this kind of merchandise; and apparently their desire was, along the line of least resistance, to sell as much as possible, as quickly as possible, to as many customers as possible. Of course, not all presentations of art can flourish in these conditions.

My manager said that he could not understand (and I absolutely approve of his attitude—as a salesman) a person who refused to be 'sold' as much as might have been possible. But I wanted rather to limit my public appearances, preferred to perform fewer times and only what I liked and where I liked to play.

Also, my manager often told me that I was a musician for musicians only. Now, I know that concerts are not given for musicians, so what sense was there in being represented by him? He even called me 'an incurable megalomaniac' when he was angry with me. I was never angry with him. Yet, finally, we separated; and I think we both felt happier.

I soon noticed that all these alleged necessities in the pursuit of a career, all these supposed prerequisites for success, are fallacies. For I am still admitted to American concert halls without a manager and without publicity. Some people with great intelligence apparently succeed in finding my address or telephone number and ask me whether I will play for their organization. And then, mostly within five minutes, we come to an agreement.

I am now always in direct contact with the president (or

117

whoever else is in charge) of the organizations which ask me to play; there is no middleman. But then, of course, all these organizations have a 'public relations director'. That is a title I have come across only in the last three years. Before that this man was always called the 'publicity manager'—but it seems the highbrows, who want to conceal simplicity, now call him a 'public relations director'—they decided that the old title sounded too simple.

So, whenever I had agreed to play on a certain date for one of these organizations, they gave my name—among the names of all other artists performing for them—to their 'public relations director' who, as part of his duty and routine, subsequently wrote to me, asking me to supply publicity material, like photographs and Press comments about my playing.

Now, I thought there must be a limit to the time in which it is necessary or useful to supply such information. It seemed ridiculous to me that a musician who has performed in public for fifty years should present evidence, in towns where he has played often before, that he can produce 'rippling scales' or has a 'beautiful tone'. I felt that those people who still did not know what I looked like or what to expect of my playing, were definitely not interested.

So whenever the public relations directors ask me for such information, I reply that unfortunately I cannot help them because I don't have a single piece of publicity material. Then I go and play and the halls are just as well attended as for the performances of artists who do supply publicity material.

I am willing to admit, however, that my attitude is rather anti-social; for less money is circulated if no publicity material is used. And that may be a very important point.

Sometimes these publicity managers ask me for the strangest things. Recently I received a letter in which I was asked to send, immediately, 8,000 dodgers. I consulted my dictionary and there I found that a dodger is an 'elusive person', a 'swindler'. Well, I thought, I know a good many crooks, but 8,000—! Eventually, of course, I discovered that 'dodger' is American slang for publicity leaflet.

And so I come to the end of my story. I hope that all the pieces I have supplied will somehow fit together and you will see that they all belong to the same picture. And I hope this picture will show you the career of a musician who always tried to do his best.

PART TWO

PART TWO

1

VOICE: *I have always wondered why one never hears Tchai-kovsky's Second Piano Concerto?*

MR SCHNABEL: I have never played even the First.

VOICE: *Is there any difference in quality?*

MR SCHNABEL: I don't think it is as successful as a composition. It is a much more uneven piece. Anyhow, no pianist can play the whole pianistic repertoire. What decides him, what forces him to go in one direction rather than another, is very mysterious. The secret of this direction of attraction is one of the most fascinating. By falling in love, we all experience this mystery. The English language says very aptly that we 'fall' into it.

VOICE: *What has made you go so exclusively into the old masters and avoid the modern? You have specialized almost exclusively in Mozart.*

MR SCHNABEL: I played much contemporary music when I was younger. I also don't know whether you refer to modern music as a quality or a quantity. And, by the way, I always thought I was labelled as the Beethoven, not the Mozart, specialist.

VOICE: *I have never heard you play anything by Debussy or Ravel at your recitals.*

MR SCHNABEL: As I indicated before, it would be wrong to think that music which is not represented in my repertoire, in my public activities, is not liked by me. But I have to limit myself. I hesitate to play Bach in public because the halls are too big for much of his more intimate piano music, for instance the incomparable 'Well-Tempered Clavier'. I have played almost all the works of Schumann; very often, Liszt's Sonata in B minor. I have played contemporary music, particularly chamber music; but when one gets older one has to live an intensive life. The extensive life, all winds blowing 'round our noses', belongs to youth. I have really enjoyed that and you will hear more of this period in my career. I have

121

been asked your last question before. My answer is that now I am attracted only to music which I consider to be better than it can be performed. Therefore I feel (rightly or wrongly) that unless a piece of music presents a problem to me, a never-ending problem, it doesn't interest me too much. For instance, Chopin's studies are lovely pieces, perfect pieces, but I simply can't spend time on them. I believe I know these pieces; but playing a Mozart sonata, I am not so sure that I do know it, inside and out. Therefore I can spend endless time on it. This can probably only be understood by one who has had the same experience. Many colleagues of mine would laugh at me. They would say: 'What is the problem? I don't see any problem.' Here we come to the absolutely uninvestigable field of *quality*—the demarcation line between quality and quantity, essence and appearance. Once I was asked by somebody: 'How is it that you speak with such reverence and awe of Mozart's profundity?' It was the wife of a star virtuoso to whom I once spoke in almost deliberately exaggerated terms of the depth of Mozart's music, the unfathomable, transcendental qualities. She said: 'We too love Mozart, but we think his music is just sweet and lovely and graceful. If your valuation,' she continued, 'is the right one, Mr Schnabel, how do you explain the fact that all children play Mozart so well?' I answered: 'Well, children have at least one very important element in common with Mozart, namely purity. They are not yet spoiled and prejudiced and personally involved. But these are, of course, not the reasons why their teachers give them Mozart to play. Children are given Mozart because of the small *quantity* of the notes; grown-ups avoid Mozart because of the great *quality* of the notes—which, to be true, is elusive!'

Aren't you content with my programmes? Have they bored you? Didn't they please you?

VOICE: *I enjoyed them thoroughly, but just wanted to know.*

MR SCHNABEL: Why should all pianists play the same type of repertoire? It is good to have two or three or more types. For instance, you never hear the charming, most effective sparkling C major Polonaise by Beethoven. You don't even know it exists. Many professional pianists have never seen that piece, but they play the march from *The Love for Three Oranges,* a piece which I think cannot compete with the Polonaise by Beethoven not even in effect.

I once played at a concert five sonatas by Beethoven. After

I had finished, one student, who apparently had prepared his question, asked me: 'Herr Schnabel, in your lonely hours, do you indulge in the pleasure of playing Friml and Baumgartner?' For me an unforgettable moment! I wondered what had happened in the mind of this young man. I was (a rather rare case in my life) speechless! Finally, I said: 'Now why don't you go to Mr Friml and ask him whether he, in his lonely hours, indulges in the pleasure of playing the Goldberg Variations?'

Let me ask you this question: who would you say is the greater—the midget on the upper level, or the giant on the lower level?

VOICE: *The giant is the greater.*

MR SCHNABEL: True, but the levels remain different.

VOICE: *I have heard things in your programme, such as the Schubert sonatas, that I have never heard anybody else play, except, perhaps, some rare soul.*

MR SCHNABEL: I was probably the first to play, again and again, Schubert's sonatas in public. They had been completely neglected. If the Schubert sonatas now appear more often on programmes, it may be partly due to my repeated performances. Aren't you enjoying the Schubert sonatas?

VOICE: *But if you hadn't played them, we would never have heard them.*

MR SCHNABEL: If you would make the effort to look in a catalogue of the works of those composers whose works mean most to you, you would find that there is a polonaise by Beethoven and sonatas by Schubert. Then you might be curious enough, if you play the piano, to look them up.

It is unfortunate that the popularity of music is chiefly determined by the activities of the 'stars', but it would be much better if we were to see the musician through music, rather than music through the musician. Of course, it is also the fault of the teachers—but to stick to Paderewski's repertoire as a standard repertoire may be considered sticking to things which are partly obsolete.

Your question didn't mean that you wish me to play Debussy and Ravel?

VOICE: *I just wanted to know why you did not.*

MR SCHNABEL: What did *you* think was the reason?

VOICE: *I didn't think about that.*

MR SCHNABEL: But why didn't you think? I don't like to

play one programme for one whole season. Of course, with our technical progress, somebody—a singer, for instance—can travel for three years, with only one programme, over all the continents of the globe. He can perform the same thing every night. I do not understand that. It is simply beyond me how a man can perform Hamlet six hundred times in succession. It is alien to me; if I play the same piece six times in two or three weeks, I already feel uneasy. Which only indicates that people are not all alike.

VOICE: *What did the pupils in Leschetizky's classes play?*

MR SCHNABEL: Leschetizky belonged to the virtuoso world of the second half of the nineteenth century, although he had studied with Czerny, who himself had been a student of Beethoven—but this virtuosity was a genuine and creative virtuosity, and not yet a mechanized one. In all my contacts with Leschetizky, which lasted until he died, I never heard him talk about money or success or the Press or the critics or society. Not a word. He was absolutely independent. The great quality of Leschetizky was his vitality; but I think he conceived of music, not, as I said before, as an exclusive sphere of personal experience, but as something which has to be presented, shown to others. He saw music as a, so to say, public function. For him it was not music itself which gave to the musician, who took. For him the musician, as a person, was the giver, and he who listened took. Nowadays, if you believe managers and promoters, the customer gives and the artist takes. The term 'to give' seems now almost inseparable from money (be it only in the form of 'applause'). When Leschetizky, as I said earlier, denied that I should ever be a pianist but said that I was, from the beginning apparently, a musician, he meant perhaps to indicate that my type 'takes' from music. There is, of course, no strict demarcation line between those innate approaches, and I do not claim a superiority for any. When I was ten or eleven, Leschetizky said to me: 'Schubert has written quite fine sonatas for piano—which nobody knows. They are absolutely forgotten. No one ever plays them. You might like them.' So I started playing Schubert's sonatas because Leschetizky said I should never be a pianist. Among the approximately 1,800 pupils he taught in the course of fifty or sixty years, I was one of a handful who never had to study Hungarian rhapsodies by Liszt. I was quite pleased with his choice for me. He did not always like me. He was very strict with me, and sometimes even hard, but yet he absolutely respected what he believed to be my musical disposition. From my tenth year on, I played in all his classes for six years. Every Wednesday night, and in the later years every alternate Wednesday night, except during the summer, Leschetizky gathered all his pupils together (perhaps seventy or eighty), and some of them had to perform. I played, as I said, each time, which gave me an inestimable training in playing before people and, moreover, only musical people. Very often he interrupted a performance and corrected the student. I am deeply grateful to him.

VOICE: *In the periods during which you don't play before an audience, do you think you lose stability?*

MR SCHNABEL: I don't think so. If one is afraid of getting nervous about playing in public, one ought to look for a listener. It doesn't matter much who it is. One may ask the janitor to come and listen, if he has time. I am sure it is now harder than ever before to find people who will listen. Why should they, when they have the radio? It was not so fifty or a hundred years ago. When somebody moved into a house and brought a piano with him, all the other tenants were proud and happy. Wonderful! Now, I need not tell you of the difficulties in regard to 'natural' and 'professional' musical noises, in apartment houses.

I think that the most productive way of higher teaching in music is to have all pupils present at all lessons. That is possible only if one has a very small number of pupils. If you have only six or seven pupils, you can do it, but if you had fifty or sixty pupils—a factory—it would be very difficult! Leschetizky had very many pupils and gave them all private lessons. Most of them studied for long periods with one of his many assistants. By the way, there is no Leschetizky method. It is a mere legend—an absolute fallacy. He never spoke, at least I never heard him speak, of technique. Several of his assistants and some of his pupils have published books on his method which are all diametrically opposed. Don't be misled by them. There was no method. His teaching was much more than a method. It was a current which sought to release all latent vitality in the student. It was addressed to imagination, taste, and personal responsibility, not a blue print, or short cut to success. It gave them a task but no prescription.

VOICE: *Didn't Leschetizky have a certain way of producing a tone, or is that something we hear of only in this country?*

MR SCHNABEL: He produced the tone, whichever in the endless variety of musical sonorities he wanted, with his ear, and not with his fingers. To try to serve music successfully with fingers is quite hopeless. Music does not care for fingers. He never discussed this problem.

VOICE: *Did his assistants?*

MR SCHNABEL: His assistants taught as I told you before. Madame Prentner's and Madame Bree's devices were diametrically opposed. Leschetizky never once wrote a study or exercise in his life. In that he is quite different from Matthay or Philippe. Leschetizky was another kind of teacher altogether. He was always an artist—a *grand seigneur,* an inspiring personality. He wanted his pupils to materialize that which he considered beautiful and spontaneous.

VOICE: *When they didn't produce what he thought was beautiful, did he think it didn't come from within, or did he think they weren't prepared enough?*

MR SCHNABEL: He thought your ears were untrained (or not talented) if your tone was not adequate. Also, much depends on one's standard of measurement. There are those who can't stand a vigorous fortissimo; they are too touchy or too soft for it. Other people, if they hear a real *pianissimo,* miss the big, lush tone. Music, as I said before, requires thousands of tones and not one standard sonority. That would ruin music. Technique is never an end, you know that. Mere dexterity is not sufficient—I can try it with any street boy, he will execute a *glissando* at once—and if he has enough sitting capacity, he will thunder octaves as rapidly as possible for a full hour. That has almost nothing to do with music. It is athletics. The blending of tones, the articulation of tones, has to be directed by the inner ear. Great physical efforts are not conducive to musical performance. Anyhow every physical accomplishment should be achieved with a minimum of effort.

VOICE: *I have heard from several sources that Leschetizky never played a piece for his pupil, to demonstrate what he wanted done. He just told him what to do.*

MR SCHNABEL: I never heard him play a whole piece, but parts he would play in every lesson, and when a concerto was performed, he played the orchestra part on the other piano.

He succeeded in his teaching the way mountain guides do in climbing. One does not know how they always find where to go; yet, they take you to the goal.

2

VOICE: *Do you think having perfect pitch is an advantage or a disadvantage?*

MR SCHNABEL: It is an advantage, but not indispensable. I suppose you refer to absolute pitch. Relative pitch is, however, sufficient and even more important. If you know with what tones a piece of music starts, you ought to know also all relations and modulations which follow. This does not fully apply to what is—wrongly—called 'atonal' music. I had absolute pitch as a child. Ever since my childhood pitch has been permanently raised in favour of string instruments which thus gain in brilliancy, to the disadvantage of human voices which become strained to a dangerous point. I have still in my ears the standard 'A' of my boyhood, and accordingly I hear things played nowadays tones higher than their notation would present them to my mental ear. For instance, if I did not know that the Prelude to the *Meistersinger* was written in C major, I might in a performance today easily hear it as D flat major. To have absolute pitch is, I repeat, a musical asset, but by no means the sign of a good musician.

VOICE: *Yesterday you mentioned Chopin's studies. You thought they were perfect pieces, yet they didn't offer you problems any longer, whereas the Mozart sonatas do. You said that some colleagues of yours think just the opposite. How do you account for differences like that among musicians?*

MR SCHNABEL: I believe the content of profundity in a piece of music remains there, whoever looks at it. It is communicated to him who is equipped with the adequate receiver. He knows it is there. There is, however, no device by which to prove that it is there to those who deny that it is. Is there any guarantee that two wanderers walking along the same path will both see everything that grows there? Do you think that, where there are flowers, everybody must see them?

VOICE: *Yes, if you are speaking in a pragmatic way.*

Mr Schnabel: Not even in a pragmatic way is that the case. I, myself, am an example of the truism that not everything which is attractive must be attractive for everybody. Attraction is a mystery, so is repulsion, even indifference. There are hundreds of things I don't see which other people see. In the physical as well as in the mental region; details, or the total. Chopin's lovely studies are for some performers fascinating because of the opportunities they give for showing how they master the keyboard. Another type of performer is less interested in the keyboard as such. His desire is to project music purely—to let the mediator disappear. To succeed he must, needless to say, have full command of his instrument. There are performers who are almost equally gifted in both directions, and attracted to both. If it comes to the one-sided ones, it should not be a problem to decide who has got the better part. I have always objected to the use of the term 'artist' as indicating excellence of performance, irrelevant of the field of activity. An artist is one who devotes his life to occupation with art. Naturally not all art can be supreme. Relatively inferior or mediocre art is still art. In usage these notions became badly confused. If I spend the same amount of time with a Chopin study or with some Beethoven bagatelle, I get tired of the Chopin piece sooner; its demands on me become, after a while, merely external. And I, slave of my disposition, can simply see no reason why I should produce sounds without inner participation in them. Due to the astonishing variety in musicians' dispositions, unity of judgement can never be expected. Some piano teachers recommend their pupils to read books, or newspapers, while playing. This seems to me absolutely futile, but it has been and is often done even today.

Voice: *What makes them say that?*

Mr Schnabel: A misconception. It is hardly ever said to beginners, rarely to amateurs, mostly to advanced students (professionals). To them it is recommended as a prescription for a lifetime. It is based on the conviction that so-called exercises, daily finger-hand-arm training for hours—and undisturbed by the interference of musical intentions—are indispensable for the acquisition and preservation of technique. The first teacher who ever thought of reading during these music-less motions has apparently himself experienced how deadly boring they are, even after a *short* time spent on them.

128

Yet, they are not meant to be music. The counsel holds, unfortunately, also for practising the fast parts of what is meant to be music. These fast parts, isolated and endlessly repeated, become degraded to exercises again. The whole procedure, as I said before, is useless. To project music, the technique employed has to be a technique which from the outset is used exclusively in the service of this projection.

In the past almost every musician was composer, teacher and performer. Then the enormous expansion of musical activities led to an unfortunate separation of these functions. Teaching, with multitudes of students not very gifted and only moderately ambitious, was gradually simplified. I think this is an inescapable consequence of collectivism. The teachers who, naturally, were not all on the same level, had to face new tasks. Rules, conventions and standards, intelligible for persons without a helpful background, had to be established. The growing emphasis on the mechanical, on methods, formulas and standardization, is symptomatic of this development. It is, for instance, characteristic that the traditional fingering of the C major scale (on the piano) which is still adhered to with the greatest reverence—uses with the right hand the thumb, the strongest finger, on the sub-dominant, with the left hand on the dominant. The right-hand movement, in the range of one octave upwards, is 3 plus 5, left hand 5 plus 3; back 5 plus 3, 3 plus 5. This is certainly ingenious. But musical only for the left hand; musical by accident. As it is built, the left hand starts with the fifth finger, which in the case of the C major scale is a 'priority'. The right hand should compensate its disadvantage by the heroic sacrifice of its fifth finger and execute the scale with only four fingers, thumb on 'G'. If played as ordered, right hand alone—or, worse, in unison with the left—the subdominant, touched with the strongest finger, might easily get a musically unintended accent on it, and thus lead to a crime against the harmonic system of centuries and make music the victim of standardization. Not ingenious, but just silly, is the order never to use your thumb on a black key. Why not, if the position of the hand makes it by far the best fingering? All such pedantries exist, of course, in general education also. Notions, ideas, knowledge, have to be simplified, reduced to formulas, further and further removed from the goal. Truth is lost, or forgotten. The individual will find it again—if he has the light. I shall not be disappointed if our

129

talks here inject a little scepticism in those of you who have none. I am sure most of you, already now, don't take everything which is printed as sacred, just because it is printed. To be confident, makes one rich; to be gullible, poor.

VOICE: *What do you consider the best way of preparing for a concert career? Attaching yourself to a well-known teacher or school, or what?*

MR SCHNABEL: Talent is the premise. It may be released, but cannot be supplied by a teacher. Neither can he guarantee world fame to his students. He is no magician; the student is more important than he. What can a teacher do? At the best open a door; but the student has to pass through it.

In a recent broadcast the idea was sold to uncounted listeners that a great artist can never be a good teacher. Did any of you hear that programme? What did you think of it?

VOICE: *There are exceptions.*

MR SCHNABEL: I see, you are inclined to believe it, though with some reserve. It was said on the radio by someone who, according to his position, should know. You do not like to think that such a person might be far off the truth? I think it is an untenable statement. That could easily be proved. It would be better to assume that even 'stars' might be wrong, occasionally.

VOICE: *Is not teaching entirely apart from playing? Someone might try both and excel in both, but the functions would still be apart.*

MR SCHNABEL: True, not every great performing artist is attracted to teaching. You apparently think only of performers when you say artists. To be a good teacher he *has* to love his work. Yet to say that a great artist can never be a good teacher is obviously thoughtless.

VOICE: *In another broadcast, the same person made a statement that seemed rather strange to me. He said that good music is the music you love. He apparently was trying to make everyone feel good.*

MR SCHNABEL: This is a dangerous, nihilistic line. It says: value depends on your own reaction. Everything you like is good food. Both meat and poison.

VOICE: *You have edited many of the compositions of Beethoven. How do you go about editing the music of a man who is dead?*

MR SCHNABEL: The *œuvre* of a man who is still alive is

rarely edited. I edited Beethoven's thirty-two sonatas in the 'twenties. Maybe I would proceed differently now. When I first tried my hand at editing, in 1912, I was not yet as conscientious, and much less experienced than in the 'twenties. For the Beethoven edition which, as a whole, I think to be still usable, I tried to get hold of as much original material as possible—manuscripts, copies corrected or seen by Beethoven, first and second editions of which Beethoven had seen the proofs. In the case of different versions in the manuscripts and in the printed editions which Beethoven had seen in proofs, I decided on the printed version, because Beethoven was not always too careful in his manuscripts, knowing that he would see the proofs. All my markings are distinguishable from Beethoven's own by smaller print. All references to problematic points are given in footnotes. The metronome markings—with the one exception of Opus 106 where Beethoven has provided them—are my choice and responsibility, but never intended to be more than suggestions. Fingerings, in my edition, have been chosen very often with the idea of forcing the student to stop and think a while. They are occasionally meant to be very difficult, in order to indicate that, where they are, special attention is advised. With an easier fingering the meaning of some important but hidden element might have escaped the student.

3

VOICE: *What do you think should be the ideal of an artist in performing music?*

MR SCHNABEL: I don't understand your question.

VOICE: *I mean in the interpretation of music, what should be his ideal?*

MR SCHNABEL: His ideal is to materialize all he wants to materialize. He wants, of course, only as much as he at a given time *understands* of what music as a whole and music in a single example demands. How much this is, depends on his talent alone, in each phase of its development. The same holds true for his capacity to judge whether he is doing what he wants to do. Whatever his gifts, he ought to make, all his life long, the greatest efforts to reach the maximum of his capabilities—which requires one more gift.

VOICE: *You say, 'as much as he understands'. What do you think should be the basis of his understanding?*

MR SCHNABEL: I am not telling you anything new in telling you that, as far as my knowledge goes, nothing in the world has ever grown from the exterior to the interior. The interior is the basis for understanding. There is the desire, the force, the gift. If somebody who has no talent whatsoever for music, and no desire either, were to undergo a scientific treatment for the chemical production of musicality in him, I wonder whether a good musician would emerge. Your question seems to me mechanical. It ought to be taken for granted that one who undertakes to perform a piece of music has, even before he performs it, some idea of it. The idea may not be his own and he may change that idea, whether his own or borrowed, yet an idea of what he wants remains the premise. Yesterday I was asked how it is that for me some pieces of music seem inexhaustibly fertile terrain for discoveries, a never-failing source of joy, a perpetual challenge, while others are comparatively limited, hedged in, get stale, rusty, or shabby. Now, it can well be that someone else sees only a province where I divine a universe, and vice versa, of course.

VOICE: *Do you think it all comes from within a person?*

MR SCHNABEL: Love has to be the starting point—love of music. It is one of my firmest convictions, that love always produces some knowledge, while knowledge only rarely produces something similar to love.

VOICE: *Can there be a standard by which to evaluate a performance?*

MR SCHNABEL: You admit that a difference exists between quality and quantity. There is, however, no legal validity, no committing evidence, of quality in art. I remember an evening spent with a select group of boys, called the Saturday-nighters, in Harrow. They invited 'experts' in all fields to talk to them informally. There was, as we are having here, also a discussion. The boys had prepared traps with tricky questions for me. One of the questions was, 'What is it that creates beauty in a work of art?' I had not time to think. I simply let my tongue go, and said, 'Your reaction to it.' Nobody can convince you that a piece of music is beautiful if to you it is *not*. I would not even try to convince you. I can't prove it. Cause and effect are both within yourself.

VOICE: *Is there no other measure to apply to art? Is it impossible to say objectively whether it is good or bad, except in the case of a few technical components of performance?*

MR SCHNABEL: This freedom from an obligatory standard of tests and terminology is a drawback—or maybe, a privilege—of music. If an actor pronounces words wrongly, if, for instance, he says beau-*tee*-ful, everyone who speaks his tongue would know it and that would finish his career. Not so with musicians. Wrong pronunciation is common among celebrated performers, but only a small minority of listeners notice it. It is a technical defect. Yet, the musician's career will not be finished, for music expresses something different to everyone who hears it. The same music does not express the same thing, as I have already said before, to the same person each time he hears it. It is wrong when it deviates conspicuously from the written text in regard to time-values and dynamics, but this is only a technical defect, the result of inattentiveness, or slovenliness, not a sign of an inferior musical quality. The meaning and the essence of music can only be communicated by music. It is hopeless to try it with words, or colours, or movements.

And the reaction to music can never be objective. To say that 'rain is dry' is nonsense, is not true. Such categories do not exist in music.

Each time I read annotations in programmes I wonder what their *raison d'être* and what their consequences may be. I should have listed them among the articles unknown in my boyhood. I think they are unnecessary, and can be very confusing, because discrepancy between the composer's or performer's and the annotator's conceptions of them is often more evident than any identity. Whether only a few or many of the persons served with the literature and with the sounds are aware of the often diametrically opposed approaches, is irrelevant. Those who are aware will become prejudiced, one way or the other. I found some unimaginable remarks in annotations to some of my own programmes. In one case the so-called second subject—in a sonata—was placed in the top voice, simply because it was the top voice, and made two measures long, though the composer had given it to an inner part and five measures' space. It took me some time to solve this enigma. Not as perverse but more bewildering was when another time I read, 'And now follows a jolly rondo', referring to a piece I thought to display unmistakably an atmosphere of despair and feverish suffering. I do not know who is right. What bewildered me and still bewilders me is that I shall never find out whether the audience heard a jolly piece, or a tragic piece. It is conceivable that for them it was jolly—for as such was it announced in print. You see, there is no art in which illusion has such force as in music. Naturally!

The one note I don't like in your question is your trust in authority. If I, or some other musician, were to give you the information for which you ask in a sufficiently scientific and intellectual make-up, you would, it seems to me, accept it as a dogma.

VOICE: *Oh, no.*

VOICE: *You haven't mentioned anything about where Leschetizky got his training.*

MR SCHNABEL: He studied with Karl Czerny. That is all I know. And Karl Czerny with Beethoven, as, of course, you know.

VOICE: *He stands out among the teachers. You said the training you got from him couldn't possibly be evaluated.*

MR SCHNABEL: You must not underrate the part nature

plays in the creation of gifted people; so I would say that what led the pupil to training, and where it led him, he got from Providence.

Do you know that the teacher of Beethoven was Mr Christian Neefe? I don't think he was a great man. He was just available in Bonn. If all good musicians required a great man as a teacher, in order to be good musicians, there wouldn't be too many of them, I am afraid. That applies to all branches of teaching. Why are you interested in Leschetizky's training?

VOICE: *Because he is still recognized as outstanding, whereas most of his contemporary teachers are forgotten.*

MR SCHNABEL: Your question reminds me of a curious scene after one of my recitals in U.S.A., at a very famous college. Many of the students, after the recital was finished, rushed to the artist's room. The first one to arrive was a very sweet girl of perhaps sixteen who, breathless, asked me: 'Are you, or have you, a teacher?' I replied: 'I do not understand.' 'I want to know whether you are taking or giving lessons.' Now I said, 'My dear child, I am too old to take lessons, but I can still learn. I am learning from you.' She disappeared like a vapour. The head of the school hurried to whisper to me: 'She was not one of ours!'

Anyhow, you can't go to the teacher of Leschetizky for lessons. Nature will continue to provide some good teachers. Are you distrustful of nature?

VOICE: *I hope this isn't a foolish question, but I was told by a pupil of Gabrilowitsch that he broke away from Leschetizky's teaching. I am curious to know what reason he could have had for that breakaway from Leschetizky.*

MR SCHNABEL: I didn't know that Gabrilowitsch ever taught piano. He never told me. He was my intimate friend, but he never discussed this subject with me. I have in many respects ideas very different from Leschetizky's, but that doesn't impair my admiration for him and his educational work. I have to be as I am. You see, we have no choice. We do our best, and have no guarantee. I am what I would call an 'active fatalist'.

VOICE: *In your edition of the Beethoven sonatas, is there any way of telling which is your pedalling and which is his?*

MR SCHNABEL: All his own pedal markings are referred to in footnotes.

VOICE: *Don't you think the difference between his and our pianos should be seriously considered?*

MR SCHNABEL: It should. But the result will not be to disavow Beethoven's very daring and revealing use of the pedal. I have played on the old pianos, I had access to the marvellous collections in Vienna and in Berlin. I have played on Bach's, Beethoven's, Weber's and other pianos. In Beethoven's case the effect of the pedalizations demanded by him was exactly the same on the old instruments as on the new ones. The old piano is different from the modern piano in that you couldn't do on the old ones all you can do on a modern piano. On that, however, you can do all that was possible on the old ones. In all his compositions for piano Beethoven made only thirty or a few more pedal marks, on thousands of pages. His pedal instructions appear only in such places where he knew that the 'normal' performer would have considered them sinful. Now I do not say that Beethoven was interested in the childish game of shocking or pleasing Philistines. He simply created, also in pedalization, the unexpected, fantastic, adventurous. The effect is often what one now labels impressionistic sonorities. The 'usual' pedalization, practically never marked by him, is part of the instrument. It belongs to piano playing. The piano is played with hands and feet. One changes the amount of pedal *ad libitum,* according to the room, to one's mood, to the occasion—but one always, automatically, employs the pedal—except in such passages as Beethoven explicitly demanded it; just there it is obligatory. The markings by Beethoven have to be observed under all circumstances, in every room or mood or company, because they are an inseparable part of the music as such, and if one does not observe these pedal marks, the music is changed.

That little story of the differences between antique and modern pianos has a tough constitution; it is again and again presented as the one excuse for the abolition of Beethoven's unambiguous orders in regard to pedalization. The story also excuses him; had he known the modern pianos he would surely have changed the orders! An equally neat story, and just as tough, ascribes to his deafness some allegedly coarse sounding measures in his later works. Now, in the case of the pedal orders, I told you it makes no difference what piano you use. I can add that even Beethoven's contemporaries tried to evade them, with similar reasoning, I am sure. In the second case, his deafness seems, miraculously enough, to have influenced just a few measures.

There remains the problem why musicians shy away from Beethoven's pedalization. They are still today deemed unpermissible, and ignored by our greatest performers. One of them enlightened me. Asked why he ignored it, his complexion turning to pallor, he answered: 'It hurts me.' Reflecting what in the world it could be that 'hurt' him, I concluded it could only be the generations-old fear of sounding two different harmonies simultaneously, even if the bass does *not* move. It is not my job to trace the originators of such superstitions. I am certain you can detect them in a library.

VOICE: *When you were giving your first lecture, you mentioned the fact that Madame Essipoff put a coin on the back of your hand and asked you to play without dropping it. You succeeded then, you said, but would fail now, for you have changed the method in the meantime. What is the difference?*

MR SCHNABEL: I don't believe in finger playing. The fingers are like the legs of a horse. If its body wouldn't move, there wouldn't be any progress; it would always remain on the same spot. If someone would strain his wits to devise, in addition to fingering, indications for handing, wristing, forearming, elbowing, upper-arming, for the feet, etc., annotation in time values and articulation, should we accept such an innovation? Definitely not, for the approach to music via our eyes, which is already now a widely cherished habit, would eventually eliminate the ears entirely, and with them the organs commissioned to direct and control what we do to music.

I am coming back for a moment to fingers. They should not be used as hammers. They require too much training and attention that way. Differentiation becomes very difficult and unreliable. The fall of weights out of a static frame is an anti-musical picture. Flexibility, relaxation, spontaneous command, combined service of all actions to the requirements of expressive musical performance, promises better results, with smaller expenditure, than fixation can arrive at. Expression means going out, and up. In and down movements, falling weights, I repeat, are self-imposed impediments, if expressiveness is the aim of a pianist. I know there is a school denying the piano the *legato,* registering it among the percussion instruments. The literature composed for it is the best refutation of that 'scientific' assertion.

137

I have no experience in teaching beginners. My pupils, who all start with me at an advanced stage of preparation, do, in general, quite well with the elasticity principle. By the way, I never—pardon me, a man my age should not use the term 'never'—hear a pupil play a piece twice. I trust him, that what he has learned in one piece will be applied to the next, and so on. I want him in a few years to go with me through as much music as possible, as many pieces as possible. When I was teaching at the Academy in Berlin, my pupils were in a certain danger. Other teachers there were the whole season preparing the piece or pieces to be performed by their pupils publicly (at the institute). My students came to me only once with their display notice. They competed nevertheless with honours.

I think that too much of education is based on pessimism. I wonder whether this is a productive basis. With my temperament I cannot believe in it and that is why I say I have changed my technique. It does not imply condemnation of the technique I abandoned.

VOICE: *What about Madame Essipoff's training?*

MR SCHNABEL: I know I can play the Czerny studies although I have never seen them since, but if I tried to play them as I played them then, with that standardized hand, I would feel very uneasy. If I do it with my way of playing, it is always relaxed and round and articulate. Also, I think the body has to be as articulate as the music. Music is modulation, so if our bodies are not modulating, and our hands are standardized, playing is much more difficult. That is why with that technique so much practising is required. As much as ten hours a day.

VOICE: *Have you done much ensemble playing?*

MR SCHNABEL: Very much. I have also composed much chamber music. Now I play it only rarely. There is no real chamber music any more in our public musical schedule, except string quartets. This is deplorable. The duo of piano and one string or wind instrument or piano and voice is misrepresented and thus misunderstood. The piano part is considered an accompaniment, though the piano, in an emergency could do the duo (though a little damaged) without the violin, or in a *Lied* play also the singer's part, together with its own. The piano provides, so to say, the symphonic substance, has the greater musical share, simply because it has a wider range and ten fingers available. Only in a lower type of music is the 'soloist' more important. The original idea of a concerto was to let all participants concertize. Each one got his say. But let us return to the duo calamity. A 'star' (singer or instrumentalist) receives hundreds of pounds for a part, his or her pianist perhaps only ten to twenty or so. He may be more musical than the 'star' but probably feels too depressed and degraded to try his best. Where he should lead, he has to obey. Almost all violin and 'cello virtuosos compel 'pianists' to subordinate the requirements of the music to their employers' vain-glory or—limitations. Nearly every fiddler tells his pianist that under all circumstances he is too loud—he does not mean he is too loud for the music, but too loud for his fiddle.

Even composers are expected to keep not too far off the traditional demarcation line. You probably know Beethoven's wonderful answer to his friend Schuppanzigh, the violinist, who complained that a certain passage in a new quartet 'can simply not be played on a violin'—not even by a man who, like Schuppanzigh, had played all previous quartets to the master's satisfaction. Beethoven snorted back: 'What do I care for your damned fiddle.'

Chamber music, including *Lieder* and small vocal ensembles, belongs to the home. It is all too rare there nowadays. Records are no adequate substitute. Yesterday I found a surprising juxtaposition in a paper, of Irving Berlin and Schubert. Irving Berlin has composed 2,000 songs, and Schubert only 600. Schubert, to be true, died at thirty-one. Statistics!

VOICE: *What did Thomas Mann and Stefan Zweig say about your playing? And were they as much as you aware of the tremendous and rapid changes taking place since they were born?*

MR SCHNABEL: Neither the one nor the other has ever said —to me—a word about my piano playing. I do not know whether they have ever heard it. But I have met both of them. I suppose that in regard to the epochal developments our feelings and behaviour had much in common. Stefan Zweig's relation to music seemed to me a bit naïve. His taste embraced too rich a *mélange*. Yet, he loved music. So did Thomas Mann. He was a staunch Wagnerite. The case of Wagner is obviously not too easy. Hanslick, Nietzsche, Shaw, and many other writers and thinkers have speculated about it. Thomas Mann was also engaged in attempts to clarify it. All this philosophical, psychological and sociological research is, to my mind, not applicable to music. Wagner's work does not consist only of music. It remains problematic and is thus perhaps the sharpest expression of the nineteenth-century spirit. I saw Zweig last in England, in Hitler's time. He was deeply depressed and without hope of the future—thus, he did not wait.

Thomas Mann is working on a story, telling of a musician's life. Writers, in general, have not such a spontaneous relation to music as painters and scientists. Especially physicists and mathematicians enjoy music without any extra-musical interference. Writers are more self-conscious, inclined to translate every experience into words. This cannot be done with music; therefore their reactions to music are often not pure enough.

VOICE: *Have you never heard music adequately described by words?*

MR SCHNABEL: Very rarely. Ernst Theodor Amadeus Hoffmann, the protagonist in Offenbach's *Tales of Hoffmann*—wrote about music, or, of music, in a manner convincing enough to make even a musician happy. He was an astonishing fellow, a wonderful, romantic, real judge, poet, painter, writer, composer, bon-vivant, and what not. Two biographies, one of Mozart, the other of Berlioz, by Walter J. Turner succeed—though his understanding of music is not quite equal to that of a good, professional musician—in transporting the reader into the region of creative genius—and that is some poetical achievement.

VOICE: *What do you think of Tovey?*

MR SCHNABEL: He was an extraordinary man. I saw him fairly often and loved those meetings. Each time I learned a lot. And had much fun too, for he would suddenly, with an absolutely unexpected twist, change from scholar to *farceur,* boyishly beaming, if I did not follow quickly enough.

VOICE: *Do you think it is possible that a close relation can exist between musicians and critics?*

MR SCHNABEL: Why not? Yet, I am not competent to talk on the subject of authors of newspaper reviews, if you mean them. They do not write to inform musicians; their job is to inform the public. I am, of course, also a part of the public, but naturally least in musical matters. I am thus not very familiar with the critics' work. There is apparently a demand for it, otherwise it would not have survived. That not all of them are equally qualified is just as certain as it is in the case of musicians, or other exacting occupations.

If you do not agree with one critic's judgement, you may be right or he may be right. Nevertheless, he has fulfilled his duty. If you read several reviews about the same event, and they are all unanimous, your information has some basis; if they are contradictory, and you do not trust one of them more than another, you have no information at all. You must—unbiased—go and find out for yourself. The critic, however, can not be criticized for criticizing.

4

VOICE: *I had the pleasure of meeting and hearing your pupil, the young Mr X, this summer and I would like to have your opinion of his work?*

MR SCHNABEL: He is a highly gifted boy. He plays, for his age, amazingly well. The real difficulties for him lie in his future, for it is more difficult to retain fame than to gain it. I feel certain of his capacity to meet them.

VOICE: *He seems very much more mature than his seventeen years warrant, though.*

MR SCHNABEL: Oh, I wouldn't use that term: mature. It would in his case sound like an objection, almost a condemnation. He plays well, convincingly, with an already manifest personality of his own. His type of talent is not too common. He has imagination and courage. He will try things and face the risk of failure. That is nowadays a rather rare quality. Courage is suppressed by the pursuit of safety.

VOICE: *Did you say it is easier to gain fame than to retain it?*

MR SCHNABEL: Well, I thought so.

VOICE: *Why is it?*

MR SCHNABEL: Perhaps I was referring to the days before paid publicity made fame. Well, you have to live up to your prestige once you have gained it. Making your début, in your young years, you are not expected to impress profoundly, to arouse passionate reaction. If you do, unexpectedly, the first time, you will be expected to repeat at least the effect of the first attempt on all following occasions.

The lazy tendency to tie artists down to pigeon-holes is getting ever stronger. This was, however, not what I meant by my previous sentence. There I referred to a once communicated level, to a whole, not to single characteristics, mannerisms, nuances. Every artist ought to be expected to develop as long as he functions, and every listener too. Development means change, progress. But it does not mean change of level.

142

Bernard Shaw, Richard Strauss, and others of great gifts were not blessed to continue on the level on which they began. Their fame dates from their initial triumphs. Early recognition has perhaps its dangers.

Fame can also, to a degree, be artificially created. It is certainly more difficult to retain *such* fame.

VOICE: *Do you think the modern American type of management is partly responsible for such conditions?*

MR SCHNABEL: I do. It favours patterns, clichés, fashions and standards. It makes the greatest efforts to direct the market, to dictate what ought to be liked best. I do not think that the musical situation in U.S.A. corresponds to the wishes of the people attracted to music The managerial force is undoubtedly responsible for some of the less appetizing supplies though, of course, they always pass the buck to the 'people's taste which they have to satisfy whether they approve or not'. In all my life I have never met a single person who could, or would, precisely tell me what he wanted; I am, however, constantly meeting people who tell me what other people want.

All this seems just not productive for art. Art is the region of co-operation, of spontaneity, directness, multiformity. The mechanical is its opposite. Quality in it cannot be proved by mechanisms or statistics. And I feel sure we all agree that not all values are suited for mass circulation. Yet, eventually, it is the artist who is accountable for the state of art.

VOICE: *Speaking of quality, I remember a magazine article about Shostakovich's Ninth Symphony. It said that the composer was afraid of comparisons with Beethoven's Ninth. He was afraid his work would not be approached for its own merits or weaknesses. Why should people be afraid of being measured with the past?*

MR SCHNABEL: Whether Shostakovich is equal to Beethoven is a question to be answered in a hundred years. You can't now say that Shostakovich is as great as Beethoven.

VOICE: *Why should one refer to the number of a symphony?*

MR SCHNABEL: We live in an age occupied, preoccupied, I would say, with quantities. But who coupled the two Ninths together? The magazine or, as they claimed, Shostakovich himself?

VOICE: *He himself.*

MR SCHNABEL: I don't believe that. Shostakovich is doing

his best and would undoubtedly be quite content to pass to posterity as only second to Beethoven. By the way, do you believe everything you see printed?

VOICE: *No.*

MR SCHNABEL: Good for you. A reporter mentioning artists or other 'stars' in public life must—that is the newest routine —put a so-called 'human touch' to his story. Now, making Shostakovich tremble for fear of being subordinated to Beethoven was fairly clever. Still cleverer, he could have pictured the young composer in tantrums, caused by the superstition that as a rule one dies after the creation of nine symphonies. Though Beethoven did not. He lived many years and wrote numerous works after the Ninth, but no other symphony, at least none which is undoubtedly his creation. From time to time compositions of the past are detected or exhumed, and some of them announced as unknown or forgotten creations of the few great ones whose products survive the ages.

Do you know when the Ninth Symphony was written?

VOICE: *I think it was about 1820.*

ANOTHER VOICE: *From 1810 to 1820.*

MR SCHNABEL: If you date it from the first sketches. When he scribbled them first and came back again and again to the material used in these first sketches, Beethoven did perhaps, or most likely did not yet, know that they would later develop into a part of that edifice which is his Ninth. He might have used this material, just as well, in another frame. This, I believe, is a very important fact, illuminating the variable usability of material.

VOICE: *You used here, or somewhere else, the term: 'extra-musical'. To what extent is the fact that Beethoven completed his Ninth Symphony in 1820 of any value? To what extent is that a* musical *and not an extra-musical fact? I am not trying to be sarcastic or critical but I just wonder how important it is to the musicians, to music lovers, or in general, to know that?*

MR SCHNABEL: The date, you mean?

VOICE: *Yes.*

MR SCHNABEL: It is not important. It is a tribute to great men to know the date of their careers. To know the day, or hour when one of their creations was completed is entirely irrelevant. It doesn't add to musical knowledge. The response to the Ninth Symphony would always be the same, absolutely independent of the day it was ready for communication.

VOICE: *You have spoken several times about competition. I would like to know whether you consider it as helpful or as worthless, a public competition in which young musicians vie with one another for some sort of award.*

MR SCHNABEL: Contests?

VOICE: *Yes.*

MR SCHNABEL: I am not too sure of their utility. By the way, do you mean contests for amateurs, for children, or for professionals?

VOICE: *Professionals.*

MR SCHNABEL: For years I was a member of the jury in such contests. It was one of my duties at the State Academy in Berlin, and I disliked no job more than that. At most of these races the contestants are treated with an automatic callousness bordering on brutality. Conditions are rather discouraging, the milieu so businesslike, that the sensitive among the competitors—and which young artist is not sensitive?—simply could not give their best. I am, moreover, afraid that more often than not these matches, now swollen to alarming numbers, are not quite honest either. I wish to emphasize that what I have just confessed to you is the point of view of one who has been exposed to the office of judge against his inclination. Maybe I was thus able to help the contestants to a hardening of their hearts, a kind of immunity against adverse circumstances.

Statistics on the results of contests, in musical and other arts, would be a great surprise. Rarely have the winners reached heights, rarely have the best in a generation been among the contestants.

Hans von Bülow, famous German nineteenth-century musician, famous also for his biting wit, once made a joke—unfortunately untranslatable—about contests. In German: *Je preiser-gekrönt ein Werk, desto durcher fällt es.* It means: the more prizes and praises are heaped on a work (in one or several contests) the surer will it turn out to be a flop. I think this is much too severe, yet, not quite wrong. Or do you think it entirely wrong?

VOICE: *The contest I had an opportunity to attend had very little first-grade talent participating and none of the first-grade talent has ever been able to win it. Those who were mechanically reliable made it, not those with personality and imagination.*

MR SCHNABEL: They were, I guess, too irritated by the loveless atmosphere, typical for examinations.

VOICE: *The judges were also soon annoyed and bored by hearing the test pieces again and again.*

MR SCHNABEL: Have the candidates never the choice of repertoire?

VOICE: *Not as far as my experience goes.*

MR SCHNABEL: That seems to me one more handicap. Nevertheless, it is apparently the prevailing practice. One of my pupils who, less with the ambition of becoming the chosen one than from a desire to get acquainted with the procedure, joined the aspirants at one of the best reported contests, told me that Schumann's fragment 'Paganini', a few measures in his *Carnaval,* was one of the items ordered as evidence. I was duly astonished, for this fragment is not even a piece but just the short interruption of a waltz; the dancers are for an instant stopped by an apparition made up as Paganini. Performed without the waltz framing it, the chance of demonstrating genius is almost nil. The chance of missing keys is better. My pupil informed me also that she was granted seven minutes for her presentation. She said that no one got more. She also received the judges' reports, in this, as well as in the case of a literary contest which, by the way, she won. I never knew that reports are handed to contestants. The musical reports were funny. One was: 'She has good hands. She should give a recital in New York.' Another one was two pages long; the *same* two pages were also received by a friend of hers who participated in the same contest. This report said, on two pages: 'She should go and study with Madame X.' I have no reason to consider this story as chimera.

VOICE: *You said last week that you never teach pupils a piece twice. What stage of preparation must they have reached when bringing it to a lesson?*

MR SCHNABEL: They come with it when it has already undergone a process of clarification in their minds and is absolutely familiar to their fingers. They don't come to be taught how to do it. They want to hear my objections and counsel, and justification of both. They take the responsibility for their performances. You should ask a few pupils of mine who are here how this works. They will tell you.

146

VOICE: *It is just as you said; we try to prepare them the best we can.*

MR SCHNABEL: You take the responsibility?

VOICE: *Yes.*

VOICE: *Some musicians become very arrogant, very conceited, very aloof, after they have gone through a certain amount of musical training. Other musicians, on the other hand, try to answer the simplest questions that anyone can ask and help to understand the most elementary things about music. This holds true also for painters, philosophers and every other art there is.*

MR SCHNABEL: And also for human beings, I submit.

VOICE: *Yes.*

MR SCHNABEL: Arrogance is not created through musical training. Neither is modesty. Both originate in a disposition and I think that in any field arrogant persons are arrogant because they are born that way.

How do human beings react, let me ask, to success or what we call success? That is a tough question because there are not only the endlessly nuanced differences between them but there are also two kinds of success. Success may be the success of approximately accomplishing what was intended. That is the success that one has with one's self, by judging the degree of fulfilment measured against one's ambition, or expectation. The other type of success comes from without and shows what other people think of us. I am never quite sure which is meant when I am asked about success.

Success with oneself is not necessarily success with someone else or with everyone. There are those who are easily satisfied with themselves and rush to the next task. Others are hypercritical and procrastinating. But success in the shape of popularity hardly affects the person at all. It is now too common and often obviously manufactured.

VOICE: *You have been asked before about the German school and the Russian school of piano playing and musical interpretation and about differences between them.*

MR SCHNABEL: The question about the Russian School must have somehow escaped me. The phrase 'German School' was supplied by *me,* in a quotation. You know my aversion to pigeon-holing and my conviction that there is only one school: namely *musical* music. Its variety seems inexhaustible. It corresponds to the uncountable differences in combinations of qualities among men. Yet, what men have in common is much more than what separates them.

Music has only one language. It cannot be translated into another one. If in word language you say 'I am hungry', it *means* the same in Norwegian and Polynesian. But it *sounds* different. Obviously a human being *must* be incapable of understanding all existing word languages. It is technically impossible for it to be otherwise. If, however, after listening to a piece of music someone complains that he does not understand *that* language, he surely has a wrong idea and he is also using the wrong term. He should have said he felt excluded from it. Surely many people are excluded from books in their mother tongue, in spite of the fact that they know what the words used in them indicate. If I hear that Johann Sebastian Bach's, Richard Wagner's and Robert Schumann's works ought to be identical because all three were Saxons, I keep, naturally, silent.

Recently I read a review of a work of a contemporary American composer. It was praised for being not only genuine American music, but Appalachian music. Well, I think we could go much further in our refinement of distinctions. We should find out in what street, on which floor, something has been composed. Why not? Certainly there must be a loftier, more elevated inspiration on the twentieth floor of a building than on the second. Noisy or quiet neighbourhoods would also count. Only imagination does not. And such 'refinement' of distinctions will more and more narrow the share of the universe in creation.

VOICE: *Do you think the virtuoso of Leschetizky's time, the virtuoso pianist you talked about the other day—the one who was not a musician—would be just as successful today?*

MR SCHNABEL: I never said that he was not a musician.

VOICE: *No? Well, would he be just as successful today as he was then, or do you think that today we expect a pianist to be a great musician as well as a great pianist?*

MR SCHNABEL: I like your 'today'. Franz Liszt, Rubinstein, and many others before yesterday, were very great musicians.

VOICE: *Why?*

MR SCHNABEL: They were creators of music. Franz Liszt was a *creative* virtuoso; he composed, he conducted, he taught, he wrote, and he kept in contact with some of the best brains of his generation. They were his intimates and their permanent exchange of ideas was evidence and promotion of culture. The virtuoso of today does not correspond to the Franz Liszt type. Our keyboard and string virtuosos do not, as a rule, either compose, or teach, or conduct, or write, or meet each other or equals in other fields. With air transport it is now technically possible to appear in public every day of the year in a different place—with the same programme. The development from local to global service of art is an event worth serious reflection. Itinerating virtuosos have, of course, existed before—and among them certainly some who had no other musical activity. Yet, they were not the highest reputed ones who addressed their work to a rather limited patronage. Twentieth-century society is not like nineteenth-century society. There are a few among us who may be considered the last radiations, faint memories of the grand old school. The majority however are more like the lesser ranks of the nineteenth century. A fresh sprout of the former many-sidedness is quite conceivable. At the moment we have representatives of a new, versatile type: the smart salesmen of any kind of tone assortments.

Do they follow a demand or a created demand? Or does their admirable adaptability come from within? Is it the expression of our generation's spirit? I am very sceptical in regard to the effect social conditions can exert on music. Speed and noise, for instance, are characteristics of the machine age *and* of savages. If, as it seems, we have not kept up with the creative level of preceding stages may it not be due to elemental forces sterilizing certain fields, condemning our years to be lean?

VOICE: *Mr Schnabel, when you talk about lean years, do you think the world runs in cycles, that we ever get back to the former stage?*

MR SCHNABEL: The same level of artistic creation has never been seen in continuity in one and the same place. After a few hundred years it seems to wander somewhere else, or to be lowered, dried out, altogether. It is in any case rather idle to speculate on what level we are. I continue composing, lean years or not!

Art music, after a very short phase of satisfying private, intimate requirements, takes now a turn towards becoming a public function. Whether all or some of the finest and most delicate creations of the comparatively exclusive period can remain a treasure and feel at home in the rougher climate of inclusiveness, is a vexing problem.

Orchestral music is now the most popular. It lends itself better to a public function than *Lieder* singing or chamber music. Home music is practically extinct as it belongs to the sphere of personal experience.

VOICE: *I know that pianists used to cart around their own pianos, their own stools and a whole trainload of their special little things. Do they still do that?*

MR SCHNABEL: It doesn't have as much publicity value as it used to have. However, the distrust or fear of not finding good pianos in certain places is quite justified.

VOICE: *Isn't it rather hard on a piano to be moved around all the time?*

MR SCHNABEL: No, there are ways to transport pianos safely. Pianos are being transported anyhow all the time and, it is true, they are often handled in an incredibly careless way. We miss, to my regret, a society for the protection of objects from cruelty. A variety of stools and chairs should not be so difficult to find in any inhabited settlement. Yet I have had strange experiences in this respect, in spite of the attention I give to such matters. Performers are generally considered steely people, who, if they only have a full house, are quite insensitive on the score of disturbances threatening them. It is my habit to inspect the hall, piano, chair, lighting, etc., the morning before a concert. Once I was going to play in a theatre: it had a glass roof, and that morning it was pouring with rain —the rain on that roof made a bigger noise than my music could ever hope to make! I said casually to the janitor how unpleasant it would be if by the evening the rain had not stopped. He clapped me on the shoulder: 'Don't worry: the audience won't hear it!'

5

VOICE: *In reference to what you said of* Lieder *singing as a now neglected art, how do you account then for the wild acclaim given Lotte Lehmann's recitals last winter?*

MR SCHNABEL: I was very happy to hear of the enthusiastic response to her *Lieder* recitals here and wherever else she presented them. By the way, I did not say that *singers* became unpopular, I said that a certain type of *Lied* culture had lost its former position in the home and in public. Lotte Lehmann is an admirable artist, yet she comes from the theatre and does not entirely correspond to the species of vocalists I referred to, when deploring the alienation from the pure *Lieder* world.

VOICE: *This* Lieder *world is what the people really want.*

MR SCHNABEL: I am not so sure, but would be delighted if you were right. The 'people', this is my deep conviction, are anyhow very little to blame in the neglect or absence of spiritual values in public life. Do you think that the very large halls where Miss Lehmann sings are adequate places for the *Lied*?

VOICE: *Definitely not.*

MR SCHNABEL: This is an intricate problem. Suppose a genuine *Lieder* singer should emerge (or more of them, and why not?), and refuse to take his beloved *Lieder* to large halls. Could he or she exist, compete, be widely known? Particularly here? I think a compromise is desirable. Better to have the *Lied* in the wrong place, presented by versatile performers, than not at all!

VOICE: *Did you ever hear Claire Dux?*

MR SCHNABEL: Yes.

VOICE: *Some people told me that her* Lieder *singing was comparable to Lotte Lehmann's and that Miss Lehmann didn't measure up to her.*

MR SCHNABEL: I don't think so. It was very charming and very musical but I think Miss Lehmann has more imagination. Have you heard Elisabeth Schumann?

VOICE: *Yes.*

MR SCHNABEL: She was very good in *Lieder* singing, but therefore most effective in smaller halls. The difficulty is that if you sell out a hall holding 800 people you will still have a deficit. Rents of halls have increased so much and publicity is so expensive that you can make some money if you play in a big hall, but not in a small one.

VOICE: *How do you rank Miss Teyte?*

MR SCHNABEL: I heard her in London and it was very charming but I wouldn't say that this belongs to the same field. It was in a joint recital I had with her and I have never forgotten it. Since then I have never given a joint concert. After I had played a Schubert sonata, Miss Teyte came on. Then she gave an encore which was a Swiss yodel and in giving the echo she sang with her hands before her mouth. She did it wonderfully; I don't mean to criticize.

VOICE: *When American jazz came to Europe, you were young enough to have a chance to look at it without discarding it as trash.*

MR SCHNABEL: How do you arrive at the idea that I discarded it as trash?

VOICE: *I have got the impression from so many other people that I assumed that it was true in your case, too.*

MR SCHNABEL: I have never studied or tried to analyse so-called 'popular' music. It is not the department I am serving. This fact—or fate, if you like—is of no consequence in regard to my attitude towards other departments. I neither hate nor despise dance music or applied music, or even mere background music. I never approach these categories condescendingly. I have, willy-nilly (for how can one escape?) heard a mass, too many, of the products in this department. Some were, and even remain, fascinating. The majority seem, as in my own department, uninteresting. This equality of inequality in all the departments does not, of course, cancel the fundamental distinctions between these departments. The best waltz by Johann Strauss is incommensurable with a Mozart rondo. I admit to having no other evidence for this statement than my own impression. Yet, this confession does not cancel the distinctions. Why is not *all* good, or *all* bad music popular? Now, even the best piece of jazz does not demand much from me, while even some rather superficial bit of 'serious' music demands already too much from someone else.

152

VOICE: *I read in a biography of Beethoven that he would often improvise at the piano and people were astounded at the beauty of his improvisations.*

MR SCHNABEL: Improvisation in the eighteenth century was a test of the craftsmanship of a professional musician. He was asked to improvise on a given theme, to improvise variations and fugues. It was, however, not an outlet for his emotions. It was not 'sitting in the twilight hour before a keyboard in trance and solitude—and let your fingers go'. The aristocratic employers or sponsors of musicians had in their cortège also a music-master and he had to examine and judge the candidates for musical services. It may well be that Beethoven and Mozart did not always improvise to the satisfaction of the music-masters. The imagination and daring of genius were probably above their reach and therefore hatefully dismissed.

The other sort of improvisation is something totally different, is probably often not more than what formerly—and less euphemistically—has been called 'strumming'. Strumming is certainly direct and may be also ecstatic, but it is not art. Art is spontaneity passed through creative conscience.

You know now of the two kinds of improvisation: the professional—technical—one, and the subconscious emotional one. The first can more or less successfully be supplied by any musician, including the trained amateur. The second one remains a sort of stammering self-expression.

Do not be misled by musicians' biographies which are rarely written by musicians. You had better not trust them too far, in musical matters. Believe me—a musician—grown-up serious people do not 'improvise'. Neither their own compositions nor their performances of compositions by others.

VOICE: *Couldn't you conceive of a direct, emotional improvisation being a work of beauty?*

MR SCHNABEL: It might be impressive as a human emanation, but it will never be what we agreed to understand by a 'work'.

VOICE: *You think a work of art has to be a studied object?*

MR SCHNABEL: No, no, no! A work of art has to be created and processed and shaped in an even stream of inspiration—of inspired concentration—from beginning to end. What is your objection to thought leading to coherence?

Do you think you can improvise books? Immediateness is only one element of spiritual action. I don't say that all works

153

of art are excellent works of art. Yet all have been produced via thought. The difference in the results comes from the uneven distribution of grace. All composers compose as Mozart or others of the towering figures did but none has as much creative power as they.

In a magazine called the *Advertisers' Digest* I saw recently a passage to the effect that prosperity is just around the corner, is so certain, so great and so close that advertising will automatically be raised from an art to a science. 'Raised from art to science.' Where will the next wave lift it to? I recommend more caution and economy in the use of terms like 'art' and 'science'.

'Improvisation' is undoubtedly a high sounding expression, much higher than 'strumming'. I repeat: improvisations by primitives can be attractive for a short time and interesting as a phenomenon. But improvisations which are performed and sold are no improvisations. The same holds for printed 'improvisations'.

VOICE: *When you played the B flat Brahms Concerto, did you learn that all by yourself? I believe at that time you had no teacher.*

MR SCHNABEL: I had played it for my teacher years before the opportunity to perform it in public. The same with three of Beethoven's concertos. There comes, however, a day when a performer must take the responsibility for his own mistakes.

VOICE: *Mr Schnabel, what did you play that day when the Princess didn't like your music? Do you remember?*

MR SCHNABEL: I think I played some Schubert and some Bach. I am not sure; I remember Schubert because one of her guests afterwards confused Schumann and Schubert. The 'Schu' was what bewildered him.

VOICE: *Was the Brahms concerto well received the first time you played it?*

MR SCHNABEL: Oh, yes, it was, and my performance was very well reviewed too—thanks to Nikisch. I believe he told the Press beforehand to be friendly towards me. I did not fare so well, however, when a little later I played the first Brahms concerto in Berlin, also with Nikisch. The leading newspaper attacked him for allowing me to play the slow movement too slow (as the paper thought). They did not understand how a man like him could participate in such a distortion of a grand work. Years later I was told that Nikisch had written a letter to the offended journalist, telling him that a young artist is entitled to do things wrong and so he did not stop me.

When in an astonishingly short time I became 'officially established', some of the great conductors such as Nikisch or Richard Strauss began to deny me rehearsals. Reasons given: 'You are a musical boy; we need no rehearsal. It will be all right tonight.'

The incomparable Nikisch was (so rumours had it) not always meticulous with rehearsals. A widely spread and enjoyed anecdote told how Max Reger at the first rehearsal of one of his symphonic works interrupted Nikisch after having listened for a few minutes, and suggested trying the Final Fugue before the rest of the piece. Nikisch agreed and started thumbing through the score, to the last bar. He couldn't discover a fugue. Nervously he turned to Reger, exclaiming: 'Where is it? I can't find it.' Reger, with a Mephistophelian grin, growled: 'There is none!' He had, naturally, noticed that Nikisch did not know his piece, and took his revenge with this trick.

VOICE: *You have probably been questioned by students in other countries. I wonder what you think about American students?*

MR SCHNABEL: I would say that many of the questions asked by the younger ones here point to the same root. They point to a belief in the existence of what I would call *a safe conduct to wisdom,* a trust in methods and books and rules to lead to the solution of problems, to settle everything. Also a belief that there is only one solution, one way, one type of experience.

If one of you tells me that the most important and productive experience in his life is listening to unorganized utterances of desire and pleasure, I would understand and respect that, though I think that listening to Beethoven's Ninth Symphony for the first or the fiftieth time would have been a different kind of experience. It is important to be aware of different levels of happiness.

It depends upon how many regions of receptivity we have in our system. It is quite a legitimate pleasure to be tickled on the surface; it is a deeper satisfaction and help to be struck or touched in your innermost region.

I can enjoy strolling along Fifth Avenue and looking at the window displays. I may be perfectly happy. I can also be perfectly happy after climbing for hours to arrive at the peak of a mountain. Only he who has derived happiness from both, the climbing and the strolling, knows that they are incommensurable and will, asked to choose, certainly decide for the mountain.

What I heard today about art and improvisation was, I suspect, an intellectualized glorification of a fashionable escape from real effort. It is neither feeling nor thought that many of your questions reveal. They reveal sometimes curiosity, mostly habit. It is apparently unavoidable to be publicity-poisoned. Be on your guard! I think I told you of the young American composer who asked whether it was advisable for an American composer to use dissonances.

We have the answer-man, a new occupation. He is not the same as soothsayers, fortune-tellers, or magicians were. He owns answers, all of them.

I admit that the only thing of which I am fairly certain is the confusion in my own mind, or to put it in another way, my acceptance of pluralism in the world of motives, intentions, and ends. I know that I am trying hard to find what I would consider suprapersonal truth, but I do not know why I try. Does this satisfy you, who are also a bit confused, I hope?

VOICE: *Sure.*

VOICE: *I think you once mentioned that you could never prove that Bach was a greater composer than Irving Berlin.*

MR SCHNABEL: I can't.

VOICE: *Then how can you disagree with the statement recently made by one of our foremost newspaper judges of music, that the best music is just the music we like best?*

MR SCHNABEL: Well, since the quality of works of art cannot be measured with a ruler, I accept his nihilistic dictum, according to which the worst is naturally what we like least. For one holding the office of a 'judge', it is an uncustomary approach. How can he expect any effect from his verdicts? And yet you quote him. A few minutes ago I warned you not to rely too much on second-hand valuations. I did not mean by that your hermetic isolation from any influence. I meant chiefly to indicate that the voice of publicity, of advertising, should not be the greatest influence.

Why have I been invited to give these talks here? What do you think? What may be the reason? Anybody else might have been invited. I don't say that I am entitled to this honour, but I have, nevertheless, been asked. Now if you were to ask

156

the persons who have invited me, 'Can you prove that this man is better suited than any other man?' what would they answer? Presumably, that they had faith in my suitability for this task. If I fail—well, they have never announced that they are infallible. Faith is, of course, a more slippery ground than so-called facts. To be literal, allegedly exact, pseudo-scientific, pseudo-realistic, statistical—etc., etc.—is comparatively convenient. Here, it seems it is something to be worshipped.

To illustrate this mentality, these examples might amuse you: one morning I said to a pupil as he entered my studio— not very originally—'It's wet out today.' His polite reply was: 'That's because it has been raining.' I reported this gem to another person: *he* said: 'Well, it might have been a sprinkler.' On another occasion a lady asked me to which of two existing schools of teaching I adhere, to that which makes you play in time or to that which makes you play as you feel. I had to think for a moment before I said: 'Can't one feel in time?'

Thousands of times I have been told that in order to live one has to eat. Each time I rise and bow, grateful for the information. Combining faith, urge, capacity of experience, idealistic efforts, and knowledge (as far as it or you can go), one ought to arrive at firm discrimination. Often what is cocksurely presented as a fact is not factual. I once heard a doctor say—and nearly fainted—that love is only a disturbance of the glandular system. Even if it were, are those who do not love doomed to an existence with never-disturbed glands? If they want to love and succeed in disturbing their glands, is the result guaranteed?

VOICE: *It is just that people go around talking. I don't think I know of anyone who has never passed a judgement. I mean if they are going to pass a judgement, either they must have a reason for it or else they shouldn't say anything at all.*

MR SCHNABEL: I would also not use the term 'judgement'. If you ask someone what he thinks of Shakespeare and he replies that this kind of work bores him, that is no judgement, it is just an answer, a communication, containing no arrogance. If he had answered: 'rubbish', you would have felt sympathy with him who is excluded from a contact which means so much to others. I might, of course, be pitied because I am excluded from prize-fighting. His exclusion and my exclusion do not however allow the conclusion that boxing and

Shakespeare are equals. Neither are the fans of different things equals simply by being fans.

Preoccupations and illusions, both much too powerful, are also not the right approach to art. At a party given in Paris for the aged Franz Liszt, one of the female guests had made up her mind to hear him play on that occasion. She insisted and insisted, was on her knees, in tears, because he refused. Finally she begged, '*One* note, please.' To get rid of her, Liszt went to the piano and softly touched one key—she dropped unconscious to the floor. So you see that the power of illusion can be truly enormous.

I refuse to participate in a discussion of the difference between Irving Berlin and Johann Sebastian Bach. I am quite sure Mr Berlin would refuse it too.

VOICE: *You have to wait a hundred years to make a judgement?*

MR SCHNABEL: Even after a hundred years you will not get a safe conduct to wisdom.

VOICE: *That is right. That is why I think you contradict yourself.*

MR SCHNABEL: I probably do.

VOICE: *You said at a previous talk to us that to judge whether Shostakovich is of the same calibre as Beethoven will be possible only after a hundred years.*

MR SCHNABEL: Yes.

VOICE: *Making a judgement now, by that token, would be entirely on your own and, therefore, impossible.*

MR SCHNABEL: You misinterpreted my remark. I meant that time and distance, posterity, longevity, acknowledgement through generations, are criteria of distinction which cannot be matched by our personal opinion and which we should not refute, even if we prefer contemporary, ephemeral, familiar output to the small *élite* of creations strong enough to satisfy and to ennoble human beings for ever.

6

VOICE: *I wanted to ask you, did you ever meet Rachmaninoff?*

MR SCHNABEL: Yes, I did, shortly after the revolution in Russia. He had left his fatherland and all his possessions there. Then, before going to U.S.A., he spent a few years in Scandinavia. That is where I met him first; I saw him then fairly often in Copenhagen. We harmonized perfectly. When I arrived in U.S.A. I tried to renew our contact. He did not respond, so I have never spoken to him in the United States. I did not speculate as to what might have caused his unexpected change of attitude. I was only sorry. Once, in 1921 or 1922, after having heard him play magnificently, I sent him, by hand, a little note of thanks—an act not too usual among colleagues and when it occurs, a special satisfaction to the receiver. Yet, he continued with his silence. Maybe my message was not delivered.

VOICE: *What do you think of musicians' unions?*

MR SCHNABEL: We would first have to decide whether the physical welfare of musicians is indispensable for the spiritual welfare of music. Music has flourished independently of musicians' hardships—or softships. This is a social problem. The unions' foremost concern is not music, but the protection of musicians from exploitation. Their actions are reactions. I am not competent to talk on and not attracted to dabbling in this subject.

VOICE: *Doesn't it affect professional musicians such as yourself?*

MR SCHNABEL: I would not think so. It is also unimportant. There are many things in public life which I resent much more. I became a member of a union by coercion. You know probably better than I what led to this coercion. AF of M against Agma, or the other way around. You know about it?

VOICE: *Yes.*

MR SCHNABEL: So I need not tell you. The American

Federation of Musicians had, before this row, never asked us solo performers to join them. They admitted, after the row, that we actually do not belong there. We are not exploited, we do not serve by the hour, we have many different employers, we do not work for fixed rates. Our activities are based on individual arrangements. After I joined the union—by compulsion—yet quite content—I was immediately sent on strike. I am quite sure that strikers just as innocent as I was, are no rarity.

The only time I ever heard anything about unions for orchestras in Europe was in Riga. Yet they existed and were, no doubt, well organized. Most orchestra musicians in Germany were civil service employees and whether they were permitted to join unions, or only to form associations, I do not know.

VOICE: *Do you think it was right for the union to make you join by compulsion? Do you have any feeling of resentment about it?*

MR SCHNABEL: They appealed—with the help of mild pressure—to my sense of solidarity. They probably thought that I as one of the musicians in comparatively privileged positions should only be glad to help in the protection of musicians who are not. That is, at least, my interpretation. It is quite sensible.

Sometimes poor musicians come and tell me that when they fall ill, or are otherwise in trouble, the union does not help them. But I don't know whether it is true, and what the union's reasons may be. I don't like some of the practices of this union. The standby practice is questionable and undignified, breeding demoralization. I am waiting for the day when a few minutes before I start performing a representative of the union will inform me that there are two unemployed pianists in the locality and I must either share my fee with them or face the consequences.

VOICE: *How did they make you go on strike?*

MR SCHNABEL: As with all their other members, we were not allowed to make records.

VOICE: *I see. But they did not put any ban on your concert performances?*

MR SCHNABEL: That was not the issue. If I remember correctly, the strike was ordered in connection with the broadcasting of records and it seems it was not unjustified. We performers or composers never get a cent from the broadcasting stations permanently using our recordings, even on commercially sponsored programmes. The strike lasted two years, I think.

VOICE: *Mr Schnabel, while we are on social questions, do you feel that there is a difference in the quality of music and the freedom of musical production in countries where there is no question of money to support symphony orchestras, plays, theatres—that sort of thing—and in America, where it is up to the people, by donations or tickets? Do you feel it makes a difference in the quality of musical production?*

MR SCHNABEL: No. I don't think it makes much difference whether the support of public artistic activities comes from the state or from private sources. Orchestra organizations here in U.S.A. seem rather overstocked with boards and committees and campaigns—junior committees and ladies' committees and boards of directors and trustees—and every year for months the same bustling promotion paraphernalia, meetings, luncheons, banquets, all stops of the publicity organs employed—is it really necessary? Or chiefly tradition, or fun, or time-killing, or business stimulation as such? Is there really not enough stability and confidence to guarantee for a long stretch the adequate, customary attendance to well-tested and always enjoyed associations? There is always a danger that the musical director of such establishments becomes distracted by so much agitation—and pessimism.

Yet America has the best orchestras in the world. We are of course lucky that an American orchestra means an international one, composed of the heirs of all European traditions. We have the greatest selection of talent.

VOICE: *Yes. Are they up to the standard, let us say, of the St Petersburg orchestra during the Czarist régime?*

MR SCHNABEL: Certainly they are. Some here are in sonority, brilliance, and virtuosity superior to all other orchestras I know. In spirit, some abroad can well compete. There are orchestras which do not play with external perfection, but with idealism and inner participation; others whose performances just tickle, thrill and 'throw' you, but miss what I mentioned before as creative conscience. Their gorgeous achievements fail sometimes with me. I hear a display, a smartly-run ensemble, a salesman streak. They serve sensations—and look bored.

I think state or municipality subsidized orchestras, on contract for several years—and not as now, several months— would flavour musical quality. They will come. There are very many, an always growing number, who cherish this idea. Some years ago everyone seemed to be against it. Each of them gave, almost automatically, the same answer when state subsidy for orchestras was recommended: 'they would be delivered into the hands of politicians'. I then pointed to the many state and municipal institutions, like hospitals, libraries, schools, museums, which to my knowledge are not more misdirected than private enterprises of the kind. And why should politicians be inferior to lady committees? This standard objection is clearly not the expression of deep thinking. And in the last few years the conviction that subsidies might be wholesome—and eventually unavoidable—has been gaining much ground. The private sponsors might gradually disappear. They have, I hear, already dwindled.

I also believe, am convinced—knowing the United States quite well in musical matters—that this country is absolutely ripe for dozens of opera houses with, let me say, a nine months' season. It would be a tremendous success. Every state might one day have its own opera. Why have we only two, with a short season? Inertia, distrust of the state? What a chance our musical talent would get! Where can singers and conductors go, as things are now?

VOICE: *In one of your books you say that you feel technical problems in piano playing should not be attacked as such, that they should be worked out as you come to them in the music. Do you mean that for the average pianist, and for a child beginning to study?*

MR SCHNABEL: Yes. I mean that one should never make any music, not even sound one musical tone, without a musical intention preceding it.

VOICE: *Most of us were taught the other way.*

MR SCHNABEL: I cannot help it.

VOICE: *Were you taught the other way, too?*

MR SCHNABEL: I really do not know what I was taught. Maybe I was taught just like you. I had no influence on my teachers' teachings. Even if they had a system I, as a child, would not have known it. We were not as system-thirsty then as one is now. The first book I saw on piano-playing problems was one written by a Mr Breithaupt in Berlin, in 1904. He was a critic for a musical monthly, a very interesting, original, fascinating man. In those first years in Berlin I saw him very often and he would always have me play for him

162

alone. I did not see why. Years later he published, with far-reaching effect, a book on piano playing. In the private seances on which he so toughly insisted, I had served him, as I knew now, as one of his guinea-pigs. Once, also before the book was out, he came to the artists' room after a concert and announced with excitement and jubilance: 'Schnabel, you play with shoulder-participation.' I and the people around me thought he was crazy. What did he mean? He had come to the concert only to watch and, as he hoped, to establish that I played with shoulder-participation. I had never speculated how much shoulder-participation is required, how much 'fall', 'weight', wrist-rolling, what elbow angles—and endlessly on. But this is a scientific age.

I believe that children and all other people who *make music* would be happiest to try just that. If I were a dictator, I would eliminate the term 'practise' from the vocabulary, for it becomes a bogy, a nightmare to children. I would ask them: 'Have you already made and enjoyed music today? If not—go and make music.'

VOICE: *Mr Schnabel, is there any special reason why seemingly you limit yourself to playing, in concerts at least, Mozart, Beethoven, Brahms and Schubert, and yet you compose in a very modern manner?*

MR SCHNABEL: I am not conscious of a reason. I follow the mysterious phenomenon of compelling attraction. Also in composition it is not a matter of choice. Technically (and theoretically) I could play any music, and compose quite other things than I do. But why should I? Did I tell you how one of my colleagues, a famous conductor, terrifically aroused by hearing a composition of mine, came rushing into the artists' room, savagely gesticulating, and shouted in the presence of many people into my face: 'Either you lie when you play, or you lie when you compose.' I said: 'Don't worry, I am lying both times.'

Now I ask you a counter-question. Do you think there is a fundamental difference between modern music—I mean contemporary music of today—and music of previous periods? Do you think that music in previous periods was never modern?

VOICE: *Oh, yes, it was. But those periods were different. Now, modern music certainly isn't like the music that was considered modern then.*

MR SCHNABEL: Do you think that their music was absolutely unlike the music which had preceded theirs?

VOICE: *No.*

MR SCHNABEL: Well, I hope you don't expect us composers of today to write music which differs from past music in nothing but the tones.

VOICE: *I thought possibly you were influenced—*

MR SCHNABEL: I am certainly influenced, but I don't exactly know by what.

VOICE: *Then another question.*

MR SCHNABEL: All right, but grant me first a few more words on this matter. I cannot see a contradiction in my playing Mozart and writing what you call modern music, for his music is also modern, as I interpret the term.

VOICE: *I see what you mean. You say that his music is modern—it can never die.*

MR SCHNABEL: I make an admittedly rather arbitrary distinction between the modern, the modish and the modernized. But what do *you* mean by modern? You certainly don't mean just 'contemporary'. Do all contemporary musicians write modern music?

VOICE: *No.*

MR SCHNABEL: And in Mozart's time, did all contemporaries of Mozart write modern music?

VOICE: *No.*

MR SCHNABEL: Was Mozart's writing much ahead of most of the people who wrote when he did?

VOICE: *It was.*

MR SCHNABEL: That is then why I call it modern. And it is the same for all periods. In regard to motivation and procedure composers nowadays compose exactly as Mozart did. I have no doubt whatsoever that Mozart's approach to music and ours now must be identical. The difference is in the amount of talent. That is the real difference. Then I am afraid you can ask me: 'If you have so much less talent than Mozart and know it—and your compositions, though they seem modern now, have hardly a chance to survive you—why do you compose?' What should I answer to that?

But now to the next question.

VOICE: *I suppose in most cases in the last decade or so, you performed at your piano recitals mostly sonatas. Why did you do that? Is it because the sonata is a piano form which*

*would show up the musician or the piano more? Maybe you
think the piano should have only larger pieces performed on
it, because it comes close to the orchestra as instrument?*

MR SCHNABEL: Please take it for granted that what I do in
music I do because I like it best. I see no reason to act otherwise and feel convinced that no one chooses his repertoire
among the works he dislikes. Why should we? Naturally, I
run the risk that my preferences are not shared by others.
Yet, my programmes have to correspond to my own taste.
You may call that sheer selfishness. True—it satisfies *me* most.
But I cannot help trying it and as long as I can exchange sonatas for bread, I shall continue. There are, however, lots of
pieces besides sonatas which I like just as much and which I
often perform when they fit my idea of a good programme.

VOICE: *You lived through a period of some of the greatest
philosophy, the greatest painting and all sorts of allied arts.
You never went to school, and you speak to us here seemingly
free from any particular influence. I just wonder if you can
tell me something about what you acquired outside of school
—I mean without school—in the way of the general thoughts
of your period and how you acquired it.*

MR SCHNABEL: I have mentioned several names—most of
them unknown to you—of brilliant people in Vienna and in
Germany with whom I had the good chance to establish contact. These contacts must have been contagious and that was
how the germs of culture must have been planted within me.
I had two very brilliant teachers and quite a number of highly
gifted co-students. In spite of that I really know very, very
little—outside of music, the field of my permanent activity.
How did I dare to accept the invitation to talk to you twelve
times?

VOICE: *Why did you accept it?*

MR SCHNABEL: Because adventures attract me.

VOICE: *I would like to convince you that you do know
quite a lot.*

MR SCHNABEL: Well, I'm glad you have this impression.
Yet, of what I guess to be knowledge, very little is in my possession.

VOICE: *You certainly would not agree to speak to us unless
you thought that even though you knew very little, we knew
even less than that!*

MR SCHNABEL: Perhaps I should talk only about music.

From my seventh year on I have been a musician. I have spent my life in music, as a composer, performer and teacher. Yet I have—and have had—little time, little inclination and, I think, little talent for analysing music and for creating or discussing systems and methods.

By disposition I am talkative. For a talkative person I have not enough time for words—I have used much less time for words and conversation in my life than for tones—and that may be the cause of my developing an inclination for expression in rather compressed form, in an aphoristic manner, and for my inability to follow if I have to listen to elaborate orations and perorations.

So I really think it is not an affectation—far from that—to admit that I have no talent for systems and methods. Maybe it is not essential to the artist to be systematic and methodical. And maybe, even if he has no analytical mind and does not know much, it might not be impossible that he could have something to tell or perhaps even to *say*.

VOICE: *Pictures by Renoir, Picasso, the French Impressionists and others are all very much accepted now and we go to museums to see them because they are considered 'art' today. But when you were a young man, these artists, like you, were they not still struggling with something that was not accepted?*

MR SCHNABEL: I remember very well when in a private home in Munich, I think it was 1901, I saw for the first time pictures by Cézanne—they were two portraits—and also some by Van Gogh. Though the beautiful Cézannes struck me at that time as being very ugly, I could not forget them—while I forgot other pictures which had pleased my eyes at once. The Cézannes grew in my memory to ever finer and more eloquent creations, gained validity and finally joined the other paintings which my consciousness treasured.

I also remember that the young professor of chemistry, whom I mentioned yesterday, spoke to me in 1900 of atom splitting and of Rutherford, and a year or two later he mentioned Einstein, saying that he seemed to be a genius. I had always some contact with people who drew my attention to something which was very promising and new, or great.

VOICE: *Did you run across a young doctor named Sigmund Freud?*

MR SCHNABEL: You mean, did I meet him personally?

VOICE: *Yes.*

166

MR SCHNABEL: No, I did not. But one of my best friends since boyhood—he belonged to my group of friends in Vienna —is a professor of psycho-analysis, teaching at Harvard. He knows however that I am very sceptical and feel uneasy about psycho-analysis. In fact, I have the idea that indirectly Freud has contributed very much, via the general, superficial interpretation of his discoveries, to the worship of irresponsibility, which is rather widespread now.

VOICE: *I remember seeing in a book of caricatures a picture of Wagner driving a quarter note into somebody's ear. When his music was first known that was the artist's impression of it and the effect it had on people—that it ruined their ear. You were alive when his music was relatively new. Was that really the impression?*

MR SCHNABEL: Wagner's music was criticized as being unbearably ugly and cacophonous. For decades it was called that, and un-understandable. Nevertheless today many of his tunes have acquired a tinge of platitude. Actually, all great composers have been criticized adversely by some of their contemporaries. One of the highest-ranking dictionaries of music in the eighteenth century says of Johann Sebastian Bach that he was a very poor craftsman in music.

That brings us back to our previous argument when I was criticized for saying that it might be better not to compare contemporary works with those which have survived a hundred years. Already those had to overcome the sum of all criticism of their own time and the following generations. To be—after all that—still very much alive, as they undoubtedly are, is certainly an important criterion—as I told you yesterday.

VOICE: *There are many works by Bach which are never performed. Would you say that just because of that, they were not good music? Of course, I realize there are other causes preventing performance—difficulties to overcome for performers—but there are so many pieces one cannot hear. Yet that would not be a reason, would you say, why it was not great music?*

MR SCHNABEL: The selection for public performance does not depend exclusively on high quality. Also the fact that some works are not performed during a certain time—like ours—or in a particular country, does not yet mean that they have failed to survive. And I told you yesterday that if you really want to get acquainted or familiar with the greater part of wonderful music, like Bach cantatas or songs by Schubert, you have to bring this about yourself by playing them at home. The public service cannot supply all of that. We have already discussed the reasons why only a small section of music can be supplied by the public service. And of this small section a considerable part belongs to inferior, ephemeral music.

On the other hand, not all creations of a great composer are equally successful, of course. It is very interesting to examine the proportion of successful works and less successful works by the same composer and see how this proportion varies between different composers. In the case of Mozart and Schubert, for instance, I think one could say that only half of their production is really successful, and the other half, by comparison with the successful half, less so; while in the case of Beethoven and Wagner, the proportion of successful works is astonishingly high.

VOICE: *By 'success' do you mean public acclaim?*

MR SCHNABEL: No! Obviously not. Did you understand it that way?

VOICE: *No. I did not think you meant that.*

MR SCHNABEL: Of course not. I spoke of that before: the two kinds of success. Here I referred to the 'success with oneself'.

VOICE: *I would like to ask whether, when you were young, you had a distinct feeling of unrest about the very new in art and music?*

MR SCHNABEL: When I first heard some works by Reger— I was very young then—and some by Strauss, I could not follow the technical procedure of that music. Later I heard the first performance of Strauss's *Elektra* and was enormously impressed; it was almost a physical sensation. There was something new in the appearance of this music. Hearing it again twelve years later, it seemed shallow to me. In the meantime it had been imitated and I had become accustomed to its procedure. Thus I was able to feel what is beneath it and that seemed rather thin to me.

I do not want to analyse a contemporary work while I am hearing it, according to rules which do not apply to it. Rules have nearly always been postulates. Great composers have not

168

created their works following rules established in books; rather have the rules been derived from their creations.

At present the listener's problem seems to be the following —as I tried to formulate it recently: while music for three hundred years has proceeded in a way in which the harmony was the basis and the melody a sequel of the harmony, during the last decades music has been created in which the harmony is a sequel of the melody. This music is called 'atonal'—a very misleading term, as its sound seems to indicate that it is a derivation of 'tone' and, obviously, tones can never be a-tonal. Actually, the term is derived from 'tonality', for this music does not refer to any tonalities or keys of the earlier harmonic system.

The new procedure is, of course, alien to ears accustomed to hearing exclusively music which employs the other procedure. Listeners expect to find the familiar procedure in every piece of music they hear and if they don't find it, they say it is not music. But that is, of course, not just. It is music, but they are still excluded from it. The fact that the unaccustomed listeners are excluded does not prove that it is not music.

The music proceeding in this way will need many more years, many more performances, and many more willing listeners before it can be said whether it will ever be generally enjoyable or not. I am accustomed to this procedure, so when I listen to such music, I listen only to the content and I find that also among works of this kind, some strike me immediately as cheap and shallow and others as very vital and inspired. So here also it is not only the appearance of music, but also its essence which can strike you. If you are interested in becoming more acquainted with this procedure, I recommend again, home consumption.

Any other questions? I hope I have not intimidated you.

VOICE: *Some of Stravinsky's music seems to me greatly inferior to other works of his. As you said a while ago, a composer composes as he has to compose. I feel that in his case many times he has composed as a pose.*

MR SCHNABEL: I would not say so. He experiments, like Picasso in the field of painting. Maybe it is a kind of parallel case—Stravinsky with his many styles, and Picasso with his. I am, however, convinced that in every case he did his best.

VOICE: *You think it was a compulsion?*

MR SCHNABEL: Yes. He could not do better. But I agree

with you that some of his works are very disappointing. Thinking of the sparkle and freshness of his *Petrouchka,* its great vitality, energy and temperament—and thinking of some of his later works of which I am very fond, I was deeply depressed and saddened when I heard a concert last year with works which were below the expected level.

7

VOICE: *Did you know a man by the name of Straube who edited the Peters Edition of Bach?*

MR SCHNABEL: Yes, I knew him fairly well. He had the highest reputation. As a performer he was perhaps a little on the sentimental side, but he was a wonderful, idealistic man, somewhat like Dr Schweitzer. I am not familiar with his editions, but am sure they are very stimulating.

VOICE: *Yes, they are.*

MR SCHNABEL: It may be that he had some typical nineteenth-century ideas about Bach interpretation. Even Busoni's Bach editions, interesting and fascinating as they are, can be dangerous in the hands of someone who is not aware of the changes in the conception of Bach style since then. The nineteenth-century conception of Bach interpretation is probably mistaken, misleading.

VOICE: *Do you have any feeling against the transcription of Bach organ works for piano?*

MR SCHNABEL: I am not fond of them. You see, I do not like transcriptions. And most of these noisy transcriptions of Bach's organ works for piano were made at a time when the conception of Bach's music, in my opinion, was false. It takes quite an effort to recognize Bach's piece in the Busoni transcription of the Chaconne. It sounds like César Franck, acquires a kind of sensuousness, impurity, or bombast which seems to be absolutely foreign to Bach's essential qualities.

There were two ideas—to approach Bach either as a cathedral or as an ink-pot. But Bach was a human being who loved to wander in the woods and sing and hear the birds, just like other people.

Hearing the orchestral transcriptions—which came later, incorporating some twentieth-century ideas—I have often felt a physical sensation—particularly those of Mr Stokowski make me feel rather uneasy, to put it mildly. When I heard the D minor Toccata, I thought a gypsy band was beginning to play; it sounded to me like Hungarian popular music.

VOICE: *Do you think that Wagner's music and the growth of the orchestra during that period changed the character of the orchestra a good deal, changed, probably, the character of conducting; perhaps affected the conducting of many older works?*

MR SCHNABEL: I think there is already a reaction. In the second half of the nineteenth century there was a development which led easily to a kind of falsification or vulgarization of the music written before Wagner. Not only by changing sonorities, but still more by the introduction of what I call 'inside dynamics', which were invented to simplify instruction in the music schools. 'Inside dynamics' were used as substitutes for genuine expressions. Let me give you an example: in a melodic succession of five tones, consisting of a crotchet, a quaver, quaver-rest, crotchet, quaver, quaver-rest and a crotchet, the second and fourth notes (quavers) will be shortened and suppressed to such an extent that the melodic line is completely lost. At the same time, the dynamic distortion creates the impression of an emotion, superficial and sentimental, which further blurs the composer's intention.

Of course, a line in music should remain a whole; whether it is marked *legato* or *staccato,* whether some note values are longer or shorter, and in whatever rhythmical arrangement it appears, it should be still the same figure, the same phrase.

However, there are still many conductors using the device of 'inside dynamics'.

VOICE: *Could you lay some of it to the effect of Wagner?*

MR SCHNABEL: Yes. But Wagner, of course, was a theatrical composer. Furthermore, even in performances of his music it was overdone. I think it is to the advantage of his music that it is now conducted much more simply than when I heard it in my youth.

VOICE: *Would you consider that Beethoven, say, belongs more to the classical period?*

MR SCHNABEL: I deplore this distinction between 'classical' and 'romantic', as there is really no line we can draw. All great expression in art contains romantic elements, and all great expression is organized into form, so you could call it classical.

It all began in the nineteenth century when we started sifting, filing, pigeon-holing, categorizing everything. Next came the classification of all works as 'Apollonic' or 'Dionysian'. All this is very unfortunate, does not correspond to reality, is handy only for school-teaching.

Every great composer was classified; like Beethoven: the eternal wrestler indiscreetly shouting out his own sufferings; Mozart: a kind of furniture exhibition and masquerade; Bach: ink-pot or cathedral; and Schubert: the charming *Lieder* king. All this is of course the sheerest nonsense. Yet it is still accepted in teaching, in many books.

VOICE: *Could you recommend any biographies of Beethoven, Bach, Brahms and the other great composers for us to read?*

MR SCHNABEL: The biographies I would recommend as best are always those which are the least readable—just dry reports; for the romanticized type of biography, like Emil Ludwig's, certainly consists of continual falsifications. In my opinion, the best book on Beethoven is one called *The Beethoven Lexicon,* or *Beethoven Dictionary*. It is alphabetically arranged, in two volumes, and wherever you open it you find something relating to Beethoven's life or work. There is no interpretation at all, just facts. As Beethoven biography, I think Thayer's is the best.

On Mozart and Berlioz I would highly recommend Walter J. Turner's books, not for what they say on music (that is often not even tenable—Turner was not a musician), but because he succeeds in taking you into the region of creative genius. His books have genuine warmth and an original approach. They satisfied me most.

VOICE: *Are all these works in English?*

MR SCHNABEL: Yes. Turner as well as Thayer wrote in English. Mr Thayer, you know, was in the diplomatic service, an American consul in Trieste, who liked music. He gathered all his material but died before finishing the work. Hermann Deiters completed it. It consists of five volumes; the last two, in German, were edited by Riemann, the musicologist of Leipzig, while the first three volumes, in English, are exclusively the American consul's work.

VOICE: *What about Dr Alfred Einstein's biography of Mozart?*

MR SCHNABEL: I like the first half of that book, the biographical section, very much. It is very readable and very moving, and perhaps there are also some new points. When it comes to dealing with music, I feel excluded, for it is very rarely that the musician and the musicologist go along together. There is a different approach which I simply do not understand. So after you have read the biography—because you want to know in what circles Mozart lived and what he thought—I feel it would be much better if you spent your time reading his letters. There is a collection of marvellous Mozart letters, translated by Miss Anderson, in three volumes. They are a sheer joy to read.

VOICE: *Isn't music a functional part of society, of our living, our enjoyment?*

MR SCHNABEL: This social function of music is only an application or effect of music, it has nothing to do with the music as such. For society consumes all kinds of music. You can never come to any valuation of music if you come with statistics proving how music is sold or circulated. That deals with the utilization of music, not with music itself.

VOICE: *Is it possible to say, then, that music itself just comes from an adaptation of absolute classical values to the ear?*

MR SCHNABEL: I think music itself comes from the desire, the ability, the necessity, to express something in tones.

VOICE: *Is all great music, all pure music, universal, or is some of it confined to nationality?*

MR SCHNABEL: Not only is great, lasting music universal; I would say that the ephemeral is just as universal—only it does not last, that is the distinction. Journalism is just as universal as eternalism, though in an age when only journalism is considered universal, I think we go in the wrong direction. But would you not agree with me that the ephemeral also is universal? Trash is just as universal as treasures are. But though both are universal, they are, of course, by no means alike.

VOICE: *By saying that even trash is universal, do you mean that peasants of a far-away, maybe underdeveloped country, would appreciate boogie-woogie, such as teen-agers here do?*

MR SCHNABEL: Such peasants will have something which corresponds to boogie-woogie here. I think these teen-agers and bobby-soxers simply behave as they do because they know they get publicity. If they were never mentioned, if nobody paid any attention to them, they would behave differently. So while some of those peasants may like boogie-woogie many of them have never heard it, but they all have something which corresponds to it. Maybe where they live there is not such a trash industry as there is in other countries. Maybe their country is 'backward' and trash has not yet been commercialized there. But they all have trash.

VOICE: *What do you think of the prevalent custom in the United States of singing songs and opera in their original languages, when we are an English-speaking nation?*

MR SCHNABEL: I am very much for the use of the language of the country in which the operas are performed. Even in songs I think it is an advantage. For though the works may then not appear quite as they were composed, it was undoubtedly the intention of the composer, when he used words in combination with music, that these words should be intelligible and understandable to the audience. I think all opera should be sung in English here.

Such was the tradition in all European countries: in Italy, everything was sung in Italian; in Germany, everything in German; in Hungary, everything in Hungarian. They never used original languages, except at Covent Garden in London, but there they had only a short season, for people the majority of whom, anyhow, did not listen—so it was not so important.

VOICE: *In opera it might not be quite so important. There is action besides the music and words. But in songs some of the texts are first-rate poetry; are beautiful, have a meaning, and if you are going to sing that kind of music, people should know what it means.*

MR SCHNABEL: I absolutely agree with you.

VOICE: *But there are difficulties. The existing translations are not good.*

MR SCHNABEL: So we should only promote and propagate the idea of making better translations. For instance, Dr Drinker in Philadelphia has translated all Bach Cantata texts. They have great merit. Then he made a new translation of the Passion text because that was not too good. I think he is now going to translate all Brahms *Lieder* texts. He is a lawyer in Philadelphia, a great music lover who has his own choir.

VOICE: *Are there many small opera companies in Germany? I mean, were there?*

MR SCHNABEL: There were hundreds of opera houses. Every little town had its own municipal or state opera house. Of course, they were all subsidized because opera can never pay for itself. When the city was not very large, it was a combined playhouse and opera house. They had a permanent ensemble, and as I said before, because of the small population of such a city, their repertoire had to be very large and wide. They had, at the most, three or four subscriber groups.

VOICE: *What type of operas did they perform? Did they do Wagner, for instance?*

MR SCHNABEL: Yes, and Puccini, but also Mozart; occasionally some light opera. It was always addressed to the same type of audience. The audiences at that time were still very homogeneous.

VOICE: *The Metropolitan Company is having a thousand-dollar contest now for an American opera.*

MR SCHNABEL: One thousand dollars is very shabby. The Detroit Symphony has a twenty-five thousand dollar prize for an American symphony. But what is an American symphony? I can imagine what an American opera is: the plot takes place in America. But what is an American symphony?

VOICE: *Mr Schnabel, would you be willing to tell us whether you prefer composing, playing or teaching—or don't you know?*

MR SCHNABEL: Oh, I know.

VOICE: *Composing?*

MR SCHNABEL: Yes, I prefer composing. Yet—it makes me very sad to think of it—twice during my life there were long intervals in which I did not compose; together they lasted nearly twenty years, from 1905 to 1914, and from 1925 to 1935. Asking myself why I did not compose, I could find only one answer, that the urge probably was not strong enough.

But all my composing was done as a kind of hobby. Officially, I am not a composer—I am labelled a pianist—so my composing was a kind of hobby, or love affair. I did it always during my vacation, in the summer time.

VOICE: *You felt you were cheating, then, when you composed?*

MR SCHNABEL: Cheating?

VOICE: *Yes.*

MR SCHNABEL: No, not exactly. I am very happy composing, am not even interested in the value of my compositions, just interested in the activity. Few of my compositions are published. That is, however, partly my own fault, for I took a rather haughty, wrong attitude towards them, when I could have had them published. They are very seldom performed,

176

too. It is getting more and more difficult to have compositions of the type I am writing performed because they are expensive in effort—and in money, as they are not promising of success.

VOICE: *Isn't that true of much good new music?*

MR SCHNABEL: Certainly. You see, music has become a circulating article. The commercialization of music has, of course, led to some improvements, to better conditions in some respects; in others, though, it has been harmful. The situation of the contemporary composer is rather difficult if his work is not easily accessible, particularly if he does not use the harmonic system which is ingrained and indoctrinated in us. We have inherited this intelligibility of music when it proceeds in a certain accepted arrangement of harmonic progressions (which is quite arbitrary, of course). Yet, one day, to some of us, it seemed exhausted. It is not that the composers who don't use it wanted to be original, for if one could be original by volition, there would be millions of original people. (One cannot even be a moron by volition, I would say.)

VOICE: *I had an argument with someone who thinks that music should be written like a scientific game, like geometry.*

MR SCHNABEL: Let him try!

VOICE: *Can one write music, not with the idea of expressing anything, but simply by making rules and seeing what one can do following those rules?*

MR SCHNABEL: Perhaps such a process exists. But if somebody has creative genius, then he may deceive himself by telling such stories.

Recently I saw the prospectus of a method of composing, published by one of the best publishers of serious music: *The Way to the Perfect Composer,* in four volumes. George Gershwin and some Tin Pan Alley geniuses were for a short time pupils of the author. This prospectus says (I am now quoting literally) that after having read these four volumes you will be equipped to compose in any desired style and to any desired degree of perfection—which implies that someone might choose to be only forty per cent perfect, another seventy-five per cent—and so forth. If you ask me, I shall not buy this book, and I would not recommend you to waste your money on it. Yet I am sure that the author is not a swindler, nor one of these genuine fanatics who believe in a system, a method to cure and solve everything. He is not like one of those men who say on billboards, 'From hell to heaven in six weeks'—in music if you take lessons from him.

VOICE: *What about Bach? Do you feel he expresses an idea or an emotion in his pieces?*

MR SCHNABEL: I think he expresses the cosmos. But I don't understand this whole problem, 'idea or emotions', 'expression or science', or whatever you call it. Every musician can compose as he likes, and every musician can also talk as he likes. But no musician can please all other musicians, particularly when he talks. So if again somebody tells you that he thinks music should be produced this and that way, tell him to try it.

8

VOICE: *People say that music transmits a message to them. But it means nothing, does it?*

MR SCHNABEL: Every individual has to decide that for himself. If somebody feels he receives a message, nobody can say that it is not so; also whether it is an emotional or intellectual message, only he himself can decide. If prepared well enough, there might be something like a mass-hypnotic effect. For instance, if people are told beforehand what effect hearing the Ninth Symphony will have on them, they may react in that way. If they are told often enough what they are likely to experience, it is very probable that they will really experience what they have been told.

However, even then it has actually nothing to do with the music. For there might be one person in the audience who does not experience it, or who experiences something completely different, and he will be just as right as the others.

I think from a musical point of view it doesn't exist. I know, though, that many musicians think they have obligations toward mankind. Many artists think that way: that they are messengers or missionaries and have to bring happiness to people and ennoble people. I don't believe that. I mean by that, I am absolutely indifferent to this problem.

VOICE: *Could you tell us the difference in construction between the piano in Beethoven's time and the modern Steinway?*

MR SCHNABEL: Ask a piano technician. It is a technical question that I cannot answer. I have played on all of these instruments, as I told you before, but I was chiefly interested in the sonorities of the instruments, their range and possibilities. I am ashamed to say that I know very little about the construction of the piano. I would not dare to take a keyboard out. I did that once when I was a boy—and many of the hammers broke. So my mother was very angry with me. Since then I have been very careful.

VOICE: *Could you tell us something more about the differences between the pianos you used in Europe and liked so much and our instruments here?*

MR SCHNABEL: As I told you, those pianos had less of a personality. I would say that the quality which distinguishes the piano from all other instruments, is its neutrality. On a piano a single tone cannot be beautiful; it is the combination and proportion of tones which bring beauty.

You are forced to produce at least two or three tones in order to create a sensuous impression or to give a sensation of music to the ear, while almost all other instruments (except percussion instruments) or the voice can give you a sensuous pleasure even from a single tone. Around 1910 it was considered very 'modern' to say that the piano is a percussion instrument and that you could play everything staccato. Stravinsky did much towards promoting these ideas along with many piano teachers, and there was a book on the subject.

Once I was told by a musician—I hope he was joking—that it does not make the slightest difference for the sonority whether you strike or hit the keyboard with the tip of an umbrella or with a finger. That was also printed in that book—and not as a joke. Of course it is sheer nonsense, for everybody who wants music knows very well all that he can do with the fingers on the piano.

He can produce all kinds of tones; not only louder or softer, shorter or longer tones, but also different qualities. It is possible on a piano to imitate, for instance, the sound of an oboe, a 'cello, a French horn. But it is not possible to imitate the sound of an oboe on a flute, or a clarinet on a violin; these other instruments always retain their own characteristics. That is why I said that the distinction of the piano is in its being the most neutral instrument.

The Bechstein piano fulfilled this demand for neutrality better than any other piano I have known. You could do almost anything on that piano. The Steinway—or rather the Steinway of twenty years ago, for it has changed somewhat since that time—was a piano which always wanted to show something. You see, it had much too much of a personality of its own.

At first, when I wanted to produce something like, let me say, the voice of a bird on a Steinway, the piano always sounded to me like the voice of a tenor instead of a bird. For many years I had the feeling that the Steinway piano did not like me. An absurd idea, but I had that feeling.

It would not take the kind of treatment I gave a piano, so I conclude that the Steinway piano is more limited. The Bechstein piano enabled me to show effects not possible on a Steinway. The tone of the Steinway vibrates much more; also there are technical reasons: it has a different action.

VOICE: *Has the Steinway changed in that regard now?*

MR SCHNABEL: Very little. You see, Steinway has a monopoly now and if somebody has a monopoly he will not see any reason for changes and improvements. Many pianists are irritated by the 'double action' of the Steinway, but the company is very obstinate in this.

VOICE: *What is this 'double action'?*

MR SCHNABEL: Do you play the piano?

VOICE: *No.*

MR SCHNABEL: Actually you can recognize it even if you don't know how to play. When you push a Steinway key very lightly and slowly down, it will stop before it has reached the bottom and requires a certain pressure, a second pressure to go down all the way.

By now I am so used to it that it hardly irritates me any more. At first, however, it disturbed me greatly: for in order to produce a *fortissimo* you can play lightly, but whenever you want to play *pianissimo* you have to use a great deal of weight as otherwise the key would not go down. It certainly seems perverse.

VOICE: *Why, Mr Schnabel, did you go on playing concerts when there was war and in the midst of a revolution?*

MR SCHNABEL: Why did I play concerts? Because Nature has made me a musician. I cannot do anything else, and since there are people who buy piano playing, I have made it my profession—that is all. That is simple, isn't it?

VOICE: *Certainly. Does it hurt you at all to know that?*

MR SCHNABEL: Does it hurt me to know what?

VOICE: *To know that you are simply an article.*

MR SCHNABEL: An instrument, not an article. I am an instrument of music.

VOICE: *Well, you know that people often go to your concerts simply to be there.*

MR SCHNABEL: I don't know. I never ask the people why they come.

VOICE: *In the face of a revolution[1] you will play for people who come to your concerts in the dark simply to show that if they have nothing else they still have culture. I question the amount of culture there is in that.*

MR SCHNABEL: At no time in Kiel did I have an opportunity to investigate who was right; I simply did my duty. I did not condemn anyone at all. I did not condemn that little soldier who asked me for my passport, nor did I condemn those very brave people who, in the dark night, walked miles to hear a concert.

VOICE: *I did not ask whether they were right or wrong; I want to know what your attitude is, how you feel.*

MR SCHNABEL: It seems you don't want to know my attitude about right or wrong; you want to know my attitude about Right or Left. Is that it?

VOICE: *I wonder how you feel. You seldom tell us how you feel about the things you do.*

MR SCHNABEL: I tell you about what I did and saw—not about what I feel. But it may be that my feelings have coloured what I was seeing. And in reporting what I saw, some of the colour in which I saw it is communicated. I hope so anyway.

However, this relation between social conditions, social movements and the art of music which can never make any statements and has no recognizable tendencies, is very difficult to discuss. It is always going to be very vague. Even in the pictorial arts it is very difficult, if somebody is painting only landscapes, to establish a relation to social movements. In music, the least descriptive of all arts, it is entirely arbitrary, simply open to personal interpretation.

All my life I have heard this talk about the power of art to bring people nearer to each other, that world peace will come only if more music is circulated and exchanged. Yet, I have seen people deeply moved—as deeply moved and affected by music as is possible—and the next morning they would go into activities which you might call criminal and inhuman.

I don't think there was ever a piece of music that changed a man's decision on how to vote. If two men voted for different people they might have loved the same piece of music with the same degree of devotion.

[1] See p. 77.

VOICE: *Yet there were a great many artists who, when war broke out, gave up painting or music or writing or whatever they were doing.*

MR SCHNABEL: And became soldiers.

VOICE: *I was not thinking of that. That is true in a number of cases, however.*

MR SCHNABEL: What did the others do?

VOICE: *I don't know. I wanted to ask you that. International catastrophe, depressions, bloodshed, make some people dislike music and others like it more intensely.*

MR SCHNABEL: What then can I do and what then could I do in the face of war, bloodshed, disaster, but continue with my music? If I were to give up my music that would not express my attitude and would not help anyone.

VOICE: *You are one of a number of people who can be objective about these things. Others can't, of course.*

MR SCHNABEL: They can be sterilized or paralysed. If the stimulus or impulse or inspiration is stopped, then probably also the person would stop; the instrument that I told you we are would stop playing. But as long as we can go on and as long as it is not physically impossible, I think we have no choice—and will continue.

VOICE: *I would like to know what happens when you feel the impulse or inspiration to compose. I have often wondered exactly what you hear, how it appears, and what your reactions are.*

MR SCHNABEL: How can I explain that in detail? Sometimes it appears and disappears again. Sometimes it comes back with great insistence and obstinacy.

VOICE: *Is it a theme, a phrase? Does it come to you all at once?*

MR SCHNABEL: It is some arrangement of tones; some assortment of tones. You see, theme, melody, phrase, are very arbitrary categories. It is some combination of tones. That would be the simplest definition for music: a combination of tones. Because a single tone, as such, is not yet music, but two tones already can be music. The cuckoo makes music.

VOICE: *Mr Schnabel, you said you doubted whether any piece of music had changed a man's vote. That certainly seems clear at the outset, but as you look into it, you see that art is a fragment of the human spirit, the human soul; something that is in all of us and that does not change.*

183

*If art has any meaning at all it lies in this—enabling us
more closely to appreciate life and to understand experiences
and thus to make us better.*

*Perhaps that is not true to the extent that I hear a sonata
now and I walk into the next room and cast a different ballot.
Perhaps it is not in that immediate sense but in the long-range
sense that art has meaning and uplift value. It certainly does
help the race and in a real sense will condition the way we feel
about each other and about the votes we ultimately will cast.
Am I clear at all or am I mixed up?*

MR SCHNABEL: Very clear, but how can you explain then
what happened with a people like the Germans, who had
really established a profound relation to music. How can you
explain that these Germans were capable of doing what they
have done in the last twelve years, were capable even of allowing it to happen, in spite of being identified in a way with art,
particularly music? In spite of the fact that average education
also was nowhere higher than in Germany?

VOICE: *I cannot explain it.*

MR SCHNABEL: They must have been motivated, urged, or
forced by some other power which infests life and is stronger,
in social life. You see, there are also collective actions which
are apparently inescapable.

In my long life as a musician and among artists with whom
I have had much contact, I have come to the conclusion that
everybody who is really related to art, to whom it is a part of
existence and an inner necessity, must feel certain things which
give him some hold.

I am now dividing the people who are related to art into
two groups. The owner group: those for whom art is simply
part of their life, has always been with them in one or the
other form—at least as desire for the possession of it. And the
others whom I call the weak opportunist group. People belonging to the owner group know and appreciate, of course,
their own relation to the art, and when they are dissatisfied
with everything else, here is something which cannot dissatisfy
them.

However, whether it will show in their actions, their social
actions, whether it can prevent their doing something which
we consider bad, that is a different question. Yet we should be
very glad that even people who act differently from us and of

184

whose actions we disapprove, can love art, are not excluded from it and cannot be excluded.

VOICE: *Mr Schnabel, you seem to have a warm spot in your heart for amateur musicians and we would be interested in hearing your distinction between the professional and the amateur musician.*

MR SCHNABEL: Well, I think first we should decide whether we are speaking about musicians related to the art of music or about those in the other departments which do not belong to the art of music. When I talk about art in music, I mean just as it is understood in literature. We would not say that everything printed is art. Neither is it the case in music, of course.

Now, do you refer to all musicians or those related to the art?

VOICE: *Include them all.*

MR SCHNABEL: I would say that in the lower regions of music-making there can hardly be any amateurs. That may impress you as an entirely wrong statement. It depends upon what you mean when you say 'amateur'. This term in its original meaning always designated a person who was trying to be active in the highest region or highest department of music. It came about only much later that somebody, already satisfied with playing a little tune or a little waltz, called himself an amateur. That, I think, was also a consequence of the industrialization and the vast commercial interests in selling sheet music and musical instruments to the greatest possible number of persons.

In the higher regions, I think Nature selects who will be professional or amateur. The professional apparently is he who feels that he is compelled to devote all his life to music. This desire or necessity is not so strong in others, yet such persons, as amateurs, may occasionally achieve something superior in quality to the professional.

Those who are professional musicians became professional, I would say, from necessity and not from choice. Some seem to be undecided, in spite of their sufficiently strong desire, because of specific conditions or their particular situation, when for instance their parents are not in favour of their becoming professional musicians.

I have known cases of amateur musicians who, up to their thirty-fifth or even fortieth year, were lawyers or doctors and then gave it up finally to become professional musicians—an activity in which they earned much less than they did as doctors or lawyers, when they had high positions. Now they had no reputation at all but they were professional musicians and for the first time in their lives they were happy.

Others desire or start out to be professionals, yet become amateurs because they are prevented, are not fit to be professional musicians.

At present, amateurs are not as numerous as before, for to be an amateur in the art of music takes time, and since so many demands are made on people, they have no time.

Also, there is that lazy excuse, 'Well, we can hear so many playing better than we can do it ourselves, why should we play?' I do not like that.

VOICE: *I think the radio and records have killed the urge within people to make music of their own.*

MR SCHNABEL: There are no statistics. I would be terribly interested to know whether the amateurs in the art of music have increased or diminished since the introduction of mechanical reproduction of music.

VOICE: *There seem to be many people now who prefer listening to the same piece of music on records or the radio at home with their shoes off, rather than be in the concert hall with an atmosphere of stiffness. I wonder whether the perfection of recording techniques and the recording of all new pieces as they are composed could possibly result in the displacing of the concert hall?*

MR SCHNABEL: I don't think so. I think that most mechanically reproduced music remains a kind of substitute. The acoustic reproduction is not quite genuine. There is always, at least for my ear, some change. Still I think it is understandable if some people are now content to listen chiefly to records, even prefer it to being present in the concert hall.

At home they have a choice of what to play. They can repeat it, and are in more intimate contact with it; while in the concert halls, programmes are generally so mixed and sometimes so questionable that the more sensitive listeners do not go.

There are very musical people, more and more of them, who go to concerts only when the programmes attract them; when something is played which they have not heard before or have not heard often and want to hear especially. Otherwise, they would rather use their gramophone or listen to the radio.

However, there is a contact, let me say a vibration, between living beings. At the concert there is a living listener and a living performer, while when a record is played there is only one living being, and one object which is, in a way, dead; so this contact, this 'vibration' is lost.

VOICE: *That is exactly how I feel. If I want to hear a particular record, I can listen to it, but I prefer a concert to listening to records.*

MR SCHNABEL: I think it should be so—it is only natural. Though music really does not address itself to your optical sense, there is something about attending an original production and being in the same room with the performer. You react differently.

9

VOICE: *Do you ever become aware of the audience during your performance, aware that the audience is appreciative, or tired, or something else? Is that tangible enough to feel?*

MR SCHNABEL: Well, I have struggled very hard during the last thirty years to secure my neutralization on the platform when I perform, for I am in the service of music each time. If, rightly or wrongly, I have the impression that the audience is not a very good one, I might become influenced by that, play badly and make music suffer.

A concert manager once told me that an artist should sense, the very second he comes out, how his audience is that night. He mentioned a famous singer and said: 'Look at this man! He feels it with his first step on the platform, and in accordance with this impression he then decides to be serious, half-serious, or non-serious.' That is a true story—all my stories are true.

So I say it is better not to be too conscious of the audience. If you are playing in a town where you have not been before, it is very difficult to judge anyhow. Only if you are very familiar with a place, have often played there, might you distinguish better. Yet I say it would always be advisable for the performer not to be dependent on that.

It should be taken for granted that the performer is in the service of music, and that the listener is in the service of music; then, if both are sufficiently in the service of music, they will meet somehow, vibrate together.

VOICE: *When people began to ride in automobiles instead of singing in choral societies, was it like this: the prestige of being in the choral society had been a very high one, but when you could have the same prestige by having an automobile, then the people were no longer interested in the choral society?*

MR SCHNABEL: Yes, that is right. Of course, we have choirs now too, but they are professional choirs. They are very good, but they are paid, not amateurs. Some schools have very good choirs. I think amateur choirs are coming in again.

VOICE: *Do you remember what you felt when Horowitz played for you?*

MR SCHNABEL: I was very impressed. He even wanted a lesson with me, but I decided that he was not in need of any. I also asked him whether he was composing and he said, very shyly, 'Yes.' He had an enormous success, was rather spoiled, and tired. He gave twenty recitals a season in one city. He was really the hero at that time. I thought it was absolutely necessary for him physically and mentally to leave Russia. I am very glad he followed my advice.

VOICE: *What caused the competition between piano makers to be so ferocious?*

MR SCHNABEL: Competition was not 'ferocious' at all. It was a business practice. When a pianist wanted to use Steinway pianos in America, he was told that he should use Steinway pianos all over the world. It was not until 1933 that this practice was given up. When I came here in 1930 to play at the Brahms Festival in Boston, I played on a Bechstein piano, sent here from Germany for the occasion. They sent a tuner from Germany too and a second piano, all at their own expense.

It is very amusing how someone, perhaps a competitor, spread the rumour that Bechstein pianos could not endure different climates. That seems not very credible, for I saw Bechstein pianos in Australia, Russia, Turkey, Greece and Norway, in tropical and in arctic climates, yet they were always the same.

VOICE: *What do you think of South American music? Do you feel that South America is too young in culture to have produced anything really good?*

MR SCHNABEL: As you should have noticed already, I do not know any music other than musical music. I refuse to admit all these special branches or types of music. I don't know German music, don't know what French music, what Austrian music is. There may be slight differences in mannerisms or embellishments, yet I cannot conceive of any other music than musical music—it may be primitive, bad, vulgar, good, noble.

There seems to be a limit drawn by Nature as to the amount of great works of music created in one generation. In some countries, musical activities may not yet have developed to a level which makes their music suitable for export. Still it is very good for home consumption.

However, if for political reasons—like 'good neighbour policy'—or for reasons of music 'business'—like the 'exchange of waste products'—you had to listen to all music written anywhere in the world, you would find, if you wanted to watch and observe it, that music is very much alike everywhere. The good pieces from one country are very much like the good pieces from other countries, and the bad pieces from one country similar to bad pieces from elsewhere. Even the use of folklore elements does not change that. When Beethoven uses a Russian theme in a quartet, it sounds like Beethoven and not like Russia.

VOICE: *In your composing, I wonder whether you have ever used the atonal system?*

MR SCHNABEL: Not strictly. I don't believe too much in being tied to any system. We are very much interested in the great achievements of Arnold Schönberg, who has supplied new material. It must have been an enormous spiritual effort to find the new medium. By now it is in general, even in popular, use; not in its entirety, but part-elements of this are in all contemporary music.

Then Mr Schönberg imposed a kind of self-punishment, for he was in danger of writing with too great ease and too quickly. So when he became afraid of his own facility, he decided to discipline himself for a certain number of years by using the twelve-tone system. Actually the twelve-tone system was first presented by Hauer. Have you heard of him? He was a schoolmaster in Vienna. But in his case it was rather a calculated system.

We always think of the twelve-tone system in connection with Schönberg. Others familiar with his music think that even in his later works there is a certain dependence on that romantic expressiveness in music created by Wagner and most conspicuous in the *Tristan* music.

Occasionally, Schönberg used to get very angry with me. We have had terrible arguments—some went on for years, but we always remained intimate friends. I liked to tease him. Thus when I read one day in a Berlin newspaper that Stravinsky had said in an interview, 'Art should be cold,' I quoted this to Schönberg. He retorted: 'That is wrong; I said that first!'

VOICE: *You mentioned before, that you did not have any system when composing. Do you believe that in teaching theory it is better not to teach definite systems to the students, let them work out their problems and rather study music with them, to get what theory they can from studying scores of good music?*

MR SCHNABEL: I think you should always make a student familiar with the technical practices of the past, with pure part-writing and the development of the harmonic system, which is a very good school and will not be lost as a discipline even on him who writes in a completely different medium or procedure. First he should be familiarized with that and then he should be asked what progress, changes, alterations or deviations he can find in later music.

VOICE: *Do you think that sometimes it is apt to kill originality in a student if there is too much technical work in theory?*

MR SCHNABEL: I don't think so, but would not deny that it could occur.

VOICE: *I wondered if he might become too factual instead of writing naturally.*

MR SCHNABEL: You have to use some form; it has to be organic, otherwise it will never take shape. It is not necessary that every composer create a new organism or new materials for every piece he writes. Do you feel that reading old poetry and learning about its form constitutes a danger to the originality of a modern poet?

VOICE: *When you were speaking about concentration on the platform, were you referring exclusively to the piano?*

MR SCHNABEL: No. You see, we all have to relax physically in order to perform with a minimum of effort and at the same time we have to concentrate mentally. I used to advise my pupils that all concentration, while they perform music, should begin above the eyes; it should not involve the shoulders, because any tension in the shoulders will make it impossible to relax arms and hands completely.

Satisfaction is chiefly provided by uninterrupted concentration. But this uninterrupted concentration is practically never achieved, even when one is alone at home. In a concert hall it is almost unthinkable, for there are always noises, sometimes adverse acoustic conditions, the unaccustomed piano which is often unsatisfactory, or for other instrumentalists and singers

191

their accompanists or partners—and the constant possibility of diversion by the presence of the audience. I have tried all my life to become independent of all this, more and more.

VOICE: *I would like to hear some more about your impressions of music in America; I mean the state of our musical life.*

MR SCHNABEL: It is a very good place for music, the general response is truly gratifying, there are wonderful orchestras. What I have found harmful, is the idea that only what pleases the 'many' is really good. I do not know whether this is generally believed, but I have heard it expressed quite frequently. I find it very important in your relation to art that you should have the courage of your own likes. You should not wait, when you are pleased by something, to see whether it pleases very many before you dare to admit that you like it.

You might live in a small place where only three or four people agree with you on artistic values. Then you should neither think poorly of yourself nor of the people who do not share your insight. There is no reason for being arrogant, just a reason for being grateful, and happy to have the privilege of understanding.

The position of music in the lives of nations has changed. I am sure that fifty or sixty years ago, here in the United States the position of music was different from what it is now, and the same change has occurred in Europe. The decrease of live music in homes—with mechanical reproduction and the automobile coming in as competitors—has been the same everywhere. Of course one difference is that in Europe there were old traditions. But there are some traditions here, too. The orchestras are fairly old, and so are the music societies. However, in Europe as well as here the whole of public life has changed. The influence of the radio, the cinema, the magazine, after the First World War was enormous, affecting even those people who never go to the films, never listen to the radio, never read a magazine. I am sure of that. There is an influence on me, and I belong to those people who very rarely enjoy those pleasures.

VOICE: *What do you think of concerts for children?*

MR SCHNABEL: Well, they also did not exist until very recently. I would not say it is not good to invite children to concerts. But, with few exceptions, I would consider it senseless

192

before they are ten years old. Taking babies to concerts, I think, is simply for publicity.

I received a letter yesterday, stating, 'I know, Mr Schnabel, that you are not interested in young pianists, but I would appreciate it if you would hear my son. He started piano lessons at the age of three.' Well, I am afraid he has been ruined.

As to children's concerts and the way they are carried out, I am more familiar with those in England than those here. My impression is that here they are not conducted in the way I should regard as the best or most advisable for children's concerts. There is too much talk—telling the children, for instance, about the different instruments of the orchestra. It may be very diverting and instructive, but the children are not directed towards listening to the music, but are expected to see if they can distinguish the oboe from the clarinet. That has no relation to music. It would be much better, in my opinion, if they were simply asked to listen, and nothing told them.

Moreover, I am not in favour of presenting special, different programmes to children, like playing only one movement of a symphony, then some other piece, then a scherzo, etc.: you see, that is all a kind of self-deception, for the complete symphony would not be longer than the three or four different pieces (or parts of different pieces) together. And there is just as much variety of expression between the movements of the symphony, as between the different pieces.

(I once read a review about a concert of mine, I think it was in Canada, which was so funny that I have never forgotten it. The reviewer said, 'When is a sonata not a sonata? When Mr Schnabel plays it.')

Concerts for children should be just like other concerts, a bit shorter, I would say. And no talk. But I see we now have even adult education. I feel very uneasy with this term. I don't quite know what is meant by it, particularly in music.

Anyhow, audiences composed of only one group or type of people are not very good—except if the distinction is that the audience consists exclusively of people who come because they love music. It is not desirable to play only for club-members, or only for workmen, or only for Jews, or only for women, or only for children!

Even subscription audiences, everywhere in the world, are considered to be rather dull. I once read an amusing story: A woman moved from her very small home-town to Hamburg, and now her dream came true that she would have a chance to go to the opera. So she went, and during the interval she talked to the lady who sat next to her, expressing her great joy and how much it meant to her to be in Hamburg now and to be able to hear the opera. The other lady who had lived all her life in Hamburg said, 'Well, I am a subscriber; this is my twenty-fifth season. I don't even listen any more.'

10

VOICE: *Were you restricted at all in Russia as to the type of music you played?*

MR SCHNABEL: No.

VOICE: *You remarked about the churches being open. That interested me, and I wondered how much of what we hear about the restrictions on music is true. Was there much restriction?*

MR SCHNABEL: As far as I know, the only restrictions concerned the texts of vocal scores. Such texts were changed, particularly when they seemed objectionable. Like the 'Ode to Joy' in the last movement of Beethoven's Ninth Symphony: a 'Loving Father dwelling above the clouds' was not admissible at that time, so that text was replaced with propaganda for their movement. What the new words meant, I did not know, of course, even after hearing a performance, since I don't understand Russian.

However, when I returned I noticed a striking change. Then I heard the first two performances ever given in all Russia of Bach's 'St John Passion', with the full Gospel text.

VOICE: *Was that in 1935?*

MR SCHNABEL: Yes, in 1935. There was no more propaganda. But in 1924–5 it was very different. I shall never forget the performance of *Lohengrin* in which two floodlights were used. One was a blue one and the other a red one. Each time the good principle was nearer to victory, the red light was projected, and when the evil principle was nearer to victory, the blue. Also, at the start of the Prelude to *Lohengrin,* the big chandelier of the Moscow Opera was dark; with every crescendo in the orchestra more and more lights were turned on, while with a diminuendo they were gradually turned off.

Now, I presume all this was meant as a device to make music attractive and intelligible to an absolutely new audience. Everything had to be visible or intelligible, and was greatly simplified. Maybe it was necessary.... Anyway, I enjoyed this

195

very much—the two floodlights for the evil and the good principles.

VOICE: *What was the quality of the musical performances at that time? The Russian orchestras, for instance? Were they good?*

MR SCHNABEL: No. They were quite rough. I also heard the conductor-less orchestra. Have you heard of that? It was a Communist idea—to have an orchestra without a conductor. It consisted of the best players in Moscow and was remarkably good. They sat in a half-circle, and one of the men was, of course, inconspicuously carrying out some of the functions of a conductor, for otherwise it would not work. When they started Beethoven's Fifth Symphony, it was truly surprising, astonishing. But soon afterwards it became monotonous and mechanical because no musician ever dared to do anything differently from the others. No imponderables were possible, everything had to go as on rails once it had started. It was not too satisfactory. I asked them afterwards—for the sake of a joke—whether they decided the tempo by vote.

VOICE: *Was Glazunov in good repute there? Was he recognized?*

MR SCHNABEL: Oh, yes. He was highly revered. He was the Grand Old Man. He left them, you know. He died in Paris.

VOICE: *I went to two of their operas. The plot had been changed for propaganda purposes. Do you suppose they still do that?*

MR SCHNABEL: No. I told you that they performed 'St John Passion' to the Gospel text, sung by Russians. 'Bourgeois' art was then admitted. They played Shakespeare's *Othello* in its entirety for two years—five-hour performances—sold out every night. The propaganda in musical and theatrical public performances had disappeared. It seems it was not necessary any more. You might have another interpretataion as to why it was stopped. I think it had become unnecessary.

VOICE: *We have had a discussion in the school where I teach as to the advisability of teaching freshmen in our school of music counterpoint or harmony first.*

MR SCHNABEL: Certainly harmony. One might very soon do both simultaneously, but I think some harmony is indispensable before starting with counterpoint.

VOICE: *There has been quite a wave of feeling in this country that it was the thing to start with counterpoint simply because contrapuntal writing came first in history, and since music began with that, that is the way we should teach it.*

MR SCHNABEL: But afterwards we adjusted counterpoint to the harmonic system which we have accepted. Apparently this harmonic system was created because the counterpoint, as it was used before, was not satisfactory.

VOICE: *We have reached a sort of a compromise, and our theory course is now called 'The melodic approach to harmony'. But we have found it very necessary that the students get a foundation in intervals and chords first; otherwise they cannot understand contrapuntal writing.*

MR SCHNABEL: I always used to say that interpretation is a free walk on firm ground. That should be applicable to composition as well, and to instruction.

VOICE: *In my piano study I very often hear the expression 'German technique' and 'Russian technique' of piano playing, and I wonder if you would explain a little what you think of that.*

MR SCHNABEL: You ought to ask your teachers who use these expressions. I don't know to what they refer. Do they use four fingers only in the one school, and in the other, five —or what? Or do they play with their knuckles? What are they doing? I have never heard of it. I would be very interested to hear from you as to what the difference is, what they say the difference is.

VOICE: *The reason I ask is because I feel, as you do, that this type of methodology cannot be used in teaching. But I have come across it in studying with Russian teachers. They speak of their approach being the Russian approach to piano playing, and they refer to playing with straighter and flatter fingers instead of round ones, resulting in more metallic or brittle playing than they associate with the German technique.*

MR SCHNABEL: I cannot accept that there is anything specifically Russian about playing with straight and flat fingers. I lived for thirty years in Germany and even so I would not be able to say what the 'German technique' is. For in Germany all kinds of piano techniques were taught—flat or round fingers, stretched out or drawn in, elbows fixed or waving, glued to the hips or far out, like a washerwoman's. Some put the tip of their nose on the keys, others looked at the ceiling. Which one was the 'German technique'?

VOICE: *These expressions are used by very well-known pianists in this country, and that is the reason I——*

MR SCHNABEL: I am sorry. I was not serious enough. But in my opinion these very unfortunate distinctions and simplifications are really absurd. There is only one good technique, whether you ride a bicycle or swim or whatever else you do, and that is to attain a maximum of achievement with a minimum of effort. That applies to all physical activity.

VOICE: *While we are on the subject of teaching, did music teachers in Europe have to be accredited, with examinations, or could anyone teach music, as it is here in the United States?*

MR SCHNABEL: After the First World War a system of licensing was introduced in Germany. In Austria, music teaching was always licensed and, I think, it was the same in Russia, before the First World War. I don't know how it was in France.

VOICE: *What do you think of that system?*

MR SCHNABEL: I think it has great merits. Too many abuses are possible where no licence is required at all.

VOICE: *I feel the condition of teaching in the United States is deplorable. There are so few really good music teachers among the very many, and for the young student who goes to a centre like New York for the first time, the musical hazards are tremendous, are terrible. There seems to be no system of controlling the quantities of instructors teaching by who-knows-what methods.*

MR SCHNABEL: Don't they all have degrees?

VOICE: *Oh, no. Any shoemaker can put up a sign and teach singing. Singing, I think, is probably most abused of all.*

MR SCHNABEL: Well, that comes just after horse-trading, in being uncontrollable.

VOICE: *Who supervised the issuing of those licences, Mr Schnabel? Was there a city or state committee?*

MR SCHNABEL: I think there was a state committee. In Germany, I think all teachers who were over thirty-five years old at the time when this regulation was introduced were not affected, but all younger teachers had to pass examinations. These examinations were held under the supervision of the directors of state or municipal music schools, who asked some of the most reliable, experienced musicians to assist them in judging the candidates.

Prussia also had a state academy of music, and a very important academy of church and school music, in which Mr Rudolf Kestenberg was the leading spirit. I have mentioned Mr Kestenberg before. This licensing of music teachers and similar projects were his life work, to which he was deeply devoted. Being a Jew, he went to Prague when National Socialism came to power in Germany. He did some very good work in Prague, chiefly in the exchange of knowledge on folklore and school music with other European countries. He is now in Palestine, I think as director of the whole musical education there. If we had some state organization in charge of this here, or a project to introduce examinations and licences for music teachers, I would highly recommend engaging this most experienced man as adviser.

VOICE: *Did you ever hear Paderewski play professionally?*

MR SCHNABEL: He played *only* professionally.

VOICE: *But did you ever hear him?*

MR SCHNABEL: Yes, I heard him once.

VOICE: *I have heard people tell how in his concerts a crew of three or four men would come out on the stage before he played to measure the height of the piano stool, its distance from the piano, and so forth.*

MR SCHNABEL: I have never heard that about Paderewski. I heard that Pachmann had a distinct inclination towards clownery in his concerts; but Paderewski was solemnity itself. He and Fritz Kreisler always appeared as if Atlas had had an easy task in comparison—as if they bore all the sorrows of mankind. At the time I heard Paderewski, in Los Angeles, he had apparently passed the peak of his pianistic career. It was after he had interrupted playing for years. I enjoyed the second half of the concert very much, the first half not so much.

I have observed that in the so-called virtuoso concert, audiences everywhere in the world behave in the same way. I noticed, as a listener to such 'virtuoso' concerts, that people are always happier at nine o'clock than they are at eight o'clock, with no exception. I call the first hour of such programmes the 'duty part' and the second hour the 'family part'. During the first hour people hardly listen, are rather indifferent, uninterested. Only when it comes nearer to the encores, do they warm up. Yet, the better pieces of music have, for the most part, been played in the first hour.

I never play this type of programme and I have, with the same audiences, quite different experiences. In my programmes, audiences often like the first piece best. Then they are fresh and impressionable, while towards the end perhaps they are a little tired.

I once wrote to my wife when I was touring in Spain that apparently some audiences in Spanish cities were so disappointed with my programmes that I felt I was cheating them. Sometimes on the platform, during my performance, I felt how unfair it was towards the audience—like in Seville while I was playing Beethoven's Diabelli Variations; I thought: 'Now, this is really unfair! I am the only person here who is enjoying this, and I get the money; they pay, and have to suffer.' They were so terribly disappointed because my concerts had been announced just like other concerts, with exactly the same size of type on posters of the same colour, in the same terminology as previous announcements—but my concerts finally turned out to be boring even during the second hour, and that was absolutely unexpected, that had never happened before.

VOICE: *Have you always had the courage to play your sort of a programme, and to refuse to play encores?*

MR SCHNABEL: It is very kind of you to call it 'courage'.

VOICE: *Or did you, as a youth, conform to other people's ideas?*

MR SCHNABEL: I played a much more varied repertoire when I was very young, but you see, when one gets older one has to turn towards intensification, towards the intensive life. I played much Liszt, for instance. But virtuoso pieces I played only for a short time because I simply had no patience to spend time with music not presenting problems of interpretation. To spend time only for mechanical work was never possible for me. I just cannot do it.

Yet I cannot accept any praise for having limited my repertoire to what it is now. I did it because my capacity for enduring uneasiness is very limited. You see, I feel somewhat uneasy with many of the pieces I don't play. That is no criticism and, certainly, it does not refer to all the pieces I don't perform. Very many of the compositions which I never play I love very much; but one cannot play everything.

VOICE: *Well, does the fact that you don't play Bach any more mean that Bach does not present problems to you?*

MR SCHNABEL: Certainly not.

VOICE: *Is it because you feel that Bach does not belong in big concert halls?*

MR SCHNABEL: That is the chief reason. The 'Well-Tempered Clavier', even the suites, are somehow wasted there and their real value cannot appear. The chief reason is the intimacy of most of Bach's piano music. And I don't play transcriptions or arrangements of any kind.

I have played toccatas, the Italian Concerto, and other works by Bach very often and have made recordings of three Bach pieces: Toccata in D major, Toccata in C minor, and the Italian Concerto. Have you ever heard these records?

VOICE: *No.*

MR SCHNABEL: I think they came out well.

VOICE: *Have you played the Goldberg Variations? Do you make an arrangement so that you can do it on one keyboard?*

MR SCHNABEL: I have not played them. But I find that without loss of any tone one can play them on one keyboard, as they are. There are only three or four awkward places. I am not very fond of the sonorities of the harpsichord and prefer this music by far on the piano.

VOICE: *Do you agree with some teachers that in playing Bach one should try to imitate the harpsichord, that is, its dynamic qualities, playing on different dynamic levels rather than with any* crescendos *or* diminuendos? *One teacher told me that if the piece is written for the harpsichord, it should be played* non-legato *throughout.*

MR SCHNABEL: I know; a war has been going on between musicologists for a long time over the issue as to whether *crescendo* and *diminuendo* is permissible in Bach's music, the Mannheim School having invented the expressions *crescendo* and *diminuendo* after Bach's time. But *crescendo* and *diminuendo* are not only expressions; they are elements of articulation and modulation, and if Bach's music were performed without articulation and modulation—or inflection, as in language—it would be unbearable, it would not be music. The same applies to *legato* and *staccato*. I am absolutely against the exclusive *non-legato* in performances of Bach's music.

You know, Bach added practically no indications regarding tempo, dynamics, phrasing, sonorities, expression, etc. to his music. Therefore an original edition—that is, an unedited text—of works by Bach consists almost exclusively of notes. Now, as I don't allow my pupils, who are all very talented and advanced, to study music from edited texts, in the case of Bach their interpretation depends to the greatest extent upon their own judgement. That is what I want. Every pupil of mine has the right to make his *own* mistakes. He should learn from those, instead of copying interpretation and mistakes from editors.

I have had amazing results. Whenever a pupil has studied from the pure, original text, he comes to his lesson playing with far fewer mannerisms or obviously wrong phrasings and dynamics than when he has studied from an edited version, being unable to get hold of the original text. This has been a most important experience for me. I feel there is little danger that a musical person, seeing a piece by Couperin, will apply the sonorities suitable for a piece by Scriabin, let me say. I think it is unnecessary to teach such things. The musical person knows them and will generally find quite good solutions as to where to play, for instance, *legato* or *staccato,* if there are no indications by the composer.

Not everyone will find the same solution, and the same person might change his solution for a new one. All this does not matter. I am not at all dogmatic about that. You see, one of the greatest attractions in interpreting Bach's music is that you have the choice.

Maybe I have my preferences even where I cannot say exactly why I have these preferences or that my preferences are right. There it may be a matter of taste. And then there are certain things which are beyond taste, of course.

There is no necessity to imitate the sonority of old instruments, for we have to assume that Bach chose those instruments only because better ones were not available. It is known that he wrote for four different instruments and that each time an improved instrument appeared he wanted even those of his works which were written for the previous instrument to be played on the improved instrument. These are facts.

Did you know that the pianoforte—the 'Hammerklavier'—was invented during Bach's lifetime? The first ones were built around 1710 in Padua, in Italy. Some musicians hailed it with great enthusiasm, but the inventor was not successful and few of these instruments were built. Bach saw an apparently poor imitation, the first one built in Germany in 1726, and found it unsatisfactory. In the last years of his life, Bach then saw a much improved model. So I think it is most important that Bach, during a substantial part of his life, knew about the invention and existence of the 'Hammerklavier' and even played on it.

VOICE: *The other day you were talking about* Lieder *singers. You said that a* Lieder *singer usually is not a great opera singer, and vice versa.*

MR SCHNABEL: As a rule.

VOICE: *Is there the same distinction between conductors of opera and conductors of other music? Is there any similarity?*

MR SCHNABEL: Hardly. It used to be that symphony concerts were performed by the opera orchestra and its conductor. Separate symphony orchestras did not exist, are of rather recent date. I would say that in the old times, the conductors were equally good for opera and concerts. Liszt, for instance, must have been equally great in both functions. Wagner conducted concerts too when he was very young. Hans von Bülow did not conduct opera very much.

Later on, the activities were always mixed. As a rule, the opera conductors preferred to conduct symphonic music. Now, in this country, there are many more symphony concerts than operas. So the conductors would love to do operas.

VOICE: *Do you think it is idle and unnecessary, or desirable, to attempt to teach audiences—audiences consisting mainly of people who don't understand, just want to enjoy music?*

MR SCHNABEL: How should one proceed? How can one gather a group of equally ignorant people, for instance? An audience is a sum of individuals and each one of them is in a different place or on a different level in their understanding, approach, or their receptivity for music. I think that if some member of the audience, a single member, wants to deepen his relation to music and to widen his knowledge of music, then he should study individually. I don't believe this is possible collectively.

On the other hand, I wonder sometimes how much the various members of an audience influence each other—for instance, what the enthusiasm of one listener in a concert does to his neighbour. Is enthusiasm really contagious? Or is boredom contagious? Which one is more contagious? When two people sit next to each other, of whom one is terribly bored and the other terribly enthusiastic and excited, what happens to these two people?

VOICE: *Nothing happens.*

MR SCHNABEL: They are just annoyed with each other?

203

VOICE: *Very annoyed with each other, because the bored one resents that the excited one wakes him up.*

MR SCHNABEL: And the excited one can't stand the bored one who chills his enthusiasm?

But to be serious, audiences are generally very good. They are unjustly blamed, again and again, for faults made by artists or managers. Audiences should not be blamed. We cannot investigate how good an audience is, collectively. 'The public'—that is one of the vaguest notions existing. The public is mute, it cannot speak, can hardly utter a sound, as a whole. It should be neither blamed nor praised for anything. It is absolutely amorphous. However, we can divide it into individuals—and that can be done with an audience too.

When I am asked, 'What do you think of our audience?' I answer, 'I know two kinds of audiences only—one coughing, and one not coughing.' That is the simplest answer. What else can I say?

That disappoints the people who ask me, for they want me to say, 'I have never had an audience like the one in your city here.'

11

VOICE: *Can you tell us more about music in Palestine?*

MR SCHNABEL: Not much. The orchestra was not yet founded at the time I was there and I know only of the conservatory in Jerusalem which was very ambitious and well directed. Its present director is a pupil of mine, Alfred Schroeder. He and his wife, Lisa Spoliansky, have many talented pupils. But at that time they were not yet there. It was still rather primitive and they had no means. Tel Aviv had no music school. I think it has changed considerably since the orchestra was formed. Also Mr Kestenberg, of whom I spoke before, is there now. His coming there was very important.

VOICE: *Can you tell us about Professor Schünemann's work in Germany's public schools? What did he do there about teaching the children the fundamentals of the theory of music, in elementary schools and high schools? Did he make them do any writing of music at all, or was it limited to singing, glee clubs, school orchestras and things of that sort?*

MR SCHNABEL: I am not familiar with their curriculum. But as far as I know, Professor Schünemann was not in charge of it. George Schünemann was the assistant director of the State Academy of Music in Berlin. He taught there, mainly history of music, and had also very much administrative work. Aside from this, he was librarian in the music department of the State Library; he and Professor Johannes Wolf. The director of the Academy for School and Church Music was Dr Hans Joachim Moser.

VOICE: *The historian?*

MR SCHNABEL: Yes, the son of Professor Andreas Moser, who was a friend and pupil of Joachim. For the reform of school music after the First World War, Mr Kestenberg was chiefly responsible. How it was done, I cannot tell you. Of course, they were teaching only teachers.

VOICE: *Do you see any tendencies in the United States that*

205

might lead us into National Socialism, as it happened in Germany about 1933?

MR SCHNABEL: I think it is not my function to talk about such subjects here.

VOICE: *Has the university limited the subjects about which you can talk?*

MR SCHNABEL: No. The limitations are chosen and set by myself.

VOICE: *Do you plan going back to Germany, and if not, what is your reason?*

MR SCHNABEL: A very simple reason. I don't want to go to a country to which I am only admitted because it has lost a war.

VOICE: *Well, I guess you know; but propaganda in the United States now is that Germany is a pretty good country, now that all the Nazis are in prison, the people welcome democracy and are sorry for everything they did.*

MR SCHNABEL: By not returning I don't punish the Germans; not at all. Moreover, the Germans are completely irrelevant. For my decision it does not matter how they feel, but rather how I feel.

Why should I go back? I am now a citizen of the United States and I think I am a good American. I was never German, you know.

VOICE: *I am just curious, whether someone who has spent so long in a certain area, whether he feels nostalgic about it.*

MR SCHNABEL: I did not feel too happy in Germany from 1912 on. But my not returning to Germany is no criticism of the Germans. And I want to make this clear: even if it were, my not returning there would mean very little; for who am I?

VOICE: *You complained about the English concert halls?*

MR SCHNABEL: I did not.

VOICE: *Well, more or less.*

MR SCHNABEL: I complained about the draught.

VOICE: *Do you refer to their air-conditioning systems?*

MR SCHNABEL: Certainly not. Just to natural, simple draughts. Fresh, ice-cold air, coming in through open windows, holes in the walls, or doors which do not close.

It is a kind of jesting question of the English when they ask: 'How do you like our climate?' I always used to answer with another question: I said: 'Do you mean your outdoor or your indoor climate?' For when I felt too unhappy in a cold, draughty British apartment, I preferred to go out, for hours. I thought this much-maligned British climate very nice —out of doors.

VOICE: *Do you feel that the playing of Beethoven is a touchstone by which any pianist should be judged?*

MR SCHNABEL: No. I think a pianist should be judged by whatever he plays.

VOICE: *Well, I heard a pianist say this summer that he felt the Emperor Concerto alone could be used as an examination for a degree, because it contains everything; and he made the statement that if a pianist could not play Beethoven, he was not a musician.*

MR SCHNABEL: I think that is going very far. I would say one should assume that somebody who performs Beethoven's music fairly well should be able also to perform any other music fairly well. Beethoven's music surely belongs to the greatest. Thus, if we agree that the greater always contains the smaller, the ability to perform Beethoven should include the ability to perform most other composers. However, it is not only the ability of a musician which decides what he performs well, but also how much he is attracted to various works or types of music. He might be very fond of some music, appreciate it greatly and nevertheless, for an uninvestigable reason, he might not be particularly attracted to performing it, occupying himself with it. Then he would not play it so well.

We love so very much music. Some of it we greatly desire to perform, some of it much less so.

VOICE: *To my knowledge, you are playing many more recitals than concertos with orchestra now. Is that because it attracts you more to play works for piano solo?*

MR SCHNABEL: No. I would prefer to keep it balanced— about the same number of recitals as appearances with orchestra. But it is not in the power of a performer to determine which engagements materialize.

VOICE: *Are there any possibilities that you will resume playing concerts of a type like your trio performances with Flesch and Becker, of which you did so many in the past?*

MR SCHNABEL: Unfortunately that seems to be a lost kind of presentation. You see, not only is the 'star' system detrimental to such concerts, but there is also the fact that this type of music is not suitable for the biggest halls; and if you arrange a concert of this kind in a smaller hall, you make a deficit even if the hall is sold out.

There is an excellent trio playing concerts in America now, but all three men have to work very hard in other activities in order to make a living. In my opinion the only way to revive this type of art on a large scale in public would be by subsidies and the creation of musical societies promoting exclusively this type of musical presentation. It would be wonderful.

It would be still better if people were to begin playing trios at home again. When I asked one of the young ladies here who recently played for me whether she has ever played chamber music, she said no—she had no opportunity. I hear this very frequently. I would like to take it for granted that all my students played chamber music, but often it proves to be impossible. They cannot find violinists or 'cellists who have time and interest for this endeavour which is, as you see, not so promising in a practical sense.

I went to a night club just once—and I did not recognize it as being a night club, for it was still evening when I was there and the place was certainly not a club. I had a meal there with a friend of mine, during which they had what they call a 'floor-show'. A singer first gave a deliberately distorted performance of an operatic aria and followed it by a jazzy kind of song, depicting her supposed life story: how she had had to sacrifice all her ambitions for her poor old mother and finally, instead of pursuing what she would have loved to do, she had landed here. The song culminated in two lines which I still remember: 'For opera I've been so passionate, but unfortunately there's no cash-in-it.'

And that is the answer to the problem of trio playing.

VOICE: *Is there an organization in Washington, started by Elizabeth Coolidge, which sponsors chamber music concerts?*

MR SCHNABEL: Not only in Washington. The organization is nation-wide. It is a magnificent scheme for circulating and spreading chamber music. I don't think it is carried out in the most practical way, for most of their concerts are hidden away and therefore somehow lost. They have concerts at the Public Library in New York, a most unsuitable place, as it is surrounded by the heaviest noises of the city, which disturb the music considerably. Also, I think it is wrong not to charge anything for admission. There should be at least a small charge because people are distrustful when it is all charity.

But it is really wonderful what Mrs Coolidge has done and continues to do. If I am correctly informed, her organization is now offering help to all concert societies in the United States which want to present more chamber music to their subscribers. If such societies are not in a position to pay the full fees for the performers, Mrs Coolidge pays the rest, which is very noble. And I think it is a much better and more effective arrangement.

VOICE: *When you spoke of the trio which you called excellent, did you mean the Albeneri?*

MR SCHNABEL: Yes. I hope they can stay together—I mean, that it will be financially possible. It is a great sacrifice.

Already, the chamber music literature is being forgotten. To the young generation most of its works are unknown. String quartets are still heard more frequently. Also compositions for piano and one other instrument are often performed. But—with the exception of the Adolph Busch-Rudolph Serkin ensemble—they are hardly ever played by two persons equally equipped. Mostly it is, as I would say, a *prima donna* and a footman.

How often have I seen or heard reports, here as well as in Europe, telling at great length and with enthusiasm about a famous violinist's or 'cellist's performance of a sonata and adding at the end: 'The accompanist played with good taste,' or something similar.

Actually, the piano part is always more substantial and the pianist should, from a musical point of view, be the leader—in chamber music as well as in songs.

But that also seems to be an economic question.

VOICE: *I think of the Weimar Republic, which I never knew, as being a place where even the delivery boys used to whistle Beethoven.*

MR SCHNABEL: Who told you that?

VOICE: *No one. It is just an idea.*

MR SCHNABEL: Delivery boys always whistled the latest jazz; or, at the best, Puccini. But now you can often hear Beethoven whistled, because the theme of the Fifth Symphony became very popular here. People often whistle without knowing what they are whistling; just tones.

VOICE: *How about something like the film of Chopin's life, or 'Fantasia' and other popular films which make music palatable? Do you like them?*

MR SCHNABEL: You remember, I told you the story of how I was asked to participate in the two-thousandth performance of *Lilac Time*, which was an operetta about Schubert's life, using his music. All that is not my world, not my department. I am definitely one-sided. You have to accept my one-sidedness. I simply have no knowledge of many things, just have heard that they exist. So I really cannot have an opinion about them.

VOICE: *I don't think you're one-sided though.*

MR SCHNABEL: I know I am. But you see, in itself, it is not yet a self-degradation to say that one is one-sided. It depends entirely on the side to which one belongs. It may even be a very arrogant statement. I leave this open.

VOICE: *I am coming back to that English concert plan you mentioned, the plan for those people who cannot afford to go to regular symphony concerts. Do you think that such a plan necessarily has to be started by someone who would endow it; or could the people themselves possibly organize it?*

MR SCHNABEL: I think that utilizing the strength and wealth of their labour unions, the people themselves could organize it very well. I hear that in New York City alone there are 800,000 unionized workers and employees. I am sure that 40,000 of them would be very glad to have a chance of getting acquainted with opera, with chamber music, with symphonies. And why they don't work out a plan like that English one, I simply cannot understand. The garment workers' union is very active in this direction, but I fear they imitate Broadway practices too much.

VOICE: *You mean like* Pins and Needles?

MR SCHNABEL: Oh, that was excellent. I meant rather another type of their activities, their musical functions. I once played with their orchestra. They have an amateur orchestra. I had a very good time playing and rehearsing with them.

I also played in Swansea, with an amateur orchestra. That concert started at eight o'clock and the rehearsal could not be earlier than at six because some of the men—those playing the brass instruments—came directly from the collieries to the performance. And this was really a democratic concert because —I saw it afterwards in Australia too—all layers of society were represented in the orchestra. I played the G major Concerto by Beethoven and did not say a word. I thought it was so moving. But the sounds those miners produced on their horns and trumpets were indescribable. My insides turned when I first heard it.

VOICE: *You said a few days ago that, in the realm of form, very little room was left for originality. Do you mean that the logical possibilities of form have been exhausted?*

MR SCHNABEL: No, I did not mean that. I think I am really not competent to speak about this. I meant to express that I feel everything which is organic is probably bound to tie up with some eternal laws. And I quoted Arnold Schönberg in connection with this, didn't I? He said, in regard to form there can be no changes.

But we already have such a great variety of musical forms, even within the same 'category' of pieces. For instance, a sonata in its original form and one of Beethoven's late sonatas, have very little in common. There are certain movements of Beethoven sonatas which are particularly worthwhile studying in regard to form. I am thinking, for example, of the first movements of Opus 101 and Opus 109.

I meant by form not something which is taught in books and fixed once and for ever, but that which really gives shape to a work.

VOICE: *In the instruction of children in piano playing, would you believe that the technical development should evolve from the study of musical pieces or do you believe that considerable emphasis should be placed upon technical material as such?*

MR SCHNABEL: I would recommend the first procedure much more. I would try to release the creative impulse and urge in the child, would try to make the child like what it is asked to do, as much as possible. Even if the child in the first half-year of its instruction does not learn much, technically, one should not worry. Also, as I have said once already: If I were a dictator, I would eliminate the term 'practice' from the vocabulary and have it called 'making music'.

VOICE: *Last week you spoke of yourself as being in the service of music. You went on to say that in performing you like to feel as isolated as possible from the audience. And then today, it seemed to me you intimated that something was missing when you could not feel the audience's response. Somehow I cannot put the two together. Could you explain what you meant in both cases?*

211

MR SCHNABEL: You mean when I said I felt music to be like a tree in the desert?

VOICE: *No, when you spoke of the audience being lifeless. You seemed to feel that something was missing when you did not feel the response of the audience.*

MR SCHNABEL: But was it not when I spoke of that experience in Folkestone,[1] that I mentioned the lifeless audience and how I felt music to be like a tree in the desert? I still felt music to be like a tree, and not like the desert. Music did not become a desert. It remained a tree; only around it was a desert.

Sometimes the boredom of an audience, intense boredom— I suppose it must be that—has such a force that it creeps up to the performer and becomes a menace to him. Isolation from the audience is a protection against that menace—which is already a good reason to strive for it.

I have very often been disturbed or interrupted in my concentration while playing. And as I was always afraid that my concentration would be interrupted, by one or the other occurrence or condition, I have struggled so intensely to secure isolation for myself.

Once when I had to play a Mozart concerto in Queen's Hall in London, for instance, the heating system did not work. It was incredibly cold. Everybody was shivering and we really discussed whether we should perform that concert or cancel it. But finally, we decided to try.

I played the Mozart concerto only mechanically, just my fingers played. I tried very hard to concentrate—but I remember that for those whole twenty-eight minutes, one insane sentence passed incessantly through my consciousness, ever repeated, and interrupting every attempt to think of anything else—'This is no climate for Mozart—this is no climate for Mozart—this is no climate for Mozart.'

Well, that was a physical reaction, you see. Sometimes it is a physical reaction. And I think with the boredom in Folkestone it was not so different. Even that produced a kind of physical reaction: finally, my senses felt it. However, on this occasion I was able to isolate myself from it. So, this time the music did not suffer. The tree in the desert remained alive.

One can give quite a good performance, outwardly, without

[1] See pp. 104–5.

212

concentrating. I demonstrate this sometimes to my students. I try to turn off my concentration and then I play for them—otherwise exactly as I would play *with* concentration. One can do that, if one has considerable experience. Yet, you would not believe how great the difference is! Not only for the performer, but also for the listener.

VOICE: *I would like to ask a question but I don't know quite how to put it. If a platform was very cold or there were draughts, then of course you felt it physically. But the boredom, that seems to me a little more difficult to feel.*

MR SCHNABEL: Of course; but it is felt. Sometimes this feeling may be a deception: as performer you might feel something which seems to indicate this boredom in the audience to you; and actually, what you feel is only created by your own tiredness or indisposition. That also can happen. But after decades of experiences, when one is an old stage-hand, as I am, one distinguishes quite easily.

VOICE: *Isn't there a sense of satisfactory communication with the audience? You named several instances in which the audience made an unfortunate impingement on the performer. But has the audience ever been of any assistance to you? Can it be, to the musician in his concentration? Isn't there also a sense of stimulation?*

MR SCHNABEL: Yes—well, generally so. What I told you, was an extreme case and I told it mainly because I thought it amusing. Normally, audiences are very good—as I have said—except if there is too much coughing. And generally, very few people in an audience cough; but unfortunately, four persons among four thousand are sufficient to disturb or at least interrupt a performance—and thus these four persons can make the difference between a disturbing and a good audience.

If you have played for the same audience very often, you might develop a feeling for their reaction and their response. But we should do better not to pay too much attention to that, for, you see, we should be fully occupied with the music. The music should occupy our whole capacity when we perform any kind of work. Music gives us enough to do, to think and to feel, and we have really no time to find out what kind of people the audience is composed of and how they react.

Sometimes it is a great surprise. You think you have performed especially well and successfully and then—not even the applause indicates any response: there is just the usual form of applause which is nothing but a convention.

All performers occasionally have had the experience of receiving the highest praise and arousing the highest enthusiasm when they themselves thought that they played badly, unconvincingly, gave a poor performance; they were thoroughly dissatisfied with themselves and everybody else loved and appreciated it more than ever. Then again it happens that the performer is unusually satisfied and thinks he came near to what he wanted to do, while the others are rather reserved and even his friends remark: 'Well, you did not seem to be at your best tonight.'

VOICE: *You said a while ago that when you heard Rachmaninoff——*

MR SCHNABEL: You all have such a good memory!

VOICE: *—when you heard Rachmaninoff, he was one of the two performers about whom you were so enthusiastic that you sent a note backstage. Who was the other one?*

MR SCHNABEL: I think the other one was Pablo Casals. And, I think, I also sent a note to Busoni once.

VOICE: *You said that often people ask you what you thought of them as an audience, and you always disappoint them because they expect you to say they were the best. Do you find very often that people like to think of themselves as a perfect audience and that only they can appreciate what you do?*

MR SCHNABEL: The audience has never asked me, just one person asked me each time and that person did not really consider himself or herself part of the audience. The person was either a colleague, a manager, a member of the society organizing the concert, a critic or an interviewer. I think audiences are not even concerned about this question. Audiences go and listen. They are not interested whether they are a good audience. They buy tickets and want to hear music or a performer. It means little to them whether the musician likes them, but more whether they like his music.

When I played the thirty-two Beethoven sonatas in London, there was a very old gentleman, a great music lover and amateur. He had heard me play once before and he bought six or seven tickets, all subscription tickets, for the whole series. Before the concerts, he invited his friends, played and explained the sonatas to them; then he came with them to my concerts. And from concert to concert he became more and more dis-

214

appointed and disillusioned about my playing. He was near despair. So, after the fifth concert, he wrote a fourteen-page letter to me—a moving letter, really—in which he said that if he had known how I played the sonatas he would certainly not have bought those tickets. He practically asked me to return the money to him. Then he went on, singling out certain places, writing for instance, 'Why did you hurry in this measure? A man with your technique!' and blaming me for many other details which were not according to his expectations, until he reached the conclusion: 'If you go on like this, you should stop playing Beethoven altogether.'

So I sat down and answered the old man. There was not a trace of irony in my letter. I assured him, for example, that he overrated my technical abilities: if I hurried, it was simply a defect of my technique; I did not want to hurry, regretted it just as much as he. But then I also wrote, in the course of this letter, that to buy a ticket is no insurance of happiness. The performer only promises to try his best, but he cannot promise to please the listener.

12

VOICE: *People say that some musicians have composed ahead of their time and some may be composing ahead of their time now. Don't you think that people say that because they don't understand this music composed in their own time and that the reason why we think we do understand the great music of the past is that we have grown up listening to it and don't have to accept it all at once?*

MR SCHNABEL: Yes, I think you are right—it is so with all really original creations, but only with those, of course. I mean creations using a new, not-before-heard idiom of expressing the same content; for I believe the content is always the same. But the possibilities of varying the expression of the same content seem limitless to me.

Obviously, the creative genius is to a certain extent always a stranger to his own generation; and there will be only a small group of people who, from the beginning, will genuinely participate in the new idiom of expressing the content. There will be people who are too lazy, people who are simply not capable of participating, and people who always want to compare it with what they like best.

VOICE: *Do you feel that contemporary composition is decadent?*

MR SCHNABEL: Well, I am one of the producers of contemporary music and I don't feel that I am decadent.

VOICE: *You said in an earlier session that an artist is half aristocrat and half anarchist?*

MR SCHNABEL: Not half and half. Rather, some of both.

VOICE: *I like that very much and was thinking about it also in terms of form and inspiration; in other words, to accept form in a composition as its necessary 'aristocratic' side, and to fill the form with ever varying, 'anarchic' inspiration.*

MR SCHNABEL: You mean: freedom within form?

VOICE: *Yes. Is that part of what you meant?*

MR SCHNABEL: Yes, it is. Freedom and form.

216

VOICE: *Then one other question: You spoke of being 'one-sided' and said that 'one-sidedness' might be a very nice thing, depending on the side on which you were?*

MR SCHNABEL: Yes, I spoke about that.

VOICE: *Which seems to me, to indicate 'many-sidedness'?*

MR SCHNABEL: I think you misunderstood what I meant. I am really 'one-sided'. I am absolutely convinced that I am one-sided and am also accepted as being one-sided. This does not mean that I have no appreciation or admiration for other sides than my own. It does not contain criticism of other sides. Conversely, the fact that I can appreciate other sides than my own does not imply that I am not one-sided. But, if you prefer the term, you can, instead, call me 'one-levelled'.

VOICE: *Then let me ask you this: I suppose that you are pretty familiar with painting, with philosophy and with the other—*

MR SCHNABEL: Not as much as you seem to believe.

VOICE: *Not as much?*

MR SCHNABEL: No. But please continue.

VOICE: *Well, this is what I wondered: whether a deeper insight into music also leads to a deeper insight into other art, or whether it means that relations to other art are neglected?*

MR SCHNABEL: That all depends upon the quality and quantity of creative gifts and of receptivities, of give and take in an individual.

VOICE: *I don't understand that.*

MR SCHNABEL: You see, if I am, as you kindly think, interested in many problems and many pleasures which are outside my actual professional activities, then I am simply grateful for being interested because I have been endowed with the gift of being interested. For I go so far as to say that one cannot even choose one's interest in things. One has to be made that way.

VOICE: *This is what I try to tell my parents!*

MR SCHNABEL: Very good. Good for you, too.

VOICE: *Was your talk in Manchester in English or was it translated for your book?*

MR SCHNABEL: In contrast to the three lectures I gave here[1] in 1940 which were written in English, I wrote my Manchester address originally in German and then it was translated for

[1] *Music and the Line of Most Resistance.* Princeton University Press. 1942.

me. It was published by the University of Manchester and later on by Simon & Schuster.[1] It is a kind of declaration of love to music. At least I meant it to be that.

VOICE: *You may not want to answer this—do you have theories of your own about memorizing?*

MR SCHNABEL: No. I let the memory do it.

VOICE: *Well, some teachers seem to feel that if a person memorizes easily and naturally without thinking about it a great deal, he should be made to think about it a great deal. And some teachers believe that only those truly memorize who write out all the music they learn.*

MR SCHNABEL: That is really very advisable. But not for the purpose of memorizing, rather to establish more and more intimacy with music. I would definitely recommend that everybody who studies music should spend at least half an hour a day copying some music. Eventually, he would do it very quickly.

VOICE: *Do it from memory?*

MR SCHNABEL: Compositions he learned, he could write out from memory. But I thought really more of copying from music. Once a gifted music student has, for instance, copied one of the string quartets by Beethoven or, let me say, the first movement of a symphony, he will have benefited much more than he ever divined. I think this is actually the quickest way to get into music. Of course, it should not only be a graphic activity. He should hear the music while he is writing it, should enjoy its beauty and greatness, and stop sometimes to delight fully in the happiness of having discovered something he had not noticed when he read or played it. He will notice much more when he writes it.

VOICE: *When you were a boy of fifteen, studying with Leschetizky, did you have to write out music a great deal? Was that part of the training?*

MR SCHNABEL: No. Leschetizky neither asked for that, nor did he recommend it. You see, that was a time when methods and systems were not yet as highly appreciated as they are now. One left very much to the pupil's talent and had great confidence in Nature. So I was really not taught very much regarding methods or systems; he taught me just music.

But I, today, wish to recommend the copying of music strongly. And I also think that every musician should try to

[1] *Reflections on Music.* 1934.

compose, even if he is so disgusted with the results that he destroys every composition immediately after he has written it. That does not matter. It is the activity and not the result which is so important.

VOICE: *Mr Schnabel, I learned a great deal when I studied from your edition of the Beethoven sonatas; and all the while I kept wondering whether you yourself learned something—I mean about Beethoven—when you were editing his sonatas?*

MR SCHNABEL: I think I did. Not from my editing, but from the sonatas; and what I learned from the sonatas I tried to put into my edition. So I rather wonder whether you have noticed in my edition, that I learned something from the sonatas while I made it. I hope it gave you that impression: I tried my best.

VOICE: *Is your relationship to the music you compose yourself, in performing it, at all similar to your relationship to the works of other composers which you perform?*

MR SCHNABEL: I never perform my own compositions, because when I have finished a composition my urge is to start the next composition. I cannot spend time practising my own compositions—and they are not too easy to play. I hardly know them: a composer does not know his compositions. He only knows his next composition—which is forming and working in him.

I am sure Beethoven did not know his sonatas as well as we know them. After he had composed a sonata, it was finished—for him.

VOICE: *Do you feel any preference, or dismay, or interest in the way your compositions will be performed?*

MR SCHNABEL: Oh, I share the defencelessness of the composer with much greater men than I am. But the fact that compositions can be interpreted in different ways, can be an asset too. If a very gifted performer feels my work differently from me, sees it in another light, and then I hear him perform it, convincingly—I might be impressed and happy and would tell him: 'You played wonderfully! How did you do it? I had a quite different conception of this work.' Music is not so definable.

Of course, when for instance I have indicated in the music that a certain place should be played softly and quietly and then the character of the performance is loud and stormy—I doubt whether I would approve of that. But as long as the text is observed faithfully, music is always open to subjective interpretations and should be so. Even further—if I had the choice between a performer who plays with inspiration and imagination but treats the text rather arbitrarily, and another performer who is absolutely reliable in his faithfulness to the text but has no imagination and is never inspired, I would generally prefer the inspired but slovenly player.

VOICE: *Once you mentioned that a programme annotator had described one of the pieces you played as being 'a jolly rondo' and you had intended to put a feeling of despair in it?*

MR SCHNABEL: Yes.

VOICE: *Would you always approach that movement with the same idea, the feeling of despair, or would that vary with your emotions?*

MR SCHNABEL: It would not vary. Certain pieces have a definite atmosphere for me. I might vary the tempo somewhat, or the sonority, but I would always keep the general atmosphere. Just as other men would keep to their atmosphere of a 'jolly rondo', I suppose.

VOICE: *What could someone who has become an adult without learning to play any instrument—what do you think he could do to participate in music?*

MR SCHNABEL: He should begin to learn now. It is never too late.

VOICE: *Mr Schnabel, you said something the other day about unevenness in the quality of works of the great masters. You even gave a percentage, I believe.*

MR SCHNABEL: In proportion to their entire work?

VOICE: *Yes.*

MR SCHNABEL: That is a very mysterious problem. In the art of music—I shall limit myself to discussing this problem within music—it is very rare that most of the works created by one man are equal in quality to his greatest creations. One can say, for instance, that in the case of Bach, Mozart, Schubert or Schumann a considerable portion of their compositions is inferior, measured by their greatest creations. On the other hand, in Wagner's work the very high proportion of equally successful creations is remarkable. One can say that, from the 'Ring' on, all his works—whether you like them or not—are of the same quality. And the case of Beethoven is most amazing, as nearly *all* his works are of equal greatness. His nine symphonies, his sixteen quartets, almost all of his thirty-two piano sonatas are actually *of the same quality,* even in spite

220

of the fact that they were composed throughout his whole life. Why is it so? Perhaps because he composed fewer works than others? I think that one explanation can be found in the fact that in each new work he wrote, he also faced—or was made by his creative disposition to face—a new formal problem. Each one of his quartets, symphonies and sonatas is decidedly different, very definitely different in form, while in that respect Mozart and Bach were rather less varied: unless you investigate their works very closely, it will seem to you that you find the same patterns, the same procedures quite often. Beethoven, I think, was the precursor of all the attempts towards more and more freedom from accepted procedures.

Now, with the separation from the harmonic system which has been employed, with many alterations, for almost 300 years, the problems of form have become still greater and more important. For, when this harmonic procedure is abandoned, the composer has fewer holds, less shelter to protect him against becoming prolix, incoherent, amorphous.

VOICE: *Do you—or did you, when you were younger—sometimes walk down the street and discover that you had been playing a certain composition entirely wrong, and that it was really meant to be played another way? Do you know what I mean?*

MR SCHNABEL: You mean the open air is necessary for this?

VOICE: *No, no. I mean that all of a sudden it came to you, maybe through an unconscious change in your own self.*

MR SCHNABEL: It does happen to me. You are absolutely right. I really do much of my work for my performances in walking. Or when I cannot sleep at night, I begin to work for my performances. I may begin, for instance, to memorize a piece which I have not played for several years, a complicated piece, perhaps some fugue; and then I am very stubborn and tough with it. Let me say, I come to a passage or to a measure of which I don't remember the continuation. Then I will not give up, sometimes for days; it will just haunt me until I find it. And in most cases I find it without consulting the music.

This is an evidence of the inner necessity in the continuation of that music: it can continue only in one way; there is no alternative.

But my conception or idea of a piece I change often and, as you said, decisively. Many pieces in the repertoire which I

221

have played from my youth are still problematic to me and I do not know whether my solution is the right one. This does not involve the question whether it is absolutely right. Rather, I mean to say that I myself don't feel right about it. It does not entirely convince me. Yet as long as I have not found a better solution, I am bound to the imperfect one.

VOICE: *Don't you think one changes one's conception of music, either while playing it or listening to it, only if it is great music? Because other music can be understood the first time?*

MR SCHNABEL: That is a very good point. I think it is absolutely true. The greater, the more profound a work of music is, the more you will find in it, the more will your conception of it grow, together with your own development—if you develop. While music which contains less and is more superficial, will become rather boring or empty to you, though you might have loved it at first.

I spoke to you earlier about the way my repertoire developed. It certainly went an unusual way. Usually you start with Bach and Mozart and, finally, the last you learn is Brahms. But I started with Brahms and now gradually I am coming to Mozart.

Initially I was labelled a Brahms player in Leipzig and a Schubert player in Munich, as I told you. So I had two labels originally, but soon I became chiefly the 'Brahms player' because Schubert has not written any works for piano and orchestra and in the first twenty years of my career I played very much with orchestras and most often the Brahms concertos.

At that time, when I ventured to play Beethoven, it was always said, of course, that I was not the right person to do it. My performances were criticized as un-Beethovenian. Was it because I did not play Beethoven so often? For later, after I began to play Beethoven most of all, I eventually received the heavyweight title of 'Beethoven player'.

Since then I have tried to become a 'Mozart and Schubert player'. But when I play Mozart and Schubert, I am told that I 'make this music greater than it is'. I read this printed— often. Now, that is in itself a wondrous statement. As if anyone could do this! I always want to recommend that this should be tried with 'small' music, to make it greater than it is.

The official musical world never admitted Mozart and Schubert to the rank, calibre, or level of Beethoven. So each time when a musician is now genuinely and spontaneously moved and impressed by a piano work by Mozart or Schubert, he is inclined to think that the performer did something wrong, for this music is not supposed to be moving and profound—you see? 'We know this music is charming and sweet and lilting—but now it sounds so important; that must be wrong.' 'He makes it greater than it is.'

VOICE: *You said several times that in order to appreciate music, you have to make music. Would you extend that to the rest of the arts? In other words, in order to enjoy pictures, you have to paint; and to enjoy literature, you have to write.*

MR SCHNABEL: I think you misunderstood me. I do not think that in order to appreciate music you *must* make music; but I would highly recommend it. You might, even if you don't make music, appreciate music and love music and enjoy music intensely; it might even be a necessity for your life. But if you were to make music, it might still enhance and improve this relation.

Therefore I recommend everyone who loves music, also to make music. But I did not say that he who does not make music is excluded from appreciating it. If this were so, concert audiences would be very small. I might have said that instead of reading books on 'how to appreciate music' and listening to lectures on 'how to appreciate music', one should spend the time better making music or listening to it.

VOICE: *Well, I did not mean exactly that. I just wondered whether you would say the same thing about the other arts.*

MR SCHNABEL: Maybe. I really cannot speak of the other arts, because I have no experience. Pictures and architecture have very often meant very much to me, have been very important in my life. But I have never tried to build a cathedral.

VOICE: *Well, supposing you had tried to build a cathedral; you might appreciate cathedrals still more.*

MR SCHNABEL: Maybe. But to be serious—the art of music and the pictorial arts are not commensurable, because the pictorial arts are not performing arts. Also, writing a poem and performing music which somebody else has written, cannot be compared. The only art which you can compare with music is the theatrical art. But since we act anyhow, all our lives, we are not so unfamiliar with that.

VOICE: *Do you think that concepts from the other arts can*

enhance our insight into music? Could they ever modify your conception?

MR SCHNABEL: I think that is not investigable. Perhaps a great impression I received somewhere has helped my music. That is absolutely possible, but I cannot investigate. Any happiness from this kind of experience might be productive for your own work. I think that every real experience is productive.

VOICE: *I did not mean just enjoying; I meant, let us say, concepts of form in the other arts.*

MR SCHNABEL: They are included in the kind of experience of which I spoke. I think 'happiness' and 'enjoyment' are very strong words.

VOICE: *But I mean whether they would be consciously applicable.*

MR SCHNABEL: I am not aware of that. I am not aware that literature or pictorial art have had, in this respect, an influence on my conception of music. Perhaps I interpret my musical conceptions into other arts and into my experiences. Maybe my experiences are influenced by my conceptions of musical form. That is probably the case. However, all this is not investigable and not very important to know.

Even if I had given you a more positive answer, what would you have made of it?

VOICE: *Well, it might be a guide to understanding any of the arts.*

MR SCHNABEL: I think that the more receptivity has been given to you for everything which is beautiful, the more you will probably, in your own work, strive for the appreciation of proportions and purity of expression. But one cannot investigate, or measure. You see, we are here in the world of qualities, and it is very difficult to approach this region with categories out of the world of quantities. It is like asking: 'How much did this influence you when you saw it for the first time?' Or: 'Which has more influence on you, works of art or Nature?' For I think Nature has a great influence—walking in the mountains, for instance. I have felt very often that musical ideas come quicker and easier to me in such surroundings. But that also is very individual. And if it was necessary to live always, let me say, in crowded quarters in a city, then one would in the course of years not be poorer in ideas; I am convinced of that. Because I think creative genius will adjust itself to any circumstances.

VOICE: *How about the productivity of this month you have spent with us—for you? I mean by that, what will you remember of us after you have left, and what do you think about the questions we have asked? Are we even sillier than the students who have often asked you silly questions in the past?*

MR SCHNABEL: I shall always remember this month. First of all, because I was afraid! While I have no 'inferiority complex' (I confess this openly), I was nevertheless quite afraid that I might be a complete failure, for I have never done this before. And whether I have been a failure, that is left to you to judge. I should better ask *you* these questions you have asked me now, because I have been more active here than you.

However, I found your questions very interesting. In the first days, questions were of that rather mechanical kind, apparently so typical nowadays, and particularly here; their characteristic is: 'Here is an expert! So I will ask him about some problems in the field of his activities. His answers must be right because he is the expert.'

As it is certain, under the circumstances, that the answers will be accepted, whatever they are, it becomes rather tempting, occasionally, to talk a little intentional nonsense. I told you that Busoni took a diabolical joy in fooling his followers, who then went around and spread his nonsensical utterances as the ultimate wisdom, as a kind of gospel. To be fooled like that may be a kind of good training for those who just believe in experts and the 'safe conduct to wisdom'. But my disposition is not like Busoni's. And then there were fewer and fewer questions of that type.

I enjoyed my discussions with you very much. I have thanked you already for the patience with which you have listened to me; I hope you will remember some of the things I have said. I would be very happy to feel that I succeeded in giving you the impression that behind all I have said in these twelve talks with you is one leading idea, one principle and one faith, and also—one doctrine. For when I spoke to you here, I wanted, above all, to encourage you—to encourage all of you in your endeavours to be related to values of a higher type—and to encourage your confidence in your own gifts of experience and judgement. Did I succeed?

REFLECTIONS ON MUSIC

Translated by César Saerchinger from an
address delivered by Mr. Schnabel at the
University of Manchester

I

LET there be tone, and there was tone. Tone has been given life in man; in him it becomes element, impulse, conception and task.

Man has the power to project tone, as sound, from within himself, without external help. Tone, with its infinite potentialities for development, has been planted in man, and demands from him the realization of these possibilities.

It was revealed to man that this gift—the gift of tone—could satisfy spiritual desires, was obviously intended, beyond all material weal and woe, to increase joy and lessen pain. And thus it became man's mission and desire to create out of this transcendental substance, out of this vibrating tone, by means of human intelligence an ever-moving cosmos, perceptible yet immaterial, an irrational reality beyond and above natural occurrence.

This creation, which is nothing but a sequence of tones, we call music. Eventually music became the most independent expression of emotional life, a symbol of feeling, intensified and ennobled without loss of its elementary qualities, spiritualized into a representative form of sovereign art.

JUST how I define art, how I endeavour to reach the most un-equivocal method of determining those attributes which distinguish art from the other emanations of the intellect (intuitively, you see, I am not in the least uncertain)—about this I shall have some things to say later on.

The organisms which until now have been produced with the material of tones, cover a wide and greatly varied field. The first two tones ever to sound one after the other were music, and Beethoven's C sharp minor quartet is music: every organized tone sequence that occurred between these two, or that came after them, is music, too. Since as yet not all human communities have reached the same cultural level, since there are still many primitive peoples, since with other peoples cultural activity was arrested and atrophied (which probably always meant retrogression and gradual decay), since, in short, the simplest and most sophisticated forms of life, as well as the intermediate ones, exist simultaneously, the lower and lowest musical orders also still exist. Most of them, moreover, are known to some of the investigators of the civilized world.

Man's ability to originate and reproduce is, as I said at the outset, incontestably present in every person.

Music, once produced, may have unlimited existence. It remains in the memory. For its lowest forms, musical notation is superfluous.

The reproduction of music has the duration of sound vibrations only; it is like a spoken word, a glance, a breath, a step. To become perceptible, music must each time be re-created from the memory. A gramophone record, the permanent reproduction of a temporary one, would have disposed of this necessity only if man would—and could—cease re-creating a composition after it had been mechanically preserved. I do not, however, believe that the aim of the gramophone record lies in that direction. And probably this would be wasted effort.

The lower and unrecorded musical forms are preserved orally, like folklore and story, from generation to generation. They are, in contradistinction to manuscript, picture and edifice, indestructible.

Probably these lowest forms are very similar to each other, whenever and wherever they occur. Bodily movements associated with work and—let us call it pleasure—executed alone or with others, as well as sound sequences perceived in nature,

230

may have induced or influenced these lower forms. I am reminded, in this connection, of bird notes, the sound of oars, the footfall of the wanderer, etc., etc.

On the most primitive level the variety of forms is naturally very restricted. But it is inherent in the nature of music that even a single form, albeit the lowest, is susceptible of differentiated expression. For instance, two tones, always equidistant from one another in pitch, may be so transformed by means of varying their metrical distance and their dynamic strength, that the faster and louder reproduction has no resemblance to its slower and softer version. By varying tone sequences in this way without changing their pitch one may, indeed, create the impression that the one is completely contrary to the other, that the one reflects utmost joy and the other utmost sorrow. This fact appears to me to be extremely important in considering the problem of the individual values of the components which go to make up a musical composition.

It is quite certain that even on its lowest plane the presentation of music was subject to conventions; and musical activity was very early one of the occupational duties of mankind. For instance, as part of religious ritual, or the watchman's service. It would be worth knowing whether all the members of a primitive community were capable of producing in sound the few lowly musical forms then in vogue; whether all of them could do it immediately and after a single hearing, some only after repeated efforts, and some not at all. To us, possessing a plenitude of musical forms, ranging from the simplest and easiest conceivable organisms to the most highly refined and complicated, to the art which seeks to attain that opposite shore, a second simplicity: to us it is difficult to conceive that not every human being should be able to solve the simplest musical problems of primitive civilizations. In our stage of civilization, to be sure, it is still a small minority that has, and seeks, the approach (he who seeks it already has it, I think)— the approach to the summits of our musical attainments. But in the valleys pretty well everybody can find his way. The simplest of our songs, dances, marches virtually everybody can sing, or whistle, or drum—at least bar by bar. Yet our simplest pieces are many degrees above the lowest forms.

The question whether the musical ascent of the individual occurs only by virtue of his talents or also by virtue of his training is of particular interest to me. The idea that education might one day become the mother of any number of geniuses, or more exactly, that every educated person could one day become a genius, seems to me the most daringly Utopian dream. I don't think we need to be afraid of that.

I began by saying that I consider everybody musical. In the primitive sense this is obviously true. I have also said that the gift so conferred demands its own enhancement—the pound its usury. How does it happen that the aptitude to fulfil this demand is not equally represented in all individuals? The German word for aptitude—Geschick—also means destiny: does not this double meaning perhaps suggest a profound truth and the correct conception?

If nature by design gave to men and women the ability to develop their aptitudes, and so brought about their utmost differentiation, it was bound, also, to assign to them duties which would lead to the division of labour. Surely Bach's Art of Fugue cannot be derived from the instinct for self-preservation alone. Hence there must be active in man an urge to change, progress and rise. He was given the obligation to grow and the possibilities of growth, but the purpose of that growth is unknown. Though his body cannot escape mortality, his work may, by comparison, be incorporeal and imperishable. When a possibility reaches maturity, it must become a reality.

The biological mechanism of the division of labour was, as we have seen, an inevitable consequence of our numerous avocations. Is man free—or was he ever free—to choose a field of endeavour which requires more than he can accomplish with the help of his primitive faculties—faculties that are bestowed on man in general? He may have the freedom to choose, but I do not think he has the ability. And I do not believe that anyone who lacks the ability for a given activity will even conceive the idea to try. Therefore it is impossible to become a genius by choice.

Already in the first stages of differentiation there must be a natural weeding-out, a selection, and a summons. No substitute for divine dispensation has ever been invented; the genius germ has not yet been discovered. Differentiation, as I said, leads to division of labour and vocational grouping. In some human communities this has hardly begun: not all have as yet been summoned; though the predisposition to become talented is surely not denied to anyone. The ways of Providence in choosing the soil for cultural development are mysterious. It first selects the individual, who may not even have formed a consciousness of his own identity. Persons become instruments. Some are created inventive; they distinguish themselves in various fields outside the merely practical. Their superiority is recognized and rewarded; their attainments are enjoyed and desired. These gifted individuals begin to exert a mutual influence on each other. The attainment of one becomes an experience to the other; he desires to repeat it. Here are the beginnings of art, and at the same time art criticism.

As you see, in my opinion artistic creation must precede a public demand. The 'order' to create the work comes from the gift—the talent—which enables its possessor to create it, though certainly not under the slogan *'l'art pour l'art'*. But a complementary order emanates from the gift which induces the demand for cultural creations. Otherwise these would not have been continuously produced.

The greater the number of creations the more exacting the demand. Thus the significance of technique constantly increased until the labour to produce a work demanded virtually all the time and concentration at the creator's command. Hence, in order to devote himself to it, his work must be exchangeable for the products which satisfy his physical needs. And these are provided by people who are gifted with receptivity, with a hunger for intellectual and spiritual food. The preservation and renewal of cultural creation, therefore, depends upon a public demand, expressed by understanding and love. This statement is not a contradiction of the previous one that creation must precede demand. A call must precede the echo. The caller who hears no echo will change his place, will utter his call from another. It may be, of course, that the dormant echo invites the call. In any case, someone must first call. Perhaps by intuition he will call only in the place where an echo awaits its awakening.

II

I HAVE hitherto avoided, as far as possible, the designation 'art'. I have said cultural creation, when in reality I meant art. That art, the sum of all art-works and artistic attainments, constitutes for me merely one of many cultural creations goes without saying. Why was I so afraid to use the word? Because I have found that common parlance includes in the collective term 'art' many things which according to my conception of the nature of art do not belong there. This is true of all branches of art; now, however, I shall try to limit myself strictly to the art of music. Wherever there exist only a few primitive musical forms, and where perhaps for centuries no increase or noteworthy change of forms occurs, I would still call these manifestations—whatever may be their purpose and effect—art. Because, in the circumstances, these forms embody a culminating stage of musical expression, and are, by their impulse and aim, art as I understand it. Music has attained individualization, and finally autonomy, later than other species of art.

Favoured by meditation and introspection in monastic seclusion, Europe began, in the Middle Ages, to erect a new art edifice from the shambles of a collapsing civilization. Man began to divine music's hidden treasures. His belief in external causes of power and weakness, in gods and heroes who provide the thriving trade and the visible florescence of the community, who could even be somewhat bribed by material sacrifices—this belief expired. In its place blossomed an idealistic faith in an esoteric glory, an indestructible power that is identical with humility, a power within the grasp of everyone, if only he is guided by love, kindliness, abstinence and the willingness to suffer. Only one misfortune was recognized: the lack of love. This communion with the soul, this spiritual human relationship, this affirmation of the individual, provided a fertile ground for the formation of a new musical art. The state of mind which fostered such feelings had great persuasive power in this age of material misery. This preoccupa-

234

tion and spiritual assurance constituted an unassailable wealth. But the demands of material existence imperilled this treasure. Hence images and descriptions were spurned, the invisible reality which is the kernel of the movement demanded other symbols. Free rein was given to the play of inspiration and fantasy. Music revealed its higher potentialities.

It is an apparent paradox that altruism strengthens the individual, but it is nevertheless true. In unselfish personal activity these men of the Middle Ages devoted their abilities to the peaceful spreading of the glory of the new faith. Fervour, united with a keen intelligence, erected a new dogma on these premises. Even temporal power was forced to reckon with this new attitude; it strove to make it serve its own ends. Obviously the new spirit had not lost all connection with the past. And its musical part, too, was connected with the previously developed forms. Man himself constituted this continuity and affinity, for man, it seems, is never to be thought of as quite new.

In the new community of faith the musical heritage, like all things cultural, was soon protected from dispersal and destruction: it was collected, sifted, studied; and useful fragments were preserved as material for a new expression. At first the cultivation of vocal music predominated. Instrumental music (instruments for the production of tone had long existed) was too worldly. In this sacred environment, subtle divisions and sub-divisions, symbols and signs, and polyphony came into being; this last possibly through the whims and enthusiasms of individuals bent on giving greater colour to the Service by means of improvisations, or in order to demonstrate their desire for liberty, or merely to overcome their own boredom.

In this circle of activity, too, division of labour, and consequently vocation, made their appearance. The congregation listened raptly, and participated (as it still does today) only in the designated places. A definite, comprehensive and teachable order was developed, yet the inner urge to enlarge it unceasingly was never suppressed, so long as the meaning was not changed. Those who were summoned by virtue of their gifts, were charged to continue their work in perpetuity.

The growing dogma became a visible reality, an influence, a power, an expanding institution. It first took hold wherever the externally directed impulses and the forces seeking intellectual solutions of conflicts were weak. When finally it invaded the regions where these intellectual forces were still effective, a conflict with the requirements and privileges of the body, the senses and the intelligence was unavoidable. Established authority could but little impair the power and intensity of the mystic flood, and vice versa. The attempt was made to let the contesting forces work together in providing the conditions of human existence, in constructing a compromise. But never again has homogeneity seemed attainable. Senses, intelligence and emotion drove forward alongside each other, often against each other, in every individual entity and in all groups: all were subjected to this struggle. Each of these forces claimed the prerogative; the effort to resolve the extremes by reason failed. Prohibitions of various kinds, designed to keep each self-assertive element in its place, became necessary in order to forestall disintegration. Dualism, or rather pluralism, became a restless but very pregnant soil for the creative individual and for all society. Every idea claimed to provide the only solution, every doctrine strove for autocracy. The end and aim of each was happiness, of which no two conceptions are alike. Champions from every direction marched toward this goal. The end justified the means. Even intelligence and love made use of violence to gain their ends. Perfect balance was possible only in personalities of a particularly harmonious kind.

The will to prevail and conquer vitalized each movement; it kindled creative genius, liberated the individual. No single effort was any longer determined by, or concentrated on, a united whole. Unprecedented progress was achieved in all fields of activity, but a unified, valid, workable, correctly proportioned mixture of all ideas did not emerge. Religion, art, science, on the one hand, technics, economics and politics on the other, may be interrelated for practical purposes. Essentially, however, they are hardly connected.

Vis-à-vis the three last named, man is an object; *vis-à-vis* the first he is the subject. He functions, as it were, in two localities. It is clear that the proselytizing, beautifying and idealizing symbols could no longer be the same in both localities. Here then was the beginning of the emancipation, individualization, specialization of art—the great transformation of music. It succeeded in becoming sovereign and absolute. Formerly the part of a whole, it now became a complete entity, standing alone by the side of other entities to whom only one thing was common—life itself. Such a transmutation into absolute music occurs when a gifted person, charged by the forces of individualism and dualism, can no longer sympathize sincerely with the established institutions for the satisfaction of spiritual desires. To such a one tradition and convention did not seem appropriate in a region which has become peculiarly personal by virtue of the always living idea of love. He discovered in music its especial fitness to become the seat of this idea.

Now music did not cease being used in the old sense; it continued to exist as a part of the other entities even after it had become a complete entity in itself. And here we have to form a new conception of music in order to divide the new from the old. The old is no longer what it was. Through the addition of a musical 'upper floor', that which formerly existed by itself becomes a structure of another category. It was art, even in its subordinate function, so long as nothing else made of the same material existed in a non-subordinate function, capable of representing the idea quite alone. Music henceforth is divided into different species, and of these I prefer to designate only one as art. 'Applied music' I no longer reckon as art.

III

Man is musical. He can produce tone sequences and reproduce them. But special aptitudes are obviously required for the projection or reception of the spiritualized refinement and shaping of the elementary product. The musicality of which normally every man and woman is possessed does not suffice to insure his or her access to the art of music.

The personal impetus toward higher intellectual levels cannot, in my opinion, be produced by outside influence; the urge must be born within him who feels it. Education and environment may give to everyone the opportunity to discover where he feels at home. Without the inborn desire, however, no true relationship to art is possible. Musical appreciation, for instance, is considered to be a part of the 'intellectual luggage' of so-called educated people; but we know that many of these have no connection even with the name of art, and that they neither pretend to it nor desire it.

The elevation of music took place in that small part of Europe which owes the colourful variety of its creations, roughly speaking, to the cross-breeding of Paganism, Hellenism and Christianity. Here music was raised from a means of private pleasure, from a secondary, servile, merely ornamental rôle to freedom of purpose, to sovereignty; it became a symbolic process, perfect within itself, subject only to its own laws and conditions; it proceeded from a recognized spiritual necessity, and by a limitless combination of means, always with the consciousness of an artistic intent, became spiritualized, condensed, formed into representative organisms guided by the direction of their intended effect toward a place which corresponds to the point of origin. From soul to soul, by way of the intellect. That expresses roughly what I understand to be the process of art.

Incidentally, the emancipation of music—the establishment of music's autonomy—seems to me the most original contribution Europe has made to the sum of human culture.

As in the case of every other product, a work of art must be preceded by the intention to make that which is to appear. Its maker must, therefore, determine it to be a work of art. The reception of a work of art, on the other hand, must be preceded by the urge to experience it (and the recipient's awareness of that urge). Absolute music is created for the purpose of being heard with complete and purely musical attentiveness —in a state of physical passivity, and intellectual passivity too, so far as association of ideas is concerned, but with a spiritual and emotional activity which awaits its release.

Not every creation in absolute music is a work of art. Strictly speaking, musical works which are connected with words and images and tangible processes do not count as absolute music, for they awaken extra-musical conceptions. In the song, the oratorio or the mass, words tend to be merely incidental. They serve the music, instead of being served by it. In opera, too, the text as such is not really a diversion from the music. What does prevent the music from being completely heard is the hearer's participation in dramatic occurrences that must be followed by the eye. Yet creations of this species are, nevertheless, art, because their authors intended them to have a symbolic significance. The operetta has no such significance; therefore it is not art, however excellent and charming it may be. Here locality, not quality, decides.

Applied music has the purpose of accompanying non-musical occupations in an animating way. There is also 'utility music', an apt expression of the day. Utility music approaches absolute music, although it often has an extra-musical tendency, since its production is for the benefit of the executants, though its performances are to be listened to. For instance, children's games, musical exercises, workmen's propaganda choruses, and music for schools. It is a way of learning music. A musical work can belong to one species only; it must lose in efficacy when drawn into a field for which it was not intended. Strauss waltzes are delightful, but they are intended for the ball-room. The B minor symphony of Schubert, when used in an operetta, is debased to prettiness, becomes mere pretty material. Works of art move, not by material, but by the spirit.

IV

ART comprises works of art and artists. The usual custom to associate quality with this designation is misleading. The expression art is abused when it is applied to a successful result of any given task. Art is a territory in itself; whatever is originated there, no matter how poor when measured by the summits, belongs to the realm of art. An artist is he who by profession and intention produces art. One must not call him an artist whose activity lies outside of art and there earns particular distinction. The best shoemaker is simply and only the best shoemaker. Even with intuition and skill and soul he is only a shoemaker. Works of art can be measured only by works of art; bad oratorios cannot be measured by good shoes. Art is not the only field of creative attainment.

As in all branches of production, there are good, bad and middling works of art, although there is no way of proving these valuations with legal validity. Possibly a claim to value may be established by the longevity of a work, and recognition by the testimony of those who are themselves recognized. Nor is there a patented method for the production of master works. No one can be intentionally original, and no one intentionally an eclectic.

All attempts to associate works of art with the private life or the philosophy of their creators, a favourite pastime of biographers, seem to me both meaningless and dangerous. The creator's attitude outside of his music is without significance for the music itself. Very simply stated, a work of art originates and lives in the space between affirmation and negation. When, where and to what we say Yes or No is entirely unimportant: the power of the statement and not its subject is what matters. It circles about the symbols Heaven, Hell, Earth; the Heaven of one may be the Hell of another, but he must feel it as such.

All emphasis on peculiarities which distinguish works of art from one another, tend to divert us from their true nature.

241

The influence of locale and Zeitgeist on the work is minimal in comparison with the similarity between all works of art. Society collaborates significantly in artistic creation only through the force of its desire for art. The undeniable fact, apparent in so many lands, that the cultivation of art flourishes now here, now there, decays again, becomes paralysed or dies —this can be explained only by the rise and fall of the demand, influenced to some extent, possibly, by political conditions. Historical events, therefore, may have influenced—stimulated or released—artistic creation; but artistic creativeness, a power belonging to all humanity, is latent within it always and everywhere. The quantitative exploitation of art works is also influenced by such propelling forces, and so is the preference for one or the other species of art. Countries and periods, therefore, may well have produced different quantities in different species, but the nature and value of art works follow only their inherent laws. Great art works and small ones have their essential qualities in common.

V

Music and musical art are mysterious, inevitable, tangible and producible realities, cosmically related and individually fashioned; impersonal, personal and super-personal. It is impossible to exhaust them. 'The rest is music', as it was in essence at the beginning. Some time I must close, and today I know of no better way of closing than by quoting Schopenhauer's definition: 'Music is the universe once again.'

INDEX

246

247

A CATALOG OF SELECTED
DOVER BOOKS
IN ALL FIELDS OF INTEREST

A CATALOG OF SELECTED DOVER BOOKS IN ALL FIELDS OF INTEREST

CONCERNING THE SPIRITUAL IN ART, Wassily Kandinsky. Pioneering work by father of abstract art. Thoughts on color theory, nature of art. Analysis of earlier masters. 12 illustrations. 80pp. of text. 5⅜ × 8½. 23411-8 Pa. $2.95

LEONARDO ON THE HUMAN BODY, Leonardo da Vinci. More than 1200 of Leonardo's anatomical drawings on 215 plates. Leonardo's text, which accompanies the drawings, has been translated into English. 506pp. 8⅜ × 11¾. 24483-0 Pa. $11.95

GOBLIN MARKET, Christina Rossetti. Best-known work by poet comparable to Emily Dickinson, Alfred Tennyson. With 46 delightfully grotesque illustrations by Laurence Housman. 64pp. 4 × 6¾. 24516-0 Pa. $2.50

THE HEART OF THOREAU'S JOURNALS, edited by Odell Shepard. Selections from *Journal*, ranging over full gamut of interests. 228pp. 5⅜ × 8½. 20741-2 Pa. $4.50

MR. LINCOLN'S CAMERA MAN: MATHEW B. BRADY, Roy Meredith. Over 300 Brady photos reproduced directly from original negatives, photos. Lively commentary. 368pp. 8⅜ × 11¼. 23021-X Pa. $14.95

PHOTOGRAPHIC VIEWS OF SHERMAN'S CAMPAIGN, George N. Barnard. Reprint of landmark 1866 volume with 61 plates: battlefield of New Hope Church, the Etawah Bridge, the capture of Atlanta, etc. 80pp. 9 × 12. 23445-2 Pa. $6.00

A SHORT HISTORY OF ANATOMY AND PHYSIOLOGY FROM THE GREEKS TO HARVEY, Dr. Charles Singer. Thoroughly engrossing non-technical survey. 270 illustrations. 211pp. 5⅜ × 8½. 20389-1 Pa. $4.95

REDOUTE ROSES IRON-ON TRANSFER PATTERNS, Barbara Christopher. Redouté was botanical painter to the Empress Josephine; transfer his famous roses onto fabric with these 24 transfer patterns. 80pp. 8¼ × 10⅞. 24292-7 Pa. $3.50

THE FIVE BOOKS OF ARCHITECTURE, Sebastiano Serlio. Architectural milestone, first (1611) English translation of Renaissance classic. Unabridged reproduction of original edition includes over 300 woodcut illustrations. 416pp. 9⅜ × 12¼. 24349-4 Pa. $14.95

CARLSON'S GUIDE TO LANDSCAPE PAINTING, John F. Carlson. Authoritative, comprehensive guide covers, every aspect of landscape painting. 34 reproductions of paintings by author; 58 explanatory diagrams. 144pp. 8⅜ × 11. 22927-0 Pa. $5.95

101 PUZZLES IN THOUGHT AND LOGIC, C.R. Wylie, Jr. Solve murders, robberies, see which fishermen are liars—purely by reasoning! 107pp. 5⅜ × 8½. 20367-0 Pa. $2.00

TEST YOUR LOGIC, George J. Summers. 50 more truly new puzzles with new turns of thought, new subtleties of inference. 100pp. 5⅜ × 8½. 22877-0 Pa. $2.50

THE MURDER BOOK OF J.G. REEDER, Edgar Wallace. Eight suspenseful stories by bestselling mystery writer of 20s and 30s. Features the donnish Mr. J.G. Reeder of Public Prosecutor's Office. 128pp. 5⅜ × 8½.
24374-5 Pa. $3.95

ANNE ORR'S CHARTED DESIGNS, Anne Orr. Best designs by premier needlework designer, all on charts: flowers, borders, birds, children, alphabets, etc. Over 100 charts, 10 in color. Total of 40pp. 8¼ × 11. 23704-4 Pa. $2.50

BASIC CONSTRUCTION TECHNIQUES FOR HOUSES AND SMALL BUILDINGS SIMPLY EXPLAINED, U.S. Bureau of Naval Personnel. Grading, masonry, woodworking, floor and wall framing, roof framing, plastering, tile setting, much more. Over 675 illustrations. 568pp. 6½ × 9¼. 20242-9 Pa. $9.95

MATISSE LINE DRAWINGS AND PRINTS, Henri Matisse. Representative collection of female nudes, faces, still lifes, experimental works, etc., from 1898 to 1948. 50 illustrations. 48pp. 8⅜ × 11¼. 23877-6 Pa. $3.50

HOW TO PLAY THE CHESS OPENINGS, Eugene Znosko-Borovsky. Clear, profound examinations of just what each opening is intended to do and how opponent can counter. Many sample games. 147pp. 5⅜ × 8½. 22795-2 Pa. $3.50

DUPLICATE BRIDGE, Alfred Sheinwold. Clear, thorough, easily followed account: rules, etiquette, scoring, strategy, bidding; Goren's point-count system, Blackwood and Gerber conventions, etc. 158pp. 5⅜ × 8½. 22741-3 Pa. $3.50

SARGENT PORTRAIT DRAWINGS, J.S. Sargent. Collection of 42 portraits reveals technical skill and intuitive eye of noted American portrait painter, John Singer Sargent. 48pp. 8¼ × 11⅛. 24524-1 Pa. $3.50

ENTERTAINING SCIENCE EXPERIMENTS WITH EVERYDAY OBJECTS, Martin Gardner. Over 100 experiments for youngsters. Will amuse, astonish, teach, and entertain. Over 100 illustrations. 127pp. 5⅜ × 8½. 24201-3 Pa. $2.50

TEDDY BEAR PAPER DOLLS IN FULL COLOR: A Family of Four Bears and Their Costumes, Crystal Collins. A family of four Teddy Bear paper dolls and nearly 60 cut-out costumes. Full color, printed one side only. 32pp. 9¼ × 12¼.
24550-0 Pa. $3.50

NEW CALLIGRAPHIC ORNAMENTS AND FLOURISHES, Arthur Baker. Unusual, multi-useable material: arrows, pointing hands, brackets and frames, ovals, swirls, birds, etc. Nearly 700 illustrations. 80pp. 8⅜ × 11¼.
24095-9 Pa. $3.75

DINOSAUR DIORAMAS TO CUT & ASSEMBLE, M. Kalmenoff. Two complete three-dimensional scenes in full color, with 31 cut-out animals and plants. Excellent educational toy for youngsters. Instructions; 2 assembly diagrams. 32pp. 9¼ × 12¼. 24541-1 Pa. $4.50

SILHOUETTES: A PICTORIAL ARCHIVE OF VARIED ILLUSTRATIONS, edited by Carol Belanger Grafton. Over 600 silhouettes from the 18th to 20th centuries. Profiles and full figures of men, women, children, birds, animals, groups and scenes, nature, ships, an alphabet. 144pp. 8⅜ × 11¼. 23781-8 Pa. $5.95

25 KITES THAT FLY, Leslie Hunt. Full, easy-to-follow instructions for kites made from inexpensive materials. Many novelties. 70 illustrations. 110pp. 5⅜ × 8½. 22550-X Pa. $2.50

PIANO TUNING, J. Cree Fischer. Clearest, best book for beginner, amateur. Simple repairs, raising dropped notes, tuning by easy method of flattened fifths. No previous skills needed. 4 illustrations. 201pp. 5⅜ × 8½. 23267-0 Pa. $3.50

EARLY AMERICAN IRON-ON TRANSFER PATTERNS, edited by Rita Weiss. 75 designs, borders, alphabets, from traditional American sources. 48pp. 8¼ × 11. 23162-3 Pa. $1.95

CROCHETING EDGINGS, edited by Rita Weiss. Over 100 of the best designs for these lovely trims for a host of household items. Complete instructions, illustrations. 48pp. 8¼ × 11. 24031-2 Pa. $2.95

FINGER PLAYS FOR NURSERY AND KINDERGARTEN, Emilie Poulsson. 18 finger plays with music (voice and piano); entertaining, instructive. Counting, nature lore, etc. Victorian classic. 53 illustrations. 80pp. 6½ × 9¼. 22588-7 Pa. $2.25

BOSTON THEN AND NOW, Peter Vanderwarker. Here in 59 side-by-side views are photographic documentations of the city's past and present. 119 photographs. Full captions. 122pp. 8¼ × 11. 24312-5 Pa. $7.95

CROCHETING BEDSPREADS, edited by Rita Weiss. 22 patterns, originally published in three instruction books 1939-41. 39 photos, 8 charts. Instructions. 48pp. 8¼ × 11. 23610-2 Pa. $2.00

HAWTHORNE ON PAINTING, Charles W. Hawthorne. Collected from notes taken by students at famous Cape Cod School; hundreds of direct, personal *apercus*, ideas, suggestions. 91pp. 5⅜ × 8½. 20653-X Pa. $2.95

THERMODYNAMICS, Enrico Fermi. A classic of modern science. Clear, organized treatment of systems, first and second laws, entropy, thermodynamic potentials, etc. Calculus required. 160pp. 5⅜ × 8½. 60361-X Pa. $4.50

TEN BOOKS ON ARCHITECTURE, Vitruvius. The most important book ever written on architecture. Early Roman aesthetics, technology, classical orders, site selection, all other aspects. Morgan translation. 331pp. 5⅜ × 8½. 20645-9 Pa. $6.95

THE CORNELL BREAD BOOK, Clive M. McCay and Jeanette B. McCay. Famed high-protein recipe incorporated into breads, rolls, buns, coffee cakes, pizza, pie crusts, more. Nearly 50 illustrations. 48pp. 8¼ × 11. 23995-0 Pa. $2.00

THE CRAFTSMAN'S HANDBOOK, Cennino Cennini. 15th-century handbook, school of Giotto, explains applying gold, silver leaf; gesso; fresco painting, grinding pigments, etc. 142pp. 6⅛ × 9¼. 20054-X Pa. $3.95

FRANK LLOYD WRIGHT'S FALLINGWATER, Donald Hoffmann. Full story of Wright's masterwork at Bear Run, Pa. 100 photographs of site, construction, and details of completed structure. 112pp. 9¼ × 10. 23671-4 Pa. $7.95

OVAL STAINED GLASS PATTERN BOOK, C. Eaton. 60 new designs framed in shape of an oval. Greater complexity, challenge with sinuous cats, birds, mandalas framed in antique shape. 64pp. 8¼ × 11. 24519-5 Pa. $3.95

THE BOOK OF WOOD CARVING, Charles Marshall Sayers. Still finest book for beginning student. Fundamentals, technique; gives 34 designs, over 34 projects for panels, bookends, mirrors, etc. 33 photos. 118pp. 7¾ × 10⅝.   23654-4 Pa. $3.95

CARVING COUNTRY CHARACTERS, Bill Higginbotham. Expert advice for beginning, advanced carvers on materials, techniques for creating 18 projects—mirthful panorama of American characters. 105 illustrations. 80pp. 8⅜ × 11.
24135-1 Pa. $2.95

300 ART NOUVEAU DESIGNS AND MOTIFS IN FULL COLOR, C.B. Grafton. 44 full-page plates display swirling lines and muted colors typical of Art Nouveau. Borders, frames, panels, cartouches, dingbats, etc. 48pp. 9⅜ × 12¼.
24354-0 Pa. $6.95

SELF-WORKING CARD TRICKS, Karl Fulves. Editor of *Pallbearer* offers 72 tricks that work automatically through nature of card deck. No sleight of hand needed. Often spectacular. 42 illustrations. 113pp. 5⅜ × 8½.   23334-0 Pa. $3.50

CUT AND ASSEMBLE A WESTERN FRONTIER TOWN, Edmund V. Gillon, Jr. Ten authentic full-color buildings on heavy cardboard stock in H-O scale. Sheriff's Office and Jail, Saloon, Wells Fargo, Opera House, others. 48pp. 9¼ × 12¼.
23736-2 Pa. $4.95

CUT AND ASSEMBLE AN EARLY NEW ENGLAND VILLAGE, Edmund V. Gillon, Jr. Printed in full color on heavy cardboard stock. 12 authentic buildings in H-O scale: Adams home in Quincy, Mass., Oliver Wight house in Sturbridge, smithy, store, church, others. 48pp. 9¼ × 12¼.   23536-X Pa. $4.95

THE TALE OF TWO BAD MICE, Beatrix Potter. Tom Thumb and Hunca Munca squeeze out of their hole and go exploring. 27 full-color Potter illustrations. 59pp. 4¼ × 5½. (Available in U.S. only)   23065-1 Pa. $1.75

CARVING FIGURE CARICATURES IN THE OZARK STYLE, Harold L. Enlow. Instructions and illustrations for ten delightful projects, plus general carving instructions. 22 drawings and 47 photographs altogether. 39pp. 8⅜ × 11.
23151-8 Pa. $2.95

A TREASURY OF FLOWER DESIGNS FOR ARTISTS, EMBROIDERERS AND CRAFTSMEN, Susan Gaber. 100 garden favorites lushly rendered by artist for artists, craftsmen, needleworkers. Many form frames, borders. 80pp. 8¼ × 11.
24096-7 Pa. $3.95

CUT & ASSEMBLE A TOY THEATER/THE NUTCRACKER BALLET, Tom Tierney. Model of a complete, full-color production of Tchaikovsky's classic. 6 backdrops, dozens of characters, familiar dance sequences. 32pp. 9⅜ × 12¼.
24194-7 Pa. $4.50

ANIMALS: 1,419 COPYRIGHT-FREE ILLUSTRATIONS OF MAMMALS, BIRDS, FISH, INSECTS, ETC., edited by Jim Harter. Clear wood engravings present, in extremely lifelike poses, over 1,000 species of animals. 284pp. 9 × 12.
23766-4 Pa. $9.95

MORE HAND SHADOWS, Henry Bursill. For those at their 'finger ends,'' 16 more effects—Shakespeare, a hare, a squirrel, Mr. Punch, and twelve more—each explained by a full-page illustration. Considerable period charm. 30pp. 6½ × 9¼.
21384-6 Pa. $1.95

SURREAL STICKERS AND UNREAL STAMPS, William Rowe. 224 haunting, hilarious stamps on gummed, perforated stock, with images of elephants, geisha girls, George Washington, etc. 16pp. one side. 8¼ × 11.   24371-0 Pa. $3.50

GOURMET KITCHEN LABELS, Ed Sibbett, Jr. 112 full-color labels (4 copies each of 28 designs). Fruit, bread, other culinary motifs. Gummed and perforated. 16pp. 8¼ × 11.   24087-8 Pa. $2.95

PATTERNS AND INSTRUCTIONS FOR CARVING AUTHENTIC BIRDS, H.D. Green. Detailed instructions, 27 diagrams, 85 photographs for carving 15 species of birds so life-like, they'll seem ready to fly! 8¼ × 11.   24222-6 Pa. $3.00

FLATLAND, E.A. Abbott. Science-fiction classic explores life of 2-D being in 3-D world. 16 illustrations. 103pp. 5⅜ × 8.   20001-9 Pa. $2.00

DRIED FLOWERS, Sarah Whitlock and Martha Rankin. Concise, clear, practical guide to dehydration, glycerinizing, pressing plant material, and more. Covers use of silica gel. 12 drawings. 32pp. 5⅜ × 8½.   21802-3 Pa. $1.00

EASY-TO-MAKE CANDLES, Gary V. Guy. Learn how easy it is to make all kinds of decorative candles. Step-by-step instructions. 82 illustrations. 48pp. 8¼ × 11.

23881-4 Pa. $2.95

SUPER STICKERS FOR KIDS, Carolyn Bracken. 128 gummed and perforated full-color stickers: GIRL WANTED, KEEP OUT, BORED OF EDUCATION, X-RATED, COMBAT ZONE, many others. 16pp. 8¼ × 11.   24092-4 Pa. $3.50

CUT AND COLOR PAPER MASKS, Michael Grater. Clowns, animals, funny faces...simply color them in, cut them out, and put them together, and you have 9 paper masks to play with and enjoy. 32pp. 8¼ × 11.   23171-2 Pa. $2.95

A CHRISTMAS CAROL: THE ORIGINAL MANUSCRIPT, Charles Dickens. Clear facsimile of Dickens manuscript, on facing pages with final printed text. 8 illustrations by John Leech, 4 in color on covers. 144pp. 8⅜ × 11¼.

20980-6 Pa. $5.95

CARVING SHOREBIRDS, Harry V. Shourds & Anthony Hillman. 16 full-size patterns (all double-page spreads) for 19 North American shorebirds with step-by-step instructions. 72pp. 9¼ × 12¼.   24287-0 Pa. $5.95

THE GENTLE ART OF MATHEMATICS, Dan Pedoe. Mathematical games, probability, the question of infinity, topology, how the laws of algebra work, problems of irrational numbers, and more. 42 figures. 143pp. 5⅜ × 8½.

22949-1 Pa. $3.50

READY-TO-USE DOLLHOUSE WALLPAPER, Katzenbach & Warren, Inc. Stripe, 2 floral stripes, 2 allover florals, polka dot; all in full color. 4 sheets (350 sq. in.) of each, enough for average room. 48pp. 8¼ × 11.   23495-9 Pa. $2.95

MINIATURE IRON-ON TRANSFER PATTERNS FOR DOLLHOUSES, DOLLS, AND SMALL PROJECTS, Rita Weiss and Frank Fontana. Over 100 miniature patterns: rugs, bedspreads, quilts, chair seats, etc. In standard dollhouse size. 48pp. 8¼ × 11.   23741-9 Pa. $1.95

THE DINOSAUR COLORING BOOK, Anthony Rao. 45 renderings of dinosaurs, fossil birds, turtles, other creatures of Mesozoic Era. Scientifically accurate. Captions. 48pp. 8¼ × 11.   24022-3 Pa. $2.50

JAPANESE DESIGN MOTIFS, Matsuya Co. Mon, or heraldic designs. Over 4000 typical, beautiful designs: birds, animals, flowers, swords, fans, geometrics; all beautifully stylized. 213pp. 11⅜ × 8¼. 22874-6 Pa. $7.95

THE TALE OF BENJAMIN BUNNY, Beatrix Potter. Peter Rabbit's cousin coaxes him back into Mr. McGregor's garden for a whole new set of adventures. All 27 full-color illustrations. 59pp. 4¼ × 5½. (Available in U.S. only) 21102-9 Pa. $1.75

THE TALE OF PETER RABBIT AND OTHER FAVORITE STORIES BOXED SET, Beatrix Potter. Seven of Beatrix Potter's best-loved tales including Peter Rabbit in a specially designed, durable boxed set. 4¼ × 5½. Total of 447pp. 158 color illustrations. (Available in U.S. only) 23903-9 Pa. $12.25

PRACTICAL MENTAL MAGIC, Theodore Annemann. Nearly 200 astonishing feats of mental magic revealed in step-by-step detail. Complete advice on staging, patter, etc. Illustrated. 320pp. 5⅜ × 8½. 24426-1 Pa. $5.95

CELEBRATED CASES OF JUDGE DEE (DEE GOONG AN), translated by Robert Van Gulik. Authentic 18th-century Chinese detective novel; Dee and associates solve three interlocked cases. Led to van Gulik's own stories with same characters. Extensive introduction. 9 illustrations. 237pp. 5⅜ × 8½.
23337-5 Pa. $4.95

CUT & FOLD EXTRATERRESTRIAL INVADERS THAT FLY, M. Grater. Stage your own lilliputian space battles. By following the step-by-step instructions and explanatory diagrams you can launch 22 full-color fliers into space. 36pp. 8¼ × 11. 24478-4 Pa. $2.95

CUT & ASSEMBLE VICTORIAN HOUSES, Edmund V. Gillon, Jr. Printed in full color on heavy cardboard stock, 4 authentic Victorian houses in H-O scale: Italian-style Villa, Octagon, Second Empire, Stick Style. 48pp. 9¼ × 12¼.
23849-0 Pa. $4.95

BEST SCIENCE FICTION STORIES OF H.G. WELLS, H.G. Wells. Full novel *The Invisible Man,* plus 17 short stories: "The Crystal Egg," "Aepyornis Island," "The Strange Orchid," etc. 303pp. 5⅜ × 8½. (Available in U.S. only)
21531-8 Pa. $4.95

TRADEMARK DESIGNS OF THE WORLD, Yusaku Kamekura. A lavish collection of nearly 700 trademarks, the work of Wright, Loewy, Klee, Binder, hundreds of others. 160pp. 8¾ × 8. (EJ) 24191-2 Pa. $5.95

THE ARTIST'S AND CRAFTSMAN'S GUIDE TO REDUCING, ENLARGING AND TRANSFERRING DESIGNS, Rita Weiss. Discover, reduce, enlarge, transfer designs from any objects to any craft project. 12pp. plus 16 sheets special graph paper. 8¼ × 11. 24142-4 Pa. $3.95

TREASURY OF JAPANESE DESIGNS AND MOTIFS FOR ARTISTS AND CRAFTSMEN, edited by Carol Belanger Grafton. Indispensable collection of 360 traditional Japanese designs and motifs redrawn in clean, crisp black-and-white, copyright-free illustrations. 96pp. 8¼ × 11. 24435-0 Pa. $4.50

CATALOG OF DOVER BOOKS

CHANCERY CURSIVE STROKE BY STROKE, Arthur Baker. Instructions and illustrations for each stroke of each letter (upper and lower case) and numerals. 54 full-page plates. 64pp. 8¼ × 11. 24278-1 Pa. $2.50

THE ENJOYMENT AND USE OF COLOR, Walter Sargent. Color relationships, values, intensities; complementary colors, illumination, similar topics. Color in nature and art. 7 color plates, 29 illustrations. 274pp. 5⅜ × 8½. 20944-X Pa. $4.95

SCULPTURE PRINCIPLES AND PRACTICE, Louis Slobodkin. Step-by-step approach to clay, plaster, metals, stone; classical and modern. 253 drawings, photos. 255pp. 8⅛ × 11. 22960-2 Pa. $7.50

VICTORIAN FASHION PAPER DOLLS FROM HARPER'S BAZAR, 1867-1898, Theodore Menten. Four female dolls with 28 elegant high fashion costumes, printed in full color. 32pp. 9¼ × 12¼. 23453-3 Pa. $3.95

FLOPSY, MOPSY AND COTTONTAIL: A Little Book of Paper Dolls in Full Color, Susan LaBelle. Three dolls and 21 costumes (7 for each doll) show Peter Rabbit's siblings dressed for holidays, gardening, hiking, etc. Charming borders, captions. 48pp. 4¼ × 5½. (USCO) 24376-1 Pa. $2.50

NATIONAL LEAGUE BASEBALL CARD CLASSICS, Bert Randolph Sugar. 83 big-leaguers from 1909-69 on facsimile cards. Hubbell, Dean, Spahn, Brock plus advertising, info, no duplications. Perforated, detachable. 16pp. 8¼ × 11. 24308-7 Pa. $3.50

THE LOGICAL APPROACH TO CHESS, Dr. Max Euwe, et al. First-rate text of comprehensive strategy, tactics, theory for the amateur. No gambits to memorize, just a clear, logical approach. 224pp. 5⅜ × 8½. 24353-2 Pa. $4.50

MAGICK IN THEORY AND PRACTICE, Aleister Crowley. The summation of the thought and practice of the century's most famous necromancer, long hard to find. Crowley's best book. 436pp. 5⅜ × 8½. (Available in U.S. only) 23295-6 Pa. $6.95

THE HAUNTED HOTEL, Wilkie Collins. Collins' last great tale; doom and destiny in a Venetian palace. Praised by T.S. Eliot. 127pp. 5⅜ × 8½. 24333-8 Pa. $3.00

ART DECO DISPLAY ALPHABETS, Dan X. Solo. Wide variety of bold yet elegant lettering in handsome Art Deco styles. 100 complete fonts, with numerals, punctuation, more. 104pp. 8⅛ × 11. 24372-9 Pa. $4.50

CALLIGRAPHIC ALPHABETS, Arthur Baker. Nearly 150 complete alphabets by outstanding contemporary. Stimulating ideas; useful source for unique effects. 154 plates. 157pp. 8⅜ × 11¼. 21045-6 Pa. $5.95

ARTHUR BAKER'S HISTORIC CALLIGRAPHIC ALPHABETS, Arthur Baker. From monumental capitals of first-century Rome to humanistic cursive of 16th century, 33 alphabets in fresh interpretations. 88 plates. 96pp. 9 × 12. 24054-1 Pa. $4.50

LETTIE LANE PAPER DOLLS, Sheila Young. Genteel turn-of-the-century family very popular then and now. 24 paper dolls. 16 plates in full color. 32pp. 9¼ × 12¼. 24089-4 Pa. $3.95

KEYBOARD WORKS FOR SOLO INSTRUMENTS, G.F. Handel. 35 neglected works from Handel's vast oeuvre, originally jotted down as improvisations. Includes Eight Great Suites, others. New sequence. 174pp. 9⅜ × 12¼.
24338-9 Pa. $7.50

AMERICAN LEAGUE BASEBALL CARD CLASSICS, Bert Randolph Sugar. 82 stars from 1900s to 60s on facsimile cards. Ruth, Cobb, Mantle, Williams, plus advertising, info, no duplications. Perforated, detachable. 16pp. 8¼ × 11.
24286-2 Pa. $3.50

A TREASURY OF CHARTED DESIGNS FOR NEEDLEWORKERS, Georgia Gorham and Jeanne Warth. 141 charted designs: owl, cat with yarn, tulips, piano, spinning wheel, covered bridge, Victorian house and many others. 48pp. 8¼ × 11.
23558-0 Pa. $1.95

DANISH FLORAL CHARTED DESIGNS, Gerda Bengtsson. Exquisite collection of over 40 different florals: anemone, Iceland poppy, wild fruit, pansies, many others. 45 illustrations. 48pp. 8¼ × 11.
23957-8 Pa. $2.50

OLD PHILADELPHIA IN EARLY PHOTOGRAPHS 1839-1914, Robert F. Looney. 215 photographs: panoramas, street scenes, landmarks, President-elect Lincoln's visit, 1876 Centennial Exposition, much more. 230pp. 8⅜ × 11¾.
23345-6 Pa. $9.95

PRELUDE TO MATHEMATICS, W.W. Sawyer. Noted mathematician's lively, stimulating account of non-Euclidean geometry, matrices, determinants, group theory, other topics. Emphasis on novel, striking aspects. 224pp. 5⅜ × 8½.
24401-6 Pa. $4.50

ADVENTURES WITH A MICROSCOPE, Richard Headstrom. 59 adventures with clothing fibers, protozoa, ferns and lichens, roots and leaves, much more. 142 illustrations. 232pp. 5⅜ × 8½.
23471-1 Pa. $3.95

IDENTIFYING ANIMAL TRACKS: MAMMALS, BIRDS, AND OTHER ANIMALS OF THE EASTERN UNITED STATES, Richard Headstrom. For hunters, naturalists, scouts, nature-lovers. Diagrams of tracks, tips on identification. 128pp. 5⅜ × 8.
24442-3 Pa. $3.50

VICTORIAN FASHIONS AND COSTUMES FROM HARPER'S BAZAR, 1867-1898, edited by Stella Blum. Day costumes, evening wear, sports clothes, shoes, hats, other accessories in over 1,000 detailed engravings. 320pp. 9⅜ × 12¼.
22990-4 Pa. $10.95

EVERYDAY FASHIONS OF THE TWENTIES AS PICTURED IN SEARS AND OTHER CATALOGS, edited by Stella Blum. Actual dress of the Roaring Twenties, with text by Stella Blum. Over 750 illustrations, captions. 156pp. 9 × 12.
24134-3 Pa. $8.95

HALL OF FAME BASEBALL CARDS, edited by Bert Randolph Sugar. Cy Young, Ted Williams, Lou Gehrig, and many other Hall of Fame greats on 92 full-color, detachable reprints of early baseball cards. No duplication of cards with *Classic Baseball Cards*. 16pp. 8¼ × 11.
23624-2 Pa. $3.50

THE ART OF HAND LETTERING, Helm Wotzkow. Course in hand lettering, Roman, Gothic, Italic, Block, Script. Tools, proportions, optical aspects, individual variation. Very quality conscious. Hundreds of specimens. 320pp. 5⅜ × 8½.
21797-3 Pa. $5.95

HOW THE OTHER HALF LIVES, Jacob A. Riis. Journalistic record of filth, degradation, upward drive in New York immigrant slums, shops, around 1900. New edition includes 100 original Riis photos, monuments of early photography. 233pp. 10 × 7⅞. 22012-5 Pa. $9.95

CHINA AND ITS PEOPLE IN EARLY PHOTOGRAPHS, John Thomson. In 200 black-and-white photographs of exceptional quality photographic pioneer Thomson captures the mountains, dwellings, monuments and people of 19th-century China. 272pp. 9⅜ × 12¼. 24393-1 Pa. $13.95

GODEY COSTUME PLATES IN COLOR FOR DECOUPAGE AND FRAMING, edited by Eleanor Hasbrouk Rawlings. 24 full-color engravings depicting 19th-century Parisian haute couture. Printed on one side only. 56pp. 8¼ × 11. 23879-2 Pa. $3.95

ART NOUVEAU STAINED GLASS PATTERN BOOK, Ed Sibbett, Jr. 104 projects using well-known themes of Art Nouveau: swirling forms, florals, peacocks, and sensuous women. 60pp. 8¼ × 11. 23577-7 Pa. $3.95

QUICK AND EASY PATCHWORK ON THE SEWING MACHINE: Susan Aylsworth Murwin and Suzzy Payne. Instructions, diagrams show exactly how to machine sew 12 quilts. 48pp. of templates. 50 figures. 80pp. 8¼ × 11. 23770-2 Pa. $3.95

THE STANDARD BOOK OF QUILT MAKING AND COLLECTING, Marguerite Ickis. Full information, full-sized patterns for making 46 traditional quilts, also 150 other patterns. 483 illustrations. 273pp. 6⅞ × 9⅝. 20582-7 Pa. $5.95

LETTERING AND ALPHABETS, J. Albert Cavanagh. 85 complete alphabets lettered in various styles; instructions for spacing, roughs, brushwork. 121pp. 8¾ × 8. 20053-1 Pa. $3.95

LETTER FORMS: 110 COMPLETE ALPHABETS, Frederick Lambert. 110 sets of capital letters; 16 lower case alphabets; 70 sets of numbers and other symbols. 110pp. 8⅛ × 11. 22872-X Pa. $4.50

ORCHIDS AS HOUSE PLANTS, Rebecca Tyson Northen. Grow cattleyas and many other kinds of orchids—in a window, in a case, or under artificial light. 63 illustrations. 148pp. 5⅜ × 8½. 23261-1 Pa. $2.95

THE MUSHROOM HANDBOOK, Louis C.C. Krieger. Still the best popular handbook. Full descriptions of 259 species, extremely thorough text, poisons, folklore, etc. 32 color plates; 126 other illustrations. 560pp. 5⅜ × 8½. 21861-9 Pa. $8.50

THE DORÉ BIBLE ILLUSTRATIONS, Gustave Doré. All wonderful, detailed plates: Adam and Eve, Flood, Babylon, life of Jesus, etc. Brief King James text with each plate. 241 plates. 241pp. 9 × 12. 23004-X Pa. $8.95

THE BOOK OF KELLS: Selected Plates in Full Color, edited by Blanche Cirker. 32 full-page plates from greatest manuscript-icon of early Middle Ages. Fantastic, mysterious. Publisher's Note. Captions. 32pp. 9¾ × 12¼. 24345-1 Pa. $4.50

THE PERFECT WAGNERITE, George Bernard Shaw. Brilliant criticism of the Ring Cycle, with provocative interpretation of politics, economic theories behind the Ring. 136pp. 5⅜ × 8½. (EUK) 21707-8 Pa. $3.95

THE RIME OF THE ANCIENT MARINER, Gustave Doré, S.T. Coleridge. Doré's finest work, 34 plates capture moods, subtleties of poem. Full text. 77pp. 9¼ × 12.   22305-1 Pa. $4.95

SONGS OF INNOCENCE, William Blake. The first and most popular of Blake's famous "Illuminated Books," in a facsimile edition reproducing all 31 brightly colored plates. Additional printed text of each poem. 64pp. 5¼ × 7.
22764-2 Pa. $3.50

AN INTRODUCTION TO INFORMATION THEORY, J.R. Pierce. Second (1980) edition of most impressive non-technical account available. Encoding, entropy, noisy channel, related areas, etc. 320pp. 5⅜ × 8½.   24061-4 Pa. $5.95

THE DIVINE PROPORTION: A STUDY IN MATHEMATICAL BEAUTY, H.E. Huntley. "Divine proportion" or "golden ratio" in poetry, Pascal's triangle, philosophy, psychology, music, mathematical figures, etc. Excellent bridge between science and art. 58 figures. 185pp. 5⅜ × 8½.   22254-3 Pa. $4.50

THE DOVER NEW YORK WALKING GUIDE: From the Battery to Wall Street, Mary J. Shapiro. Superb inexpensive guide to historic buildings and locales in lower Manhattan: Trinity Church, Bowling Green, more. Complete Text; maps. 36 illustrations. 48pp. 3⅞ × 9¼.   24225-0 Pa. $2.50

NEW YORK THEN AND NOW, Edward B. Watson, Edmund V. Gillon, Jr. 83 important Manhattan sites: on facing pages early photographs (1875-1925) and 1976 photos by Gillon. 172 illustrations. 171pp. 9¼ × 10.   23361-8 Pa. $9.95

HISTORIC COSTUME IN PICTURES, Braun & Schneider. Over 1450 costumed figures from dawn of civilization to end of 19th century. English captions. 125 plates. 256pp. 8⅜ × 11¼.   23150-X Pa. $7.95

VICTORIAN AND EDWARDIAN FASHION: A Photographic Survey, Alison Gernsheim. First fashion history completely illustrated by contemporary photographs. Full text plus 235 photos, 1840-1914, in which many celebrities appear. 240pp. 6½ × 9¼.   24205-6 Pa. $6.00

CHARTED CHRISTMAS DESIGNS FOR COUNTED CROSS-STITCH AND OTHER NEEDLECRAFTS, Lindberg Press. Charted designs for 45 beautiful needlecraft projects with many yuletide and wintertime motifs. 48pp. 8¼ × 11. (EDNS)   24356-7 Pa. $2.50

101 FOLK DESIGNS FOR COUNTED CROSS-STITCH AND OTHER NEEDLE-CRAFTS, Carter Houck. 101 authentic charted folk designs in a wide array of lovely representations with many suggestions for effective use. 48pp. 8¼ × 11.
24369-9 Pa. $2.25

FIVE ACRES AND INDEPENDENCE, Maurice G. Kains. Great back-to-the-land classic explains basics of self-sufficient farming. The one book to get. 95 illustrations. 397pp. 5⅜ × 8½.   20974-1 Pa. $6.50

A MODERN HERBAL, Margaret Grieve. Much the fullest, most exact, most useful compilation of herbal material. Gigantic alphabetical encyclopedia, from aconite to zedoary, gives botanical information, medical properties, folklore, economic uses, and much else. Indispensable to serious reader. 161 illustrations. 888pp. 6½ × 9¼. (Available in U.S. only)   22798-7, 22799-5 Pa., Two-vol. set $17.00

DECORATIVE NAPKIN FOLDING FOR BEGINNERS, Lillian Oppenheimer and Natalie Epstein. 22 different napkin folds in the shape of a heart, clown's hat, love knot, etc. 63 drawings. 48pp. 8¼ × 11. 23797-4 Pa. $2.25

DECORATIVE LABELS FOR HOME CANNING, PRESERVING, AND OTHER HOUSEHOLD AND GIFT USES, Theodore Menten. 128 gummed, perforated labels, beautifully printed in 2 colors. 12 versions. Adhere to metal, glass, wood, ceramics. 24pp. 8¼ × 11. 23219-0 Pa. $3.50

EARLY AMERICAN STENCILS ON WALLS AND FURNITURE, Janet Waring. Thorough coverage of 19th-century folk art: techniques, artifacts, surviving specimens. 166 illustrations, 7 in color. 147pp. of text. 7⅞ × 10¾. 21906-2 Pa. $9.95

AMERICAN ANTIQUE WEATHERVANES, A.B. & W.T. Westervelt. Extensively illustrated 1883 catalog exhibiting over 550 copper weathervanes and finials. Excellent primary source by one of the principal manufacturers. 104pp. 6⅝ × 9¼. 24396-6 Pa. $3.95

ART STUDENTS' ANATOMY, Edmond J. Farris. Long favorite in art schools. Basic elements, common positions, actions. Full text, 158 illustrations. 159pp. 5⅜ × 8½. 20744-7 Pa. $3.95

BRIDGMAN'S LIFE DRAWING, George B. Bridgman. More than 500 drawings and text teach you to abstract the body into its major masses. Also specific areas of anatomy. 192pp. 6½ × 9¼. 22710-3 Pa. $4.50

COMPLETE PRELUDES AND ETUDES FOR SOLO PIANO, Frederic Chopin. All 26 Preludes, all 27 Etudes by greatest composer of piano music. Authoritative Paderewski edition. 224pp. 9 × 12. (Available in U.S. only) 24052-5 Pa. $7.50

PIANO MUSIC 1888-1905, Claude Debussy. Deux Arabesques, Suite Bergamesque, Masques, 1st series of Images, etc. 9 others, in corrected editions. 175pp. 9⅜ × 12¼. 22771-5 Pa. $6.95

TEDDY BEAR IRON-ON TRANSFER PATTERNS, Ted Menten. 80 iron-on transfer patterns of male and female Teddys in a wide variety of activities, poses, sizes. 48pp. 8¼ × 11. 24596-9 Pa. $2.25

A PICTURE HISTORY OF THE BROOKLYN BRIDGE, M.J. Shapiro. Profusely illustrated account of greatest engineering achievement of 19th century. 167 rare photos & engravings recall construction, human drama. Extensive, detailed text. 122pp. 8¼ × 11. 24403-2 Pa. $7.95

NEW YORK IN THE THIRTIES, Berenice Abbott. Noted photographer's fascinating study shows new buildings that have become famous and old sights that have disappeared forever. 97 photographs. 97pp. 11⅜ × 10. 22967-X Pa. $7.50

MATHEMATICAL TABLES AND FORMULAS, Robert D. Carmichael and Edwin R. Smith. Logarithms, sines, tangents, trig functions, powers, roots, reciprocals, exponential and hyperbolic functions, formulas and theorems. 269pp. 5⅜ × 8½. 60111-0 Pa. $4.95

HANDBOOK OF MATHEMATICAL FUNCTIONS WITH FORMULAS, GRAPHS, AND MATHEMATICAL TABLES, edited by Milton Abramowitz and Irene A. Stegun. Vast compendium: 29 sets of tables, some to as high as 20 places. 1,046pp. 8 × 10½. 61272-4 Pa. $21.95

REASON IN ART, George Santayana. Renowned philosopher's provocative, seminal treatment of basis of art in instinct and experience. Volume Four of *The Life of Reason*. 230pp. 5⅜ × 8. 24358-3 Pa. $4.50

LANGUAGE, TRUTH AND LOGIC, Alfred J. Ayer. Famous, clear introduction to Vienna, Cambridge schools of Logical Positivism. Role of philosophy, elimination of metaphysics, nature of analysis, etc. 160pp. 5⅜ × 8½. (USCO) 20010-8 Pa. $2.95

BASIC ELECTRONICS, U.S. Bureau of Naval Personnel. Electron tubes, circuits, antennas, AM, FM, and CW transmission and receiving, etc. 560 illustrations. 567pp. 6½ × 9¼. 21076-6 Pa. $9.95

THE ART DECO STYLE, edited by Theodore Menten. Furniture, jewelry, metalwork, ceramics, fabrics, lighting fixtures, interior decors, exteriors, graphics from pure French sources. Over 400 photographs. 183pp. 8⅜ × 11¼. 22824-X Pa. $7.95

THE FOUR BOOKS OF ARCHITECTURE, Andrea Palladio. 16th-century classic covers classical architectural remains, Renaissance revivals, classical orders, etc. 1738 Ware English edition. 216 plates. 110pp. of text. 9½ × 12¾. 21308-0 Pa. $11.95

THE WIT AND HUMOR OF OSCAR WILDE, edited by Alvin Redman. More than 1000 ripostes, paradoxes, wisecracks: Work is the curse of the drinking classes, I can resist everything except temptations, etc. 258pp. 5⅜ × 8½. 20602-5 Pa. $4.50

THE DEVIL'S DICTIONARY, Ambrose Bierce. Barbed, bitter, brilliant witticisms in the form of a dictionary. Best, most ferocious satire America has produced. 145pp. 5⅜ × 8½. 20487-1 Pa. $2.95

ERTÉ'S FASHION DESIGNS, Erté. 210 black-and-white inventions from *Harper's Bazar*, 1918-32, plus 8pp. full-color covers. Captions. 88pp. 9 × 12. 24203-X Pa. $7.95

ERTÉ GRAPHICS, Erté. Collection of striking color graphics: *Seasons, Alphabet, Numerals, Aces* and *Precious Stones*. 50 plates, including 4 on covers. 48pp. 9⅜ × 12¼. 23580-7 Pa. $6.95

PAPER FOLDING FOR BEGINNERS, William D. Murray and Francis J. Rigney. Clearest book for making origami sail boats, roosters, frogs that move legs, etc. 40 projects. More than 275 illustrations. 94pp. 5⅜ × 8½. 20713-7 Pa. $2.50

ORIGAMI FOR THE ENTHUSIAST, John Montroll. Fish, ostrich, peacock, squirrel, rhinoceros, Pegasus, 19 other intricate subjects. Instructions. Diagrams. 128pp. 9 × 12. 23799-0 Pa. $5.95

CROCHETING NOVELTY POT HOLDERS, edited by Linda Macho. 64 useful, whimsical pot holders feature kitchen themes, animals, flowers, other novelties. Surprisingly easy to crochet. Complete instructions. 48pp. 8¼ × 11. 24296-X Pa. $1.95

CROCHETING DOILIES, edited by Rita Weiss. Irish Crochet, Jewel, Star Wheel, Vanity Fair and more. Also luncheon and console sets, runners and centerpieces. 51 illustrations. 48pp. 8¼ × 11. 23424-X Pa. $2.75

YUCATAN BEFORE AND AFTER THE CONQUEST, Diego de Landa. Only significant account of Yucatan written in the early post-Conquest era. Translated by William Gates. Over 120 illustrations. 162pp. 5⅜ × 8½. 23622-6 Pa. $3.95

ORNATE PICTORIAL CALLIGRAPHY, E.A. Lupfer. Complete instructions, over 150 examples help you create magnificent "flourishes" from which beautiful animals and objects gracefully emerge. 8⅛ × 11. 21957-7 Pa. $3.50

DOLLY DINGLE PAPER DOLLS, Grace Drayton. Cute chubby children by same artist who did Campbell Kids. Rare plates from 1910s. 30 paper dolls and over 100 outfits reproduced in full color. 32pp. 9¼ × 12¼. 23711-7 Pa. $3.50

CURIOUS GEORGE PAPER DOLLS IN FULL COLOR, H. A. Rey, Kathy Allert. Naughty little monkey-hero of children's books in two doll figures, plus 48 full-color costumes: pirate, Indian chief, fireman, more. 32pp. 9¼ × 12¼. 24386-9 Pa. $3.50

GERMAN: HOW TO SPEAK AND WRITE IT, Joseph Rosenberg. Like *French, How to Speak and Write It.* Very rich modern course, with a wealth of pictorial material. 330 illustrations. 384pp. 5⅜ × 8½. 20271-2 Pa. $4.95

CATS AND KITTENS: 24 Ready-to-Mail Color Photo Postcards, D. Holby. Handsome collection; feline in a variety of adorable poses. Identifications. 12pp. on postcard stock. 8¼ × 11. 24469-5 Pa. $2.95

MARILYN MONROE PAPER DOLLS, Tom Tierney. 31 full-color designs on heavy stock, from *The Asphalt Jungle, Gentlemen Prefer Blondes,* 22 others. 1 doll. 16 plates. 32pp. 9⅜ × 12¼. 23769-9 Pa. $3.95

FUNDAMENTALS OF LAYOUT, F.H. Wills. All phases of layout design discussed and illustrated in 121 illustrations. Indispensable as student's text or handbook for professional. 124pp. 8⅛ × 11. 21279-3 Pa. $4.50

FANTASTIC SUPER STICKERS, Ed Sibbett, Jr. 75 colorful pressure-sensitive stickers. Peel off and place for a touch of pizzazz: clowns, penguins, teddy bears, etc. Full color. 16pp. 8¼ × 11. 24471-7 Pa. $3.50

LABELS FOR ALL OCCASIONS, Ed Sibbett, Jr. 6 labels each of 16 different designs—baroque, art nouveau, art deco, Pennsylvania Dutch, etc.—in full color. 24pp. 8¼ × 11. 23688-9 Pa. $3.95

HOW TO CALCULATE QUICKLY: RAPID METHODS IN BASIC MATHE-MATICS, Henry Sticker. Addition, subtraction, multiplication, division, checks, etc. More than 8000 problems, solutions. 185pp. 5 × 7¼. 20295-X Pa. $2.95

THE CAT COLORING BOOK, Karen Baldauski. Handsome, realistic renderings of 40 splendid felines, from American shorthair to exotic types. 44 plates. Captions. 48pp. 8¼ × 11. 24011-8 Pa. $2.50

THE TALE OF PETER RABBIT, Beatrix Potter. The inimitable Peter's terrifying adventure in Mr. McGregor's garden, with all 27 wonderful, full-color Potter illustrations. 55pp. 4¼ × 5½. (Available in U.S. only) 22827-4 Pa. $1.75

BASIC ELECTRICITY, U.S. Bureau of Naval Personnel. Batteries, circuits, conductors, AC and DC, inductance and capacitance, generators, motors, trans-formers, amplifiers, etc. 349 illustrations. 448pp. 6½ × 9¼. 20973-3 Pa. $7.95

SOURCE BOOK OF MEDICAL HISTORY, edited by Logan Clendening, M.D. Original accounts ranging from Ancient Egypt and Greece to discovery of X-rays: Galen, Pasteur, Lavoisier, Harvey, Parkinson, others. 685pp. 5⅜ × 8½.

20621-1 Pa. $11.95

THE ROSE AND THE KEY, J.S. Lefanu. Superb mystery novel from Irish master. Dark doings among an ancient and aristocratic English family. Well-drawn characters; capital suspense. Introduction by N. Donaldson. 448pp. 5⅜ × 8½.

24377-X Pa. $6.95

SOUTH WIND, Norman Douglas. Witty, elegant novel of ideas set on languorous Mediterranean island of Nepenthe. Elegant prose, glittering epigrams, mordant satire. 1917 masterpiece. 416pp. 5⅜ × 8½. (Available in U.S. only)

24361-3 Pa. $5.95

RUSSELL'S CIVIL WAR PHOTOGRAPHS, Capt. A.J. Russell. 116 rare Civil War Photos: Bull Run, Virginia campaigns, bridges, railroads, Richmond, Lincoln's funeral car. Many never seen before. Captions. 128pp. 9⅜ × 12¼.

24283-8 Pa. $7.95

PHOTOGRAPHS BY MAN RAY: 105 Works, 1920-1934. Nudes, still lifes, landscapes, women's faces, celebrity portraits (Dali, Matisse, Picasso, others), rayographs. Reprinted from rare gravure edition. 128pp. 9⅜ × 12¼.

23842-3 Pa. $8.95

STAR NAMES: THEIR LORE AND MEANING, Richard H. Allen. Star names, the zodiac, constellations: folklore and literature associated with heavens. The basic book of its field, fascinating reading. 563pp. 5⅜ × 8½.   21079-0 Pa. $7.95

BURNHAM'S CELESTIAL HANDBOOK, Robert Burnham, Jr. Thorough guide to the stars beyond our solar system. Exhaustive treatment. Alphabetical by constellation: Andromeda to Cetus in Vol. 1; Chamaeleon to Orion in Vol. 2; Pavo to Vulpecula in Vol. 3. Hundreds of illustrations. Index in Vol. 3. 2000pp. 6⅛ × 9¼.   23567-X, 23568-8, 23673-0 Pa. Three-vol. set $37.85

THE ART NOUVEAU STYLE BOOK OF ALPHONSE MUCHA, Alphonse Mucha. All 72 plates from *Documents Decoratifs* in original color. Stunning, essential work of Art Nouveau. 80pp. 9⅜ × 12¼.   24044-4 Pa. $8.95

DESIGNS BY ERTE; FASHION DRAWINGS AND ILLUSTRATIONS FROM "HARPER'S BAZAR," Erte. 310 fabulous line drawings and 14 *Harper's Bazar* covers, 8 in. full color. Erte's exotic temptresses with tassels, fur muffs, long trains, coifs, more. 129pp. 9⅜ × 12¼.   23397-9 Pa. $8.95

HISTORY OF STRENGTH OF MATERIALS, Stephen P. Timoshenko. Excellent historical survey of the strength of materials with many references to the theories of elasticity and structure. 245 figures. 452pp. 5⅜ × 8½.   61187-6 Pa. $9.95

Prices subject to change without notice.

Available at your book dealer or write for free catalog to Dept. GI, Dover Publications, Inc., 31 East 2nd St. Mineola, N.Y. 11501. Dover publishes more than 175 books each year on science, elementary and advanced mathematics, biology, music, art, literary history, social sciences and other areas.